The
Wars of the
Roses
in Fiction

Recent Titles in
Bibliographies and Indexes in World History

The
Wars of the
Roses
in Fiction

❖   ❖   ❖

An Annotated
Bibliography,
1440–1994

Compiled by
Roxane C. Murph

Bibliographies and Indexes in World History,
Number 41

GREENWOOD PRESS
Westport, Connecticut • London

Library of Congress Cataloging-in-Publication Data

Murph, Roxane C.
    The Wars of the Roses in fiction : an annotated bibliography,
    1440–1994 / compiled by Roxane C. Murph.
        p.   cm—(Bibliographies and indexes in world history, ISSN
    0742–6852 ; no. 41)
    Includes index.
    ISBN 0–313–29709–6 (alk. paper)
    1. Great Britain—History—Wars of the Roses, 1455–1485—
    Literature and the wars—Bibliography.   2. English literature—
    Bibliography.   3. English literature—Middle English, 1100–1500—
    Bibliography.   4. Great Britain—History—Lancaster and York,
    1399–1485—Historiography—Bibliography.   5. Great Britain—History—
    Tudors, 1485–1603—Historiography—Bibliography.   I. Title.
    II. Series: Bibliographies and indexes in world history ; no. 41.
    Z2017.M87   1995
    [PR25]
    016.823008′0358—dc20   95–12746

British Library Cataloguing in Publication Data is available.

Library of Congress Catalog Card Number: 95–12746
ISBN: 0–313–29709–6
ISSN: 0742–6852

First published in 1995

Greenwood Press, 88 Post Road West, Westport, CT 06881
An imprint of Greenwood Publishing Group, Inc.

Printed in the United States of America

The paper used in this book complies with the
Permanent Paper Standard issued by the National
Information Standards Organization (Z39.48–1984).

10 9 8 7 6 5 4 3 2 1

❖

Contents

❖

Preface

Few periods in history have engendered as much dispute as the one known as the Wars of the Roses, a term which came to be used to describe the 15th century conflict between the houses of Lancaster and York for the throne of England. Indeed, to this day both historians and writers of fiction engage in heated debate about the characters and events of the period, the partisans on both sides tending to dismiss their opponents either as unscholarly romantics or deluded believers in myths.

There is even disagreement among historians about the date of the start of the Wars of the Roses, with some arguing for 1399, when Henry Bolingbroke seized the throne from his cousin Richard II, thus becoming the first Lancastrian monarch, and others for 1455, the date of the first battle of St. Albans, when Richard, Duke of York, first took up arms against Henry VI. There is disagreement as well about when the conflict finally ended. Some see the execution of Perkin Warbeck and the young Earl of Warwick in 1499 as the end of the wars. Other historians note, however, that Henry VII was again plagued by a Yorkist pretender in the person of Edmund de la Pole, Duke of Suffolk, the younger brother of the Earl of Lincoln who was killed at Stoke in 1487, in support of the pretender Lambert Simnel. After Tudor's death, his son, Henry VIII, executed all surviving possible Yorkist claimants, including Suffolk and the elderly Margaret Pole, Clarence's daughter, who went to the block in 1541. Their deaths removed any further Yorkist threat to the Tudors, and by anyone's reckoning the Wars of the Roses were ended.

For the purpose of this bibliography I have confined myself, with a few exceptions, to works written in English during and/or about the years 1440, the time of Humphrey of Gloucester's ascendency, to 1499 and the death of Perkin Warbeck.* A few of the works begin before or after these years, but are mainly concerned with the period under discussion. Those works which are set in the period, but which take little or no notice of the political events of the time, have been omitted. Only the first edition of each work is noted, since many have gone into numerous editions. The only exceptions are cases in which there have been nearly simultaneous publications by both English and American publishers, or those in which the work appeared under a different name in subsequent editions. I have read most of the works included in this bibliography, but a few were impossible to obtain, and I have so noted them.

This bibliography is written for both students and general readers with an interest in 15th century history. Since it is not intended as a work of criticism, I have generally refrained from offering an opinion of the literary or historical merit of the works. In certain cases, however, when they have value both as literature and history, or when the authors' lack of understanding of the period makes their writing valueless, I have made note of this, but generally I have left it to the reader to judge their merits. Some of them are very good indeed, true works of art. Others fail to meet any but the lowest standards, while more than a few fall between the two extremes.

The critical enjoyment of any work of historical fiction depends to some degree on the reader's knowledge of the period. Those who are unfamiliar with the Wars of the Roses would benefit by reading any of the following general histories of the period: E. F. Jacob's *The Fifteenth Century* (London, 1961); John Gillingham's *The Wars of the Roses* (Baton Rouge, La., 1981); Anthony Goodman's *The Wars of the Roses* (New York, 1981); or Charles Ross' *The Wars of the Roses* (London, 1976). All present a balanced view of the conflict.

I am indebted to many people who brought to my attention and/or helped me to obtain many of the works in this bibliography, among them Mary Bader of the Library of Congress; the staff of the reading room of the Folger Shakespeare Library; Joyce Martindale, head of the inter-library loan department, and the staff of the reference department of the Mary Coutts Burnett Library, Texas Christian University; Carolyn Hammond, librarian of the Richard III Society, London; Mary Miller, fiction librarian of the American Branch of the Richard III Society; Myrna Smith; Mary Donermeyer; and Jim Morris of UMI; Doyle Williams for sharing his computer expertise so generously; and my husband, for his infinite patience during the research and writing of this bibliography.

*Most of the works about this period were written in English, but more than a few are in French, Spanish, Italian, German, and Dutch.

The
Wars of the
Roses
in Fiction

Introduction

The Wars of the Roses, so I have heard,
Was caused by too many children of Edward the Third.

This little doggerel verse, recited by generations of school children, contains, like many simplisms, more than a grain of truth. Although the dates of the Wars of the Roses, a dynastic conflict between the houses of Lancaster and York, are generally given as 1455, the year of the first Battle of St. Albans, to 1485, the date of the Battle of Bosworth Field, the roots go back more than fifty years. In 1399, Henry of Bolingbroke, the eldest son of Edward III's third son, John of Gaunt, seized the crown from his cousin Richard II. In so doing, he passed over the childless Richard's heir, Edmund Mortimer, the great-grandson of Edward III's second son, Lionel of Clarence, thus setting in motion a bitter dispute that lasted for nearly a century, and resulted in the virtual destruction of the houses of Lancaster and York, and many of their supporters as well.

Henry of Bolingbroke, Duke of Lancaster, took the throne as Henry IV, the first Lancastrian king, and he was succeeded, more or less peacefully, by his son, Henry V. That god-like monarch of romantic memory succeeded in winning for England both a great deal of French territory, and the princess and crown of France. It was a legacy which would cost England dearly. When Henry V died in 1415, he left a nine-month-old son, who became Henry VI, in the care of his quarrelsome and ambitious relatives, including his brothers, John, Duke of Bedford, and Humphrey, the "Good Duke" of Gloucester, and his uncle, Henry Beaufort, the rich and worldly Bishop of Winchester.

When the young king was taken from his mother, Catherine de Valois, to be raised by his father's relations, the young widow found solace in the arms of Owen Tudor, a Welsh gentleman in her employ, and one of the children of this liaison was the father of Henry Tudor. There is some dispute about whether or not Owen and Catherine were married, but no proof exists either to prove or disprove the point. As Henry VI grew to manhood, it became apparent that he had inherited the madness of his maternal grandfather, and he became the pawn of rival factions seeking to control him; first his uncles, and later his wife, Margaret of Anjou, and her favorites, and their opponents, Richard, Duke of York, and his supporters. Henry's wife, a penniless French princess, whose marriage settlement included the cession of Maine and Anjou to the French, was a strong-willed, arrogant woman whose intense friendships and enmities split the country into ever more warlike factions. She surrounded herself with Beaufort supporters, the descendents of John of Gaunt and Katherine Swynford, who married after the birth of their children. With these men, and the Duke of Suffolk, she attempted to govern the country, with the pious, kind-hearted king content to retire to his prayers, away from the quarrels of the court. Margaret and her supporters became ever more unpopular as the country descended into near anarchy, and many people looked to the Duke of York to reform the government.

Richard of York was the son of Anne Mortimer, the grand-daughter of Lionel of Clarence, and Richard, Earl of Cambridge, who was a descendant of Edward III's fourth son, Edmund, Duke of York. Cambridge was accused of plotting to seize the throne, and executed by Henry V in 1415. After his father's death, Richard, now the Duke of York, was brought up as the ward of Ralph Neville, Earl of Westmorland. He married the earl's daughter Cecily, thus joining two of the most powerful families in the country. Although York was able and ambitious, it is unlikely he would have pressed his claim to the throne had circumstances not forced him to the action.

Since the marriage of Henry VI and Margaret of Anjou had been supported and arranged by Suffolk and Somerset, it was natural that she should be guided by their opinions and advice, and she accepted without question that their enemies were hers. Margaret's new friends both feared and hated the Duke of York, both for his popularity and position as the first lord of the realm, and his possible danger as a claimant to the throne. Had the queen used some tact in her dealings with York, it is possible that he would have become, if not an ally, at least a loyal opponent. Her treatment of him, and the mismanagement of the country by her and her supporters, however, left him little choice but to oppose her.

During the king's frequent and lengthy bouts of madness, York served as Protector, despite the Lancastrians' attempts to prevent it. In 1455 feelings between the two factions became so bitter that armed conflict was inevitable. In May of that year the opposing armies met at St. Albans, and after a short battle, during which Henry VI was slightly wounded, and Somerset, Northumberland, and Clifford were killed, the victorious Yorkists brought the captive king to London. During the following five years of intermittent strife, first one faction and then the other gained the ascendency. The Yorkist lords insisted that their only purpose in opposing the king was to remove his evil counselors, but these same men, with the support of the queen, were determined to retain their power and influence.

In 1460 York, in a move that surprised and dismayed even his closest supporters, laid claim to the throne, but under the terms of an agreement reached between the parties, Henry was to retain the crown for life, and York was to be his heir. The duke then withdrew to his castle of Wakefield in Yorkshire, but the queen, who could not accept the setting aside of her son, attacked the Yorkist forces, and York, his son Rutland, and his brother-in-law Salisbury were killed. To mock York's pretensions, the queen had the heads of the three leaders set up over the Micklegate Bar in York, with a paper crown adorning the head of the late duke.

The Yorkist title then devolved on the duke's eldest son, nineteen-year-old Edward, and within months he and his cousin Warwick, Salisbury's son, had defeated the Lancastrians and forced Henry VI and his queen into exile. The heir of York was then crowned King Edward IV. Warwick, who had been instrumental in placing Edward on the throne, expected to be the power behind it, but the new king proved to be independent and strong-willed. Warwick, who believed that a French alliance was in England's best interest, went to France to negotiate a marriage between Edward and the sister-in-law of Louis XI, but in his absence the king secretly married Elizabeth Woodville, a Lancastrian widow with two children. His disclosure of the marriage several months later humiliated Warwick and, like the unpopular marriage of Henry VI and Margaret of Anjou, this union had long-lasting and disastrous repercussions for the country.

The new queen had a large family, and she lost little time in securing for them honors, offices, and advantageous marriages. As the king turned more and more to his new in-laws for support and advice, and rewarded them lavishly, the old nobility, especially Warwick and his family, felt angered and betrayed by what they perceived as their diminished importance. It was not long before Warwick rebelled, joined forces with Margaret of Anjou, and succeeded in forcing Edward from the throne and replacing him with Henry VI. This so-called 're-adoption' lasted less than a year. Edward returned from exile in Burgundy, defeated and killed Warwick at Barnet in 1471, and weeks later destroyed the remainder of the Lancastrian forces at Tewkesbury. Margaret of Anjou was taken prisoner, her son was killed in the battle, and Henry VI died in the Tower, "of pure melancholy and displeasure," according to the official Yorkist story. In the Tudor version of the incident, he was murdered by Edward's brother Richard of Gloucester, later Richard III.

In 1483 Edward IV died, probably worn out by years of inaction and debauchery. He left his widow, several children, including two young sons, Edward and Richard, his brother Richard of Gloucester, whom he had named Protector, and a court full of quarrelsome and ambitious sycophants. The

Woodville faction, led by the queen and her brother Anthony, moved quickly in an attempt to forestall Gloucester by having the young king, Edward V, crowned before his uncle knew what had happened.

Gloucester, warned by Hastings, the late king's close friend, and aided by the Duke of Buckingham, prepared to circumvent the queen's plans. The young king had been living at Ludlow under the care of his maternal uncle, Anthony Woodville, Earl Rivers, and Gloucester intercepted them on their way to London. He arrested Rivers and Richard Grey, the queen's son by her first husband, and took control of the king. The queen learned of the failure of her plans before Gloucester and the king reached London, and she fled into sanctuary with her other children.

Gloucester announced his intention to have his nephew crowned as quickly as possible, and made preparations accordingly. There is little doubt that opposing factions were at work, and that the Protector feared that his life was in danger, for on June 10, 1483, he wrote to the city of York, asking for men to protect him against "the Queen, her blood adherents and affinity, which have intended, and daily doth intend, to murder and utterly destroy us and our cousin the Duke of Buckingham, and the old royal blood of this realm."

Whether or not this was the case, on June 13, at the meeting in the Tower so dramatically described by Sir Thomas More, Gloucester accused Hastings, Bishop Morton, and others of plotting with the queen and Jane Shore, the late king's mistress, to destroy him. Hastings was summarily executed, and the others were arrested.

A few days thereafter the queen reluctantly allowed her younger son Richard to leave sanctuary and join his brother in the Tower, so that he could take part in the coronation. Less than a week after that, however, Bishop Stillington of Bath and Wells revealed that Edward IV and Elizabeth Woodville were not legally married, since the king had previously been contracted to Eleanor Butler, the daughter of the Earl of Shrewsbury. The children of the Woodville marriage were therefore illegitimate, and unable to succeed to the crown.

The council accepted the story, possibly on being shown proof which is no longer extant. It is equally possible that the members of the council dreaded the rule of a minor controlled by the unpopular Woodvilles, and so chose to believe the story without proof. On June 25 a de facto parliament met at Westminster and drew up a petition asking Richard of Gloucester to take the crown, and on the following day he accepted. He was crowned on July 6, 1483, as King Richard III, and his nephews were lodged in the Tower as virtual prisoners.

The question central to any discussion of Richard III is "Did he murder his nephews, the Princes in the Tower?" No one has ever been able to answer this question satisfactorily, but a heated debate has been going on since Richard's death in 1485, and shows no sign of abatement to this day. Many other candidates have been cast in the role of the murderer of the princes, including

Buckingham and Henry VII, and there is a significant number of writers both of history and fiction who have accepted the theory that they were not murdered at all, but that at least the younger of them escaped or was sent to safety, to reappear years later as Perkin Warbeck.

On August 22, 1485, just over two years after he took the throne, Richard III was defeated and killed at Bosworth Field by Henry Tudor, the last Lancastrian claimant to the throne. His claim was dubious at best, since he was descended on his mother, Margaret Beaufort's, side from the illegitimate union of John of Gaunt and Katherine Swynford, and on his father's side from the questionable marriage of Catherine Valois and Owen Tudor. During his exile in Brittany and France Tudor had secured the support of disaffected Yorkists by promising to marry Elizabeth of York, the eldest daughter of Edward IV. Determined to claim the throne in his own right, he married her belatedly, to show that he had no need of her title.

Henry Tudor's reign was disturbed by several uprisings in favor of pretenders who claimed to be the rightful heirs to the Yorkist crown. In 1487 Lambert Simnel claimed to be first Clarence's son Edward, whom Henry had locked up in the Tower, and then Richard, Edward IV's younger son. Simnel was supported by Richard III's nephew, the Earl of Lincoln, and Francis Lovell, one of the late king's closest friends. They were defeated at the Battle of Stoke, Lincoln was killed, Lovell escaped, and Simnel was captured. In a show of mercy, and proof that he had a sense of irony, Henry spared the young man's life, and gave him a job in the royal kitchens.

The next rebellion was longer lasting, and frightened the king sufficiently that all who were involved lost their lives. Perkin Warbeck, claiming to be Richard of York, was sponsored, like Simnel, by the Dowager Duchess of Burgundy, the sister of Edward IV and Richard III. The Lancastrians declared that he was the son of a merchant from Tournai who happened to bear a striking resemblance to Edward IV, and that the duchess had coached him carefully. Others believed, as many, including Horace Walpole, have since then, that he was who he claimed. Warbeck had the support of both the French and Scottish kings, both ever eager to cause trouble for England, and he invaded the country, expecting the people to rise to his support. He was disappointed. Henry Tudor may have been unpopular, even hated, but the English were tired of war and cared not at all who sat on the throne as long as they were left in relative peace. When Warbeck was finally captured, he was put under house arrest until Henry could find, or manufacture, an excuse to put him to death. The king was negotiating for a Spanish marriage for his son Arthur, and Ferdinand and Isabella were reluctant to marry their daughter to a young man who might not succeed to the throne. As long as there were any claimants, however remote their chances of success, the marriage would not take place. Henry, therefore, arranged that Warbeck should be caught in a plot with young Warwick, who was simple, if not retarded, and the two were tried and found guilty of treason, and executed. The Tudor succession was secured, and the Wars of the Roses were at an end.

Long before the conflict between the houses of York and Lancaster was termed the Wars of the Roses, it was the subject of writers of popular fiction, who dramatized, romanticized, and trivialized its characters and events, and occasionally even portrayed them accurately. The earliest writings were ballads and poems, usually anonymous, written during or shortly after the events they portrayed, and always showing a strong bias toward one side or the other. Since they were contemporary with their subjects, ballads were the only fiction form whose writers were not influenced by the chronicles of the sixteenth and seventeenth centuries.

Some of the earliest ballads of the period under discussion express support for the popular Dukes of Gloucester and York, and are bitterly critical of their enemies, especially Suffolk and Somerset. These favorites of Margaret of Anjou were blamed, along with the queen, for the mismanagement of the government, while the weak Henry VI, who was generally loved, if not admired, escaped the worst censure. Several ballads, such as the "Ballade Set on the Gates of Canterbury," "The Day Will Dawn," and "The Bisson Leads the Blind," lament the hard times and the perceived fall from greatness suffered by the country during the period between 1445 and 1450.

Others, however, target those Lancastrian lords who were blamed for the poverty, loss of territory and prestige, and breakdown of order. "Advice to the Court, I," written in 1450, attacks Suffolk and his friends, and suggests that any man, no matter how powerful, should be punished for giving evil counsel, by the loss of wealth and position. A sequel, "Advice to the Court, II," charges these same advisors with beggaring the king and oppressing the commons, and urges the king to control and punish the traitors. The Duke of Suffolk, the man deemed most responsible for problems at home and in France, was the target of two of the most blatantly anti-Lancastrian ballads. In the "Arrest of the Duke of Suffolk," the author gloats over the duke's downfall, caused by his responsibilty for the unpopular marrriage between Henry VI and Margaret of Anjou, the loss of English possessions in France, the death of the popular commander John Talbot, Earl of Shrewsbury, and the embezzlement of treasury funds. Suffolk was widely believed to be the queen's lover and the father of her son, and the favoritism she showed him, at the expense of both Gloucester and York, only increased his unpopularity with the commons. Both the queen and Suffolk, as well as Cardinal Beaufort and Somerset, were blamed for the mysterious and sudden death of the popular Humphrey, the "Good Duke" of Gloucester. In "The Death of the Duke of Suffolk," another ballad dating from 1450, the author, who was probably a cleric and undoubtedly a Yorkist, describes the horrible death of Suffolk at the hands of sailors who were taking him to exile in France. There is little sympathy for the murdered Suffolk, whom the writer calls Jackanapes, but rather a fervent hope that England will never again see his like.

While the Yorkist ballad writers were attacking the queen and her favorites, the Lancastrian writers were just as busy fighting back in such poems as "The Five Dogs of London," in which five servants of the Duke of York are killed by their faithless master. A few of the writers, more concerned with the country than with faction, prayed only for peace, and celebrated, prematurely, as it turned out, the reconciliation of the two sides in 1458. In "Reconciliation of Henry VI and the Yorkists," the Lancastrian writer gives thanks for the end of civil war and prays that peace might continue.

Humphrey of Gloucester, an idol to the commons and gadfly to the queen and her friends, was the subject of several early ballads and many later poems and novels. As the king's uncle and regent in England during his minority, Gloucester expected to be the ruling power behind the throne. His quarrels with Cardinal Beaufort, his opposition to the king's marriage, and his own frequently erratic behavior, destroyed his influence at court, although he remained popular with the commons. As the last surviving brother of Henry V, Humphrey was heir to the throne, and when his second wife, Eleanor Cobham, was accused of using witchcraft to encompass the death of Henry VI and make Humphrey king, she was exiled and he was disgraced. His vehement opposition to a truce with France typified his policy of opposing whatever Beaufort, Suffolk, and the queen supported. In 1447 a parliament was summoned to Bury St. Edmunds, and shortly after his arrival, Gloucester was put under house arrest. The following day he died, and immediately rumors to the effect that he had been murdered by his enemies swept the country.

Several contemporary ballads memorialize the "Good Duke," among them the "Epitaph for the Duke of Gloucester," which was at one time erroneously attributed to Lydgate. The poem is a prayer for the soul of Humphrey, murdered despite all the good he had done for his country. A later poem, from about 1460, uses the unhappy ends of both Humphrey and his wife to show the fickleness of fortune. The author of "Examples of Mutability" asserts that Humphrey had made confession to a treacherous bishop (Beaufort), who reported what he had learned to the king. Henry had his uncle arrested, and the shame and anguish of his arrest caused Humphrey's death.

The anger that swept the country after Gloucester's death was directed not at the king, but at the queen, Beaufort, Suffolk, and Somerset. Henry was loved for his gentleness and piety, but few of his subjects respected him. The general feeling seemed to be that he and the country would be happier and more at peace if he could retire to a monastery to lead a life of contemplation. "A Prayer to Henry VI," written during his lifetime, is a plea to that "blessed king so full of vertue" to intercede with Jesus and Mary for help in times of trouble.

As the troubles mounted, more ballads in support of the Yorkists appeared. The writer of "Prelude to the Wars" laments the decline or defeat of the heroes of England's past glory, the dismal state of the country in 1449, and the uncertainty of York's future. After York's death and the accession of his son as Edward IV, there were many ballads written to celebrate the glory of his house. The writer of "The Rise of the House of York," celebrating Edward's coronation, compares England to a garden overgrown with weeds, meaning the House of Lancaster, which would now be put right by the heir of York, whom God has helped to overcome his enemies. "A Political Retrospect" celebrates Edward's victory over the usurping Lancastrians, while "Twelve Letters Save England" sings the praises not only of Edward, but his father, Warwick, and Salisbury, who helped to achieve his victory. "The Battle of Towton" tells of Edward's great victory as the "chief flour of this lond," who saved England from Margaret of Anjou and her army of savage men from the north.

Lancastrian sentiment found few expressions during the first years of Edward's reign, but Warwick's exile in 1470, during which he joined forces with the Lancastrians, elicited "Willikin's Return," in which the author looks forward to the restoration of Henry VI with the earl's help. The restoration was short-lived, and Yorkist sentiment, always strong in London, is expressed in "The Battle of Barnet," where the author exhorts the English to accept the return of Edward IV, who had been unjustly deprived of his inheritance by Henry VI, and to live in peace and reconciliation.

Verse continued to be a vehicle for partisan sentiment throughout the centuries following the Wars of the Roses, although few voices were raised in support of the Yorkists until fairly recent times. The Tudor version of history, articulated so convincingly by Shakespeare, had its precedents in the works of lesser authors. Humphrey Brereton, a retainer of the Stanley family, is credited with at least two early sixteenth century ballads, both of which are designed as much to glorify his patrons as the Tudors. "Ladye Bessiye" is a paeon to Elizabeth of York, who is portrayed as the moving force behind the plot to bring Henry Tudor to England so that he can wrest the crown from the murderous usurper Richard III. She is aided by the Stanleys, using Brereton as the messenger between the conspirators. "Bosworth ffeilde" relates the role of the Stanleys in securing Tudor's victory and the crown, and although it is a song of celebration of the outcome, the author concedes that Richard III had attempted, against the advice of evil counselors, to be a wise ruler.

Ballads and songs dealing with historical subjects, blatantly political as most of them were, were considered by later generations to be an excellent way to teach people about the great events of their country's past, but how much confidence can be placed in their historical accuracy? There is little doubt that they were a good barometer of the sentiments of the various factions of both nobility and commons, and some writers believed that they give an accurate account of the history of the period. The compiler and editor of the three volume *Collection of Old Ballads*, for example, wrote in his introduction, "I have known children who never would have learn'd to read, had they not took a delight in poring over *Jane Shore*, or *Fair Rosamund*: and several fine historians are indebted to Historical Ballads for all their learning. For had not Curiosity and a Desire of comparing these Poetical Works with Ancient Records, first incited them to it, they never would have given themselves the Trouble of diving into History." Unfortunately, some writers, and by no means all of them writers of fiction, seem to have been influenced more by these poetical works, than by those ancient records. Both Bishop Thomas Percy and J. O. Halliwell, who published versions of "The Song of the Lady Bessie," accepted parts of that fantastic tale which are unverified and unverifiable by any other source, as the truth.

James Gairdner, the 19th century historian whose biography of Richard III was considered the standard until well into the 20th century, while noting that the poem contained many anachronisms and "fantastic additions which the author has made to the plain and simple facts," still believed that "There is certainly a great deal of truth in the poem."[1]

Charles Ross, the author of highly regarded biographies of Edward IV and Richard III, writing of Brereton's other poem, "The Ballad of Bosworth Field," declares that "on both historical and literary grounds, the ballad deserves most serious consideration as a major historical source."[2] The author, he notes, was a well-informed contemporary, who, although he was probably not present at Bosworth, nevertheless was able to supply the names of many of those who fought on both sides. It should be noted, however, that Gairdner, and to a much lesser extent Ross, accepted the Tudor version of the life and character of Richard III.

The sixteenth century saw a flowering of long narrative poems, many concerning themselves with the Wars of the Roses, particularly the role played by Richard III. William Baldwin's *Mirror for Magistrates*, which appeared first in 1559 and went into several expanded editions, contained poems by different authors, who expounded at length on the actions and motives, not only of Richard III, but Clarence, Lord Clifford, Warwick, Anthony Woodville, and others. They are all cautionary tales, designed to point out the pitfalls of too much pride and ambition, and the perils of life at the top.

Both villains and victims are represented, not infrequently in one and the same person. Each of the tragedies is narrated by the ghost of the title character, and since the subjects were chosen for their value as object lessons, rather than for their historical importance, facts are changed or distorted to make a point. The sources employed by the authors of the *Mirrour* tragedies were the same as those used by Shakespeare.

In 1610 Richard Niccols published a revised edition of the *Mirrour* entitled *A Winter Night's Vision*, which contained ten new tragedies written by Niccols, including two about Richard III; "The Lamentable Lives and Deaths of the Two Young Princes, Edward the fifth, and his brother Richard Duke of Yorke" and "The Tragical Life and Death of King Richard the Third." Both owe much to Thomas More and Shakespeare. Michael Drayton, the author of several works about the period, also contributed one tragedy to this collection.

Drayton was also the author of *England's Heroical Epistles*, a collection of verse letters, purportedly from historical figures. The collection includes several from the period of the Wars of the Roses, including Katherine of Valois, Owen Tudor, Suffolk, and Edward IV. Drayton took the period for his subject in a later work, *Poly-Olbion*, a historical and topographical description in verse of England and Wales, in which he gives an account of the Wars of the Roses, and a description of the terrain on which the battles were fought.

Other epic poems written by Samuel Daniel (*The Civile Warres betweene the Howses of Lancaster and Yorke*), Christopher Brooke (*The Ghost of Richard III*), historian Sharon Turner (*Richard the Third*), and novelist Anne Radcliffe (*St. Alban's Abbey*), show a continued interest in the subject by both poets and other writers from the 16th through the 19th centuries. Although the epic form is infrequently employed by 20th century poets, the subject of the Wars of the Roses continues to engage their interest. Alfred, Lord Douglas' "Perkin Warbeck" laments the tragic fate of the unfortunate pretender, while science fiction/fantasy writer Ursula Le Guin, in "Richard," describes the betrayal and death of Richard III, and the destruction of his reputation.

When one thinks of plays written about the Wars of the Roses, Shakespeare's name is the first, perhaps the only, one that comes to mind. Certainly no writer has had more influence on the way we view the characters and events of the period, despite the distortions of fact, the near caricature portrayal of Richard III, and the anachronisms which abound in the three parts of *Henry VI* and *Richard III*. In his play *Richard and Anne,* Maxwell Anderson makes much of the idea that, although what Shakespeare was writing was drama and not history, people preferred his version to the truth, because it was much more interesting. At the end of the play Richard notes sadly:

Maybe when a great poet takes over history--
Whether it's lies or truth--and writes his vision
Into such blazing words, that's reality-- What really happened has no chance against it.--
Beware of great poets, then.
What they say is final, can't be contradicted.

Although Shakespeare is the best, and best-known of the playwrights who wrote in English about the wars between Lancaster and York, he was neither the first nor the last. *The True Tragedy of Richard III*, an earlier anonymous play, inspired and influenced Shakespeare, who borrowed several of its ideas and lines. He, in turn, inspired others, like John Crowne, whose two plays about Henry VI closely follow Shakespeare's in some respects, notably in his portrayal of "Good Duke Humphrey' and Richard of Gloucester. He adds some fantastic details of his own, however, including Warwick's blighted passion for Elizabeth

Woodville, which causes him to rebel against Edward IV.

John Caryll, John Ford, Nicholas Rowe, Thomas Heywood, and others, while writing on different aspects of the Wars of the Roses, all accepted Shakespeare's interpretation of the character of Richard III, Henry VII, and other figures of the period. This is not surprising, since at that time few voices had been raised to dispute its truth. In the 18th century Colley Cibber's, and to a lesser extent William Macready's, version of *Richard III*, which altered, omitted, and added to Shakespeare's text, increased the popularity of the play, and many of the great actors of the day made their reputations playing the hunchbacked murderer. Many of these actors, who frequently doubled as manager/playwrights, wrote and produced their own versions of Shakespeare's *Richard III* and parts II and III of *Henry VI*, as well as his other plays, to suit the talents of their companies and the tastes of their audiences. The practise continues to this day, and it is seldom that a production of either *Richard III* or *Henry VI* is done without some cuts or revisions.

During the 18th century Cibber's version of *Richard III* was the inspiration for more than a few parodies and burlesques. These works, by F. C. Burnand, William By, Charles Selby, and others, were music hall comedies, with songs set to popular tunes of the day, numerous puns and topical references, and, of course, many alterations to the text.

Several playwrights in the 19th and 20th centuries presented a point of view in direct opposition to Shakespeare's, and portrayed Richard III as the hero and Henry Tudor as the villain of their works. Caroline M. Keteltas, the author of *The Last of the Plantagenets* (1844), noted in her preface to the play that her purpose in writing it was to rescue Richard's reputation from the calumny heaped on it by Shakespeare. Richard III had other defenders in Stuart Vaughan (*The Royal Game*, 1974), and Gordon Daviot, a pen name of Elizabeth Mackintosh, who writing under the name Josephine Tey, wrote *The Daughter of Time*, one of the best known novels about the last Plantagenet. Her play *Dickon*, like the novel, portrays Richard in a most sympathetic manner. There have been several other plays which present Richard III in a kindlier light than did Shakespeare and his early followers, but the genre has not been as popular as either verse or novels.

Almost all of the significant, and some historically insignificant figures of the period were the subjects of verse, plays, and novels, either as heroes or villains. With the exception of Richard III, who was virtually always portrayed as a villain until the late 19th century, the most popular literary subject was Edward IV's 'Merry Mistress,' Jane (nee Elizabeth) Shore. Although there is very little reliable historical evidence of Jane's background or life before she became the king's mistress, Sir Thomas More has fixed her indelibly in the imagination as a kind, generous young woman, whose morals may well have raised concern among the clergy, and eyebrows among the commons, but who was ever ready to help those who petitioned her to intercede with the king. Her cruel treatment at the hands of Richard of Gloucester after Edward's death is movingly described by More, who probably exaggerated both her influence on the late king, and the extent of her fall.

Jane Shore, as viewed by the poets, playwrights, and novelists, had a variety of maiden names. She was Jane Wainstead in the various versions of *The History of Jane Shore*, Jane Winstead in Mrs. Bennett's novel, and Jane Milverton in William Harrison Ainsworth's novel about her. Her name in fact may have been Elizabeth Lambert.[3] Jane is frequently referred to as "The Goldsmith's Wife," but although it is generally believed that her husband was one William Shore, a mercer, there is no evidence to indicate that he followed the goldsmith's trade.

Whatever Jane's maiden name or her husband's occupation, she has emerged as one of the most popular, and frequently appealing, figures of the period. Perhaps this is because her life is legend, and there are few facts to contradict it. More claims that she was still alive, though ancient, when he wrote his history, but that even then vestiges of her great beauty remained. Her reputed charm, wit, and beauty, and her meteoric rise and fall, made her an irresistible subject, and an example of the wages of sin, for poets, novelists, and playwrights from the sixteenth century to the present. She is the pathetic heroine of many poems, novels, and plays, and figures importantly in others.

In the earliest works she is generally shown to be a repentant woman, intent on warning others to avoid the pitfalls which led to her downfall. As her legend grew, so did her character, from a merely pathetic symbol of a fallen woman, to a forceful, even domineering influence at court. In Ainsworth's *The Goldsmith's Wife*, Jane begins as a flighty young woman, but develops into a skilled diplomat who helps the king make important political decisions. Both Jean Plaidy (*The Goldsmith's Wife*) and Philip Lindsay (*The Merry Mistress*) portray Jane as the victim of the queen's son Dorset, who seduced her into treason against the Duke of Gloucester, but Lindsay saves her from the penury she is reduced to in the first novel, by having her marry Richard Lynom, Richard's solicitor. Whatever her character or fate, and whether she was viewed as the victim of Richard III, Hastings, or Dorset, she continues to fascinate both writers and readers.

Humphrey of Gloucester has almost as many partisans and detractors as his nemesis, Margaret of Anjou. Humphrey had many enemies during his lifetime. They ranged from the impotent Katherine of Valois, who hated and feared him for separating her from her son, Henry VI, and forbidding her to marry Owen Tudor, to the powerful Margaret of Anjou and her supporters. These included Bishop Beaufort, Somerset and Suffolk, who all opposed Gloucester's plans for war with France. Humphrey was the darling of the commons, a generous and learned patron of the arts, and an unstable and quixotic leader. Even those writers who admired his learning and fidelity to his brother Henry V, fault him for his impetuous and ill-considered policies. His mysterious death is attributed by those writers who support the Yorkist cause to Margaret of Anjou, Beaufort, and Somerset. Those writers sympathetic to the queen and her faction believe it to be a fortuitious accident, and deplore the implication that there was foul play involved.

Henry VI is accounted by most writers, even those with Yorkist sympathies, to be an innocent, saintly man who had the great misfortune to be born to a position for which he had no talent, and little taste. He would, both his supporters and detractors agree, have been happier living the life of a monk, and England would no doubt have enjoyed more peace and security if he had retired quietly to a monastery. Henry was weak, ineffectual, subject to periodic bouts of madness, and was completely dominated by his vengeful and arrogant wife, Margaret of Anjou. Margaret was both the pawn and the leader of her faction, and her policy tended to be based on her passionate hatreds and her desire to reward her favorites, rather than on what might benefit her new country, and as a result, she has had few defenders among either historians or writers of fiction. The chronicler Hall declared that the marriage "semed to many, bothe infortunate, and unprofitable to the realme of England, and that for many causes." He notes that, instead of bringing a dowry, the Marquis of Suffolk gave both money and lands to her father, and that the marriage so alienated the Earl of Armingnac, that he expelled the English from territory that they had won at great cost in France. "But," Hall concludes, "most of all it should seme, that God with this matrimony was not content. For after this spousage the kynges frendes fell from hym, both in England and in Fraunce, the Lordes of his realme, fell in division emongest themselfes, the commons rebelled against their sovereigne Lorde, and naturall Prince, feldes wer foughten, many thousands slain, and finally, the kyng deposed, and his sonne slain, and this Quene sent home again, with asmuche misery and sorowe, as she was received with pompe and triumphe, suche is worldly unstableness, and so waveryng is false flattering fortune."[4]

The queen's show of favoritism toward Somerset and Suffolk did not go unremarked by either nobles or commons, and as her unpopularity grew, and her vengefulness towards the Yorkists increased, scandalous rumors about her and her favorites began to circulate. These were fed as much by Henry's monkish piety and periods of madness, as by the queen's behavior, and when their son Edward was born, there were many who believed, and a few who said openly, that he was not fathered by the king. The scandal was fed inadvertently by Henry himself, who was suffering from one of his mad spells, and could not be roused sufficiently to acknowledge his child. When, months later, he recovered his wits and was shown the young prince, he declared that the infant must have been fathered by the Holy Ghost.

The death of Humphrey of Gloucester, which many blamed on the queen and her faction, brought matters to a head, and Henry was forced to exile Suffolk. The duke was forcibly taken from the ship that was carrying him into exile, and murdered. The Lancastrians, and especially the desolate queen, blamed the Duke of York, but the commons rejoiced at the death of the hated Suffolk. Very little sympathy has been extended to either Margaret of Anjou or her supposed paramours by writers of succeeding generations. Shakespeare implies an intimate realtionship between the queen and Suffolk, and makes her an instigator of Gloucester's murder. In John Crowne's play, which owed much to Shakespeare, Margaret and Suffolk are admitted lovers who connive at both Humphrey's murder and Eleanor Cobham's downfall. Later writers have accepted many of these suppositions, portraying the queen as singleminded in her determination to destroy the hated Yorkists, and save the throne for her son.

Margaret has had defenders as well, although they are not as numerous as her detractors. Lady Georgianna Fullerton's *A Stormy Life* shows a proud, spirited, intelligent woman, who believes from childhood that she was born to be a queen, but who is destroyed by the cruel buffetings of fate and hostile political forces. In Barnaby Ross's *The Passionate Queen.*, Margaret is the brave, loyal wife and mother, who attempts to protect her mad husband and her innocent son from the intrigues of the English court. Betty King, the prolific writer of novels with a pro-Lancastrian slant, treats the queen with great sympathy in *Margaret of Anjou*, but shows her to be a sexually passionate woman, frustrated by her monkish husband, and generous with her favors to other men she finds attractive.

Elizabeth Woodville, Edward IV's queen, has aroused much the same feelings among writers as has Margaret of Anjou, and for similar reasons. Their marriage, performed in secret, and not revealed until months later, alienated the powerful Earl of Warwick and the nobility, as well as the commons. The new queen had a large family, and it quickly became apparent that they were to be the beneficiaries of both titles and wealth, at the expense of the old nobility. The king probably had two goals in mind in implementing this policy; he was proving to Warwick and his faction that he would not be ruled by them, and he was diffusing the power of the nobles. The idea may have been sound, but the results were disastrous, for the civil wars, which he hoped his reign would end, continued. Warwick defected to the Lancastrians and died fighting against his former protege at Barnet. The queen and her family took much of the blame for this turn of events, and the uncontrolled greed of the Woodvilles, as well as Elizabeth's vindictiveness toward her enemies, or supposed enemies, so reminiscent of that of Margaret of Anjou, alienated all classes of society.

Although Elizabeth Woodville cannot compare with either Jane Shore or Anne Neville in the number of novels, plays, or poems in which she is a sympathetic heroine, she does have her defenders. Jan Westcott, in *The White Rose*, portrays Elizabeth and her family in the kindliest light possible, S. R. Bridge endows her with humility and kindness in *The Woodville*, and other authors, mostly during the 19th century, found the romantic courtship of an innocent and injured widow irresistible. To the vast majority of writers, however, she was an ice-queen, cold and scheming, who had no interest except to increase the wealth and power of her family.

Two bizarre eighteenth century plays are exceptions to the general view of Elizabeth Woodville, and her role in the lives of Edward IV and other members of the court. The earlier of the two is Paul Hiffernan's *The Earl of Warwick, or The King and Subject; a Tragedy*, written in 1764, and the second is *The Earl of Warwick, a Tragedy*, by Thomas Francklin, written in 1766, which follows Hiffernan's work closely. The theme of both plays is the great love between Warwick and Elizabeth Woodville, and the bitter quarrel which it engendered between the earl and the king, who was also in love with Elizabeth. Margaret of Anjou persuades the proud and embittered Warwick to join with her to replace Edward with Henry VI, intending to destroy him when her goal is accomplished. Elizabeth attempts to heal the rift between the two men, but the reconciliation comes too late. Warwick leads his men against the king, but regrets his action and decides to return to his Yorkist loyalty, whereupon Margaret stabs him. In the Hiffernan play, the distraught Elizabeth then stabs herself, and throws herself on her dead lover's body. Francklin ends his play with Edward and Warwick asking each other's forgiveness, and the earl asking Elizabeth to marry the king. Edward promises, over his friend's corpse, to pattern himself on the great Warwick, and he and Elizabeth are married.

Both playwrights admired both Elizabeth Woodville and Warwick, Hiffernan calling the earl the "born enemy to oppression of every sort, and strenuous asserter of the 'Rights and Liberty of Man'." Francklin, at least, realized, and apologized for the lack of historical accuracy in his play, excusing it on the grounds that he wrote of the distant past, in apparent ignorance of the widely available 16th and 17th century chronicles.

Warwick's younger daughter, Anne Neville, who succeeded Elizabeth as queen, is a much more sympathetic figure in fiction than her predecessor. Although she was virtually ignored by the poets, Shakespeare made up for this neglect by portraying her as a spirited and intelligent heroine in *Richard III*. She suffered another long period of neglect following this play, only to be re-discovered during the 20th century. She has since been portrayed as Warwick's mistreated pawn (Evelyn Hood's *The Kingmaker's Daughter* and Frances Irwin's *The White Pawn*), the long-suffering wife of the villainous Richard III (Francis Leary's *The Swan and the Rose* and Jan Westcott's *Set Her on a Throne*), and as the happy and contented, though sickly wife of her adored and adoring husband (Margaret Davidson's *My Lords Richard*, Sharon K. Penman's *The Sunne in Splendour*, and Hilda Brook Stanier's *The Kingmaker's Daughter*).

Elizabeth of York, the eldest child of Edward IV, and the wife of Henry Tudor, has been the subject of as many differing interpretations of her life and character as has Anne Neville or Richard III. She was the doughty heroine of Humphrey Brereton's "Song of the Ladye Bessie," a young woman of fierce loyalty to her family and then to her chosen husband Henry Tudor. Elizabeth masterminds the plot to remove her wicked uncle Richard III from the throne and turn it over to Henry. This imaginative work was the basis for Blanche Hardy's *Sanctuary*, and one or two other novels.

Novelists of both Lancastrian and Yorkist leanings have generally been very sympathetic to Elizabeth, the former viewing her as the loving and beloved wife of Henry VII, and their marriage as the joining of the red and white roses to bring peace and prosperity to England. Yorkists also favor the first Tudor queen, but they see her more as a victim of Henry VII than the willing recipient of his bounty. In their view Elizabeth was a pawn whom Henry most reluctantly agreed to marry in order to secure the support of disaffected Yorkists in driving Richard III from the throne. Elizabeth had little say in the matter, and indeed she, according to many of these writers, was in love with her uncle, and hoped to marry him after Anne's death. Her marriage to the cold, crafty Henry was one of necessity, and he neither loved nor trusted her, and indeed was in no hurry to fulfill his promise, or to have her crowned. Henry's shabby treatment of his wife, the daughter of his hated enemy, as described by Francis Bacon in his *Reign of Henry VII*, forms the basis of several novels, including Hilda B. Stanier's *Plantagenet Princess* and Brenda Honeyman's *Richmond and Elizabeth*.

Cecily of York, the mother of Edward IV and Richard III, and Margaret Beaufort, Henry Tudor's mother, were both fairly important players in the games of power during the Wars of the Roses, and both have attracted their fair share of attention from novelists. Indeed, each has been the heroine of at least one series of novels, Proud Cic of Eleanor Fairburn's quartet, and Margaret Beaufort of several of Betty King's.

Cecily Neville has generally been treated kindly by fiction writers, and although her excessive pride has been noted and criticized by authors of both Yorkist and Lancastrian sympathies, and her purported, but unproven affair with the archer Blackburn frequently noted, she seems to have aroused little antipathy and much sympathy. Her relations with her ambitious husband and sons are, of course, a matter of speculation, since it is impossible to determine with any degree of certainty how she felt about the their determination to seize the crown. She was, after all, a member of the powerful and ambitious Neville family. The Earl of Salisbury was her brother, and Warwick the Kingmaker her nephew. She married the Duke of York, the heir of arguably the most powerful family in the realm. Whether her husband was nothing more than a greedy and over-mighty magnate whose lifelong ambition it was to wear the crown he believed rightfully his, or a normally ambitious man whose only interest, aside from his family, was to ensure that the country was run in an orderly manner, is subject to dispute.

To writers of Lancastrian sympathy, York was a cruel, power-mad baron, disloyal to his king and careless of all but his own faction. Anne Radcliffe, in *St. Albans's Abbey*, portrays him as cruel, deceitful, and devious, while Guy

Paget, in *The Rose of Raby*, views him as a reluctant would-be usurper, forced into the leadership of the faction which abhors the misgovernment of Margaret of Anjou and her favorites. Whatever the view of York and his actions, most writers agree that he had the full support of his wife, and that after his death she encouraged her son Edward to continue his father's pursuit of the crown.

Most authors, following Hall, note that Cecily objected to her son's marriage to Elizabeth Woodville, and it is true that after that event she retired in seclusion, rarely appearing at court. Her relations with her two other surviving sons, George of Clarence and Richard of Gloucester, have also been the subject of much dispute. Some writers aver that the feckless George was her favorite, and that she pleaded with Edward to spare his life. Others insist that Richard, her youngest, was also her dearest. Thomas More, however, accused Richard of slandering his mother by implying that he was the only true son of the Duke of York. If More was correct, the duchess was the most forgiving of mothers, for Richard was staying with her at Baynard's Castle, her London home, at the time, and remained there even after the supposed accusation, delivered by Friar Shaa in his speech at Paul's Cross.

There is no doubt that Margaret Beaufort gave her wholehearted support to her son Henry Tudor's claim to the throne. Indeed, she dedicated her life and considerable intelligence to plotting on his behalf, and was rewarded for her successful efforts by Henry's complete devotion and trust. With the possible exceptions of Jasper Tudor and Bishop Morton, she was the only one who could claim them.

The brilliant and pious Margaret, daughter and heir of John, first Duke of Somerset, married three times. Her first husband was Edmund Tudor, the eldest son of Henry V's widow Catherine of Valois and her husband or lover Owen Tudor. Edmund died before their son was born, and Margaret subsequently married Henry Stafford, and then Lord Thomas Stanley, but she may have taken an oath of celibacy after Edmund's death. In any event, Henry was her only child. She was a woman of formidable learning, and a great patron of both Oxford and Cambridge Universities. Her character, however, depends on which author one reads. To the Lancastrians she was a paragon of virtue, a warm and loving mother and mother-in-law, and a loyal friend. They portray her as a woman so dedicated to helping her son gain his rightful crown, that she denied herself the love and comfort offered her by her brother-in-law Jasper, whom she loved in return, in order to stay in England and work to achieve her goal.

Writers sympathetic to the Yorkists present a very different Margaret, a cold, deceitful plotter, who would stop at nothing to destroy Richard III, the man who stood in her son's way. One writer, Jean Evans, in *The White Rose of York*, even goes so far as to suggest that it was Margaret who encouraged Buckingham to murder the princes in the Tower, hoping that he would be executed for the deed, and thus leave the way clear for her son to seize the crown.

Perkin Warbeck, the pretender whose claim to be Richard of York, the younger son of Edward IV, presented the most serious threat to Henry Tudor's throne, has been the subject of many novels, plays, and poems, either as hero or dupe. Writers from Horace Walpole to the present have accepted Warbeck's claim as genuine, arguing that his intimate knowledge of the court and family of Edward IV proved that he was no imposter. Others insist that his strong resemblance to the late king proved only that Edward, known for his philandering, had left his bastards on the continent as well as at home. These writers believe that Henry Tudor was correct in his judgment that Warbeck was nothing more than the son of a Flemish merchant who had been carefully coached by Margaret of Burgundy, Edward's sister, who planned to use him to dethrone the man who had killed her brother Richard. Historical proof to settle the question conclusively is lacking, but the romantic story of the handsome youth, who so charmed and convinced so many who met him that he was the son of Edward IV, continues to attract both writers and readers.

Perkin Warbeck's claim to be Richard of York points up one of the most persistant and puzzling historical mysteries; what was the fate of the Princes in the Tower? Were Edward V and Richard, Duke of York, the two young sons of Edward IV, murdered by their wicked, hunchbacked uncle Richard of Gloucester, so that he could seize the throne? Sir Thomas More's version of the story, which was followed and accepted without question by generations of chroniclers, historians, and writers of fiction, tells a tale of the pitiless, corrupt, and deformed Richard, who hires Sir James Tyrell and his henchmen, Dighton, Greene, and Slaughter, to smother the boys in their beds, and to hide the corpses. More's history, which was printed in the chronicles of Fabyan, Hall, and Holinshed, among others, was used by the writer most responsible for the portrait of Richard III familiar to nearly everyone since the 16th century. Shakespeare, in his plays *Henry VI, Parts II and III*, and *Richard III*, portrayed the king as the personification of evil, a "heap of wrath, foul indigested lump, as crooked in [his] manners as in [his] shape." So monstrous is he that not even his own mother can love him, and so he makes a conscious effort to become as evil in character as in appearance, declaring, "Since the heavens have shaped my body so, Let Hell make crook'd my mind to answer it." This is somewhat of a twist on the idea prevailing at the time, that a misshapen body was the outward manifestation of an evil mind, a notion that still had wide acceptance until fairly recent times.

Shakespeare stressed, but did not invent, the difference between the evil, deformed Richard and the angelic Henry, whom Hall described as "a man of no great stature, but so formed and decorated with all gyftes and lyniamentes of nature that he seemed more an angelical creature than a terrestriall personage."[5] Shakespeare, following the chroniclers and More, took up the theme of the physical and moral differences between the men, portraying Richard as the personification of evil and Henry Tudor as God's instrument to destroy him.

More importantly, however, they introduced the idea, with virtually no basis in fact, that Richard was the usurper and Tudor the rightful heir to the throne. This theme gained wide acceptance only by virtue of the fact that few men were willing to dispute Henry's shaky claim after he had secured the throne, and had succeeded in defeating the last Yorkist claimants. He and his son, Henry VIII, between them also used judicial murder to root out the last Plantagenets with any claim, however remote, to the throne. How very fortunate they were to have had the genius of Shakespeare to impress on men of the late Tudor and early Stuart periods, and all future generations, the history of Richard III that they wanted the world to believe.

This view, often called the 'Tudor Myth,' was accepted by poets, playwrights, and novelists well into the 19th century, in the beginning, at least, because it was politically the safest course, and later, because this version had been around so long few people had any interest in challenging it. Although a few writers, notably Horace Walpole, had published works in which they attempted to rescue the reputation of Richard III by attacking the Tudor version as false and self-serving, they were largely ignored or discounted as gadflies. In the latter half of the 19th and early 20th centuries, however, a slight, but significant change can be seen in the historical and fictional treatment of both Richard III and his successor. Although Henry Tudor's image had changed quite early from Hall's 'angelicall creature' to the more accurate one of the cold, miserly, and vindictive man portrayed by Francis Bacon, he was still generally seen as the hero who had saved England from the clutches of the villainous Richard III. In his 1849 novel, *The Woodman*, G. P. R. James refers to Henry as 'a cold and greedy Prince,' but nevertheless finds him preferable to his predecessor, 'a murdering usurper.

Although Henry is still accorded high marks for his political and financial acumen, and his skill at bringing peace and prosperity to England, his personality and character were no longer viewed as exemplary. To be sure, he still has his champions, including some modern novelists who seem to agree with Hall's assessment of him, but his reputation has generally declined since Bosworth.

Richard's reputation, which changed much more slowly, has nevertheless undergone a more dramatic metamorphosis. Early in this century several novelists, taking their view of Richard from Walpole, Sir Clements Markham, and Caroline A. Halsted, his passionate admirers, and Sharon Turner and J. H. Jesse, who were more temperate, but generally favorable to him, published works in which the traditional roles of hero and villain were reversed. Some authors, such as John Reed Scott, declared him innocent of the murders of the princes. In *Beatrix of Clare*, his 1907 novel, Prince Edward kills his brother Richard and then commits suicide.

Dora Greenwwell McChesney, whose 1912 novel, *The Confession of Richard Plantagenet,* is very sympathetic to Richard, also absolves him of the murders of the princes, but he is nevertheless a limping misshapen man who is guilty of the deaths of Clarence and Edward of Lancaster. Patrick Carleton, in *Under the Hog*, portrays Richard as a just and hard-working king, who nevertheless orders the deaths of his nephews in order to forestall an uprising in their names. Other novelists, like Marion Palmer in *The White Boar*, and Francis Leary in *Fire and Morning*, support the theory that Buckingham was responsible for their murders. In *The Swan and the Rose*, an earlier novel, however, Leary portrays a different Richard, an evil, misshapen tyrant who forces Anne Neville to marry him. Four years later, in *Fire and Morning*, he is merely hard and ruthless, but just.

It was Josephine Tey, in her 1951 novel *The Daughter of Time*, who went the farthest in rehabilitating the reputation of Richard III, and it is this work, in which the maligned monarch is portrayed as positively saintly, that has been most responsible for the changed perception many people have today. Tey attempted to demolish More's and Shakespeare's portrayal of Richard as a cunning, heartless monster, who carried out his plan to seize the throne by the systematic murders of everyone who stood in his path. In this work More, Polydore Vergil, and especially Henry Tudor are the villains whose treachery and deliberate lies, in the service of their own ambitions, contrast markedly with the nobility and loyalty of the king whose reputation they destroyed. The truth, no doubt, lies somewhere between these two poles.

Many of the novels included in this bibliography were written in the last fifteen or twenty years, during the time when the 500th anniversary of the Battle of Bosworth Field reawakened interest in the period. Unfortunately, the majority of these are of the paperback romance variety, despite the fact that some of them were published in hardcover. Although some of these romance writers have apparently done some research on the 15th century, most show only a superficial knowledge of the politics and personalities of the time. Without exception, they are passionately partisan, on one side or the other, and the characters tend to be metaphors for virtue or vice, rather than human beings.

It is impossible to say with certainty what influences a writer to adopt the cause of either York or Lancaster, but religion is apparently one factor. This holds true more for 19th and early 20th century writers than for more recent ones, who tend not to be quite so open about their religious bias. In general, the earlier Catholic writers tend to favor the Lancastrian cause, and this is most evident in their treatment of Henry VI and Margaret of Anjou. Some, like Sophie Maude, the author of *The Hermit and the King*, Enid Dinnes, author of *The Three Roses*, and Robert Hugh Benson, the author of *The History of Richard Raynal, Solitary* and a Roman Catholic clergyman, wrote specifically for Catholic young people, while others, like Lady Georgianna Fullerton, the author of *A Stormy Life*, were just influenced by their faith. All of these writers viewed Henry as a Christian martyr, who should have been canonized.

Protestant authors, on the other hand, are not always to be found in the

Yorkist camp, but those that are, frequently endow their characters with Lollard sympathies. John Reed Scott, for example, in *Beatrix of Clare*, has Richard III reading an English language Bible. The hero of W. S. Symonds' *Malvern Chase* is a member of a Lollard family, which supports the Yorkists because they believe that Edward IV will support their cause. Hildebrande, the young heir, becomes disillusioned, however, when he realizes that he will get no support from the king, but although he leaves the court, he continues a loyal Yorkist.

Although Catholic clerics are frequently portrayed as villains in works by Protestant writers, few can equal the blatant bigotry of the authors of two 18th century plays. In his *King Henry the VII, or The Popish Imposter*, written in 1746, Charles Macklin portrays the Papal legate to Scotland as the evil plotter who, acting under orders from Rome, attempts to use Perkin Warbeck to drive Henry VII from the throne. Henry, it appears, has proved himself insufficiently respectful toward the pope, and must be replaced by a ruler who will accept without question all orders from Rome. In its distortion of historical fact this play is not so very different from many others, but the blatant anti-Catholic propaganda which informs it sets it apart.

Another, earlier play, *Humfrey of Gloucester* by Ambrose Philips, follows John Crowne's *Henry the Sixt; The First Part, or The Murder of the Duke of Glocester,* which itself followed Shakespeare quite closely, in that Cardinal Beaufort is the evil genius behind the duke's downfall and murder, but there is no overt anti-Catholic bias in the play itself. This comes in the author's preface, in which he refers to Gloucester as "a great Opposer of the oppressive usurpation of the See of Rome." In the Prologue to the play, written by Bartholomew Paman, Humphrey is described as a supporter of Wyckliffe, who was murdered for his opposition to priest-ridden Henry VI and his ministers.

The nineteenth century novelist Emily Sarah Holt also used her works as vehicles to express both her anti-Catholicism and anti-Semitism. In *The Tangled Web*, her novel about the Perkin Warbeck rebellion, several of the minor characters are secret Lollards, the plight of the Lollard martyrs is brought into the plot throughout, and the Catholic characters she portrays sympathetically are shown to be deluded in matters of religion. The dissolute character and irresponsible behavior of her anti-hero, Piers Osbeck, known to the English as Perkin Warbeck, is explained by the fact that he is the son of converted Jews, and when his widow, Katherine Gordon, learns of his Jewish blood after his death, her remaining affection for him turns to revulsion.

Religion, however, is just one of the factors which influence an author's defense of one side or the other in the conflict between the Houses of Lancaster and York. In most cases it is a minor consideration. More important is the almost unchallenged acceptance of the Tudor version of the life and character of Richard III. Although some authors, like Robert Louis Stevenson in *The Black Arrow*, espouse the Yorkist cause and still agree with More and

Shakespeare that the last Plantagenet was a thoroughgoing villain, many blame Edward IV and his queen for the troubles of their house. Edward's licentious-ness and inattention to the business of government in his later years, and the queen's ambitions for her large family, were without doubt contributing factors to the tragic events which followed the king's death. These themes are explored in many novels dealing with the period, including Jean Evans' *The Divided Rose,* Eleanor Fairburn's *The Rose at Harvest End,* and Mrs. Bennett's *Jane Shore.*

Many of the 19th and early 20th century novels about the Wars of the Roses were written for young people, with the aim of instilling in them an understanding and appreciation of the ideals of chivalry. The fact is, however, that chivalry on the order of that supposedly practiced by the Knights of the Round Table bore not the remotest resemblance to the way most of the nobility, either Lancastrian or Yorkist, behaved during the Wars of the Roses. But the heroes, generally Lancastrian, of books by Evelyn Everett-Green, Charlotte M. Yonge, Hawthorne Daniel, and others, were men of the highest ideals, who were willing to die in defense of their cause and their honor. To be sure, there were some few members of the nobility on both sides of the conflict who sacrificed all they possessed, including their lives, to defend the cause they believed in, but generally the partisans were defending the side which promised them the greatest material rewards, and that, on more than one occasion, was subject to change. One has only to look at the career of Richard Neville, Earl of Warwick, for an example of mutability. So rare were the instances of unswerving loyalty among the nobility, that those who calumniated Richard III after his death, yet took pains to praise him for his loyalty to his brother, while Edward lived, as well as his courage in battle.

The fact remains, however, that all of these works of fiction, whether verse, play, or novel, reflect a bias on the part of the author, and although many, especially the later ones, are well-researched, almost all omit any fact that would tend to weaken or discredit the author's argument. Some authors are more guilty than others in this regard, and they carry their bias to such lengths that their characters are not flesh and blood, but metaphors for good and evil, and they change or distort facts to suit their whim. Does this really matter? Their works are, after all, fiction, to be enjoyed for their entertainment, not their educational value, although, if the author has researched the period well, the reader can learn a good deal about it. Unfortunately, however, many novelists have only the most superficial knowledge about the events and characters, using them merely as pegs on which to hang their plots, and readers need at least a basic knowledge of the period to tell if what they are learning is accurate.

There can be little doubt, that from Tudor times until the present, many writers of both fiction and history, and those who read their works, have accepted almost without question the truth of Shakespeare's version of the Wars of the Roses, especially of the character and actions of Richard III. The Duke of Wellington's oft quoted remark that he never read history, and that the only history he knew he learned from Shakespeare, shows the great influence that works of fiction have on our beliefs. *Caveat lector.*

NOTES

1. Gairdner, James. *History of the Life and Reign of Richard the Third.* Cambridge: Cambridge University Press, 1898. p. 345.

2. Ross, Charles. *Richard III.* Berkeley and Los Angeles: University of California Press, 1981. p. 235.

3. *Ibid.* p. 138, n. 32.

4. Hall, Edward. *Chronicle.* Edited by Sir Henry Ellis. London: J. Johnson; F.C. & J. Rivington, et al., 1809. p. 205.

5. *Ibid.* p. 416.

Novels and Short Stories

1. Abbey, Anne Merton [Jean Brooks-Janowiak]. *Katherine in the Court of the Six Queens*. New York and Toronto: Bantam Books, 1989. 454pp.

Katherine Chase, grandaughter of both Edward IV and John Howard, Duke of Norfolk, becomes a lady-in-waiting to Katherine of Aragon, and serves in turn all the queens of Henry VIII. Married to one of her Howard cousins, she nevertheless falls in love with the mysterious John de Gael, who is also a Plantagenet. Mysteries of inheritance, blackmail, and mistaken identity abound, and the author offers an interesting solution to the fate of the Princes in the Tower.

2. Abbey, Margaret [Margaret York]. *The Warwick Heiress*. Vol. III: *In the Shadow of the Tower*. London: Robert Hale and Company, 1970. 190pp.

Piers Langham, the orphaned son of a man killed at Wakefield, saves the life of Alicia Standish, a lady-in-waiting to Anne Neville, and becomes a retainer of the Duke of Gloucester. The courtships of Richard and Anne, and Piers and Alicia, are set against the background of the quarrel between Warwick and Edward IV. This author knows the period well.

3. _____. *The Crowned Boar*. Vol. IV: *In the Shadow of the Tower*. London: Robert Hale and Company, 1971. 205pp. Published in the United States as *Son of York*. (See entry 4.)

In this sequel to *The Warwick Heiress*, (see entry 2) Charles Beaumont, a former squire to the Duke of Gloucester, returns to England from Burgundy, where he has been exiled for nine years. He rescues Meg Wollatt, the step-daughter of an inn-keeper, who tries to rape her, and asks Gloucester to place Meg in the duchess' charge. When Richard takes the throne after Edward's children have been declared illegitimate, he asks

Beaumont to take the younger prince to safety in Burgundy. Meg and Beaumont have fallen in love, and they marry so that she can accompany him on his secret mission.

4. _____. *Son of York*. New York: Pinnacle Books, 1973. 190 pp.

See entry 3.

5. _____. *Brothers-in-Arms*. London: Robert Hale and Company, 1973. 223pp.

Catherine Newberry, a Lancastrian orphan, swears revenge against Edward IV, Clarence, and Gloucester for the death of her father at Tewkesbury. Her plans for vengeance are forgotten when she meets and falls in love with Richard of Gloucester.

6. _____. *The Heart is a Traitor*. London: Robert Hale and Company, 1978. 189pp.

In this sequel to *Brother-in-Arms* (see entry 5) Catherine Newberry is made a ward of Richard of Gloucester. She marries Sir Hugh Kingsford, who is jealous of her love for the Duke. After the death of Edward IV, Catherine fears that her husband's jealousy will lead him to support the Woodvilles against the Protector.

7. _____. *Blood of the Boar*. London: Robert Hale Limited, 1979. 192 pp.

In this sequel to *The Heart is a Traitor* (see entry 6) Catherine Newberry's husband Hugh is banished from court for conspiring with Hastings and Stanley. Anne Neville summons Catherine to court, where she must endure the hostility of Elizabeth of York. While the king awaits the invasion of Henry Tudor, Catherine must protect her son Richard, the illegitimate son of Richard III.

8. Ainsworth, William Harrison. *The Goldsmith's Wife*. London: Tinsley Brothers, 1875. 3 Vols.

Jane Milverton, an empty-headed young woman, marries the goldsmith Shore, becomes the mistress of Edward IV, and a master of diplomacy, suggesting and negotiating the Treaty of Pequigny, and singlehandedly attempting to save Clarence's life. The plot and characters of this historically inaccurate novel by a prolific and popular Victorian writer strain credulity.

9. Akerman, John Yonge. *The Adopted Son; a Legend of the Rebellion of Jack Cade*. New York: Wilson & Company, 1842. *(Brother Jonathan. Extra. Vol. 2, no. 5. July 25, 1842).* 47pp.

In 1430, when the daughter of a wealthy merchant, who has secretly married a law student, gives birth to a baby boy, her enraged father orders his steward to dispose of the infant. The steward, unable to carry out the cruel order, places the child on the doorstep of merchant John Furnival, the father of Anna and Richard. Furnival names the baby Valentine, and brings him up as his own son. Valentine and Anna fall in love, but Richard envies and hates his foster brother, and attempts to have him murdered. Valentine joins the army and goes to France, returning on the eve of Jack Cade's rebellion. Richard, a supporter of the Duke of York, is one of the rebels, and he and Valentine settle their differences during the battle on London Bridge.

10. Allison-Williams, Jean. *Cry 'God for Richard.'* London: Robert Hale Ltd., 1981. 191pp.

After Warwick's rebellion against Edward IV in 1470, the king and his brother Richard flee into exile to Bruges. Richard meets Elinor Lovell, the sister of his friend Francis, whom he had known when they were children. They fall in love, and Elinor gives birth to their son John. The story, told by Elinor and Francis, follows Richard's life until his death at Bosworth Field.

11. _____. *Mistress of the Tabard*. London: Robert Hale Limited, 1984. 191pp.

Lucy Crosby, daughter of the owner of the Tabard, the inn in Southwark made famous by Chaucer, and niece of the builder Sir John Crosby, who designed the Duke of Gloucester's London house, is seduced by a gentleman claiming to be in service to Lord Hastings. When she discovers that he is really the married Duke of Buckingham, she is devastated, but finds comfort in the friendship of Simon Verney, a sign painter. They are befriended by Gloucester, and when Simon discovers the whereabouts of Anne Neville, who has been placed as a scullery maid by her brother-in-law Clarence, Gloucester is so grateful that he takes the young couple under his protection, and commissions Simon to paint his portrait.

12. _____. *Simon of the Tabard*. London: Robert Hale Limited, 1984. 190pp.

Simon Verney, the sign painter turned court portrait painter, (see entry 11) is sent by Hastings to Middleham to inform Richard of Gloucester of his brother's death. Rising ever higher in the Duke's confidence, Simon supports Gloucester as he takes the crown, fights off his enemies, and attempts to govern wisely. Simon is painting the king's portrait, the only one done in his lifetime, during Richard's terrible ordeal of losing his only son and his beloved wife. The painting is finished just before Richard leaves London to plan his defense against Henry Tudor's invasion.

13. *The Amours of Edward IV. An Historical Novel.* London: Printed for Richard Sare, 1700. viii + 120pp. Reprinted. New York: Garland Publishing Company, 1973.

One of the earliest novels in English, the *Amours*, according to the title page, was the work of the author of *The Turkish Spy*, but this was merely an attempt to capitalize on the name of a popular writer, and the actual author is unknown. The heroine, Elizabeth Woodville, tells her daughter the story of her life to pass the time in sanctuary. She describes the great passion that the widowed Earl of Warwick conceived for her after the earl had killed her first husband in battle. She spurns him, and when he goes to France to negotiate a marriage for the king, she arranges to meet Edward IV to beg him not to force her to marry the earl. Edward falls madly in love with her, and persuades her to marry him, so enraging Warwick, that he rebels against the king. The plot, based more on the author's imagination than historical fact, was probably the inspiration of entries 525, 531.

14. Anand, Valerie. *Crown of Roses.* London: Headline Book Publishing PLC, 1989. 404pp.

Fourteen-year-old Petronel is brought home from the convent to marry fifty-year-old Lionel Eynesby, in order to mend a quarrel between their families. She falls in love with Lionel's nephew, an illegitmate son of Richard, Duke of York, and bears him a son, whom she passes off as Lionel's. After the death of Richard III, the Yorkists attempt to use the boy to impersonate the younger son of Edward IV.

15. _____. *Women of Ashdon.* London: Headline Book Publishing PLC, 1992. New York: St. Martin's Press, 1993. 373pp.

Susannah Whitmead, the daughter of yeomen, is sent to live with wealthy relatives to be educated and make a good marriage. Although she loves Giles Saville, she is forced to marry James Weston, the owner of Ashdon.

When James is killed fighting for Richard III, Susannah marries his cousin and heir Arthur Trefusis, so that she can keep Ashdon. Arthur, angry that he has not been sufficiently rewarded by Henry Tudor, on whose side he had fought at Bosworth, joins the Perkin Warbeck rebellion, and is executed. Susannah then marries Giles, and her grand-daughter Christina inherits the debt-ridden Ashdon. Christina marries her cousin Henry Whitmead, to whom she has sold her home, so that she can keep it, and her obsession with the place nearly destroys her marriage.

16. Andrew, Prudence. *A Question of Choice*. New York: G. P. Putnam's Sons, 1962. 272pp.

   A disputed election for the position of Abbot of Woodchester Abbey in Gloucestershire in 1478 pits candidates sponsored by Edward IV and Warwick against each other. The interesting concept is marred by several factual errors and one-dimensional characters.

17. Appleyard, Susan. *The King's White Rose*. Toronto and New York: Paperjacks, Ltd., 1988. 416pp.

   Jane Shore is the king's white rose in this historical romance, in which the emphasis is more on romance than on history. Richard of Gloucester is a sinister presence, but the Marquis of Dorset is the real villain of the book.

18. Armitage, Alfred. *Red Rose and White: relating the Experience of Ralph Mortimer, Son of a Knightly House, during the Stirring Times of Richard III*. London: Shaw & Co., Ltd., 1901. 334pp.

   Not available for review.

19. Ashton-Jinks, Cicely. *Child of Promise*. London and Toronto: Cassell and Company Ltd., 1944. 266pp.

   The twelfth child born in sixteen years to the Duke and Duchess of York is weak and frail, and fearing for his life, the duchess christens him immediately. Richard of Gloucester is born as a result of the mending of a rift between the duchess and her unfaithful husband, who has sacrificed his family to his ambition. The novel follows the lives of Richard and his family until the death of his beloved wife Anne, when his mother has a premonition of the imminent destruction of the Plantagenet line.

20. Bailey, H. C. *Knight at Arms*. New York: E. P. Dutton & Company, 1925. 309pp.

In 1483 Silvain de St. Lo, a bold, adventurous French knight whose father had been deprived of his title and lands by Louis XI, returns to claim his birthright after the king's death. He captures a renegade Englishman named de Richemont, who is accused of raiding the border between France and Brittany, and decides to return him to England. When the unprepossessing de Richemont informs Silvain that he is Henry Tudor, the true king of England, he realizes that he cannot turn him over to the hunchbacked Richard III, and he saves his life and returns him to France.

21. _____. *The Merchant Prince*. London: Methuen & Company Ltd., 1926. 281pp. New York: E. P. Dutton & Company, 1929. 281pp.

During the Wars of the Roses, Hugh Camoys, a poor Southampton youth, markets his mother's embroidery work. Refusing to declare himself either Yorkist or Lancastrian, Hugh, like the other merchants, cares little for politics as long as he is left to trade in peace. When Henry VI passes an edict against the export of wool, Hugh becomes first a bootlegger, and then a wealthy and respected merchant.

22. Barnes, Margaret Campbell. *The Tudor Rose*. London: Macdonald & Company Ltd., 1952. 313pp. Philadelphia: Macrae Smith Company, 1953. 313pp.

Richard III is the reluctant villain in this story of the life of Elizabeth of York. He orders the murder of his nephews out of necessity, but the author leaves the reader with the near certainty that the younger prince escaped and reappeared as Perkin Warbeck. Henry Tudor is portrayed as a cold, conniving, and grasping man, who engineers the murder of Warbeck and the young Warwick.

23. _____. *The King's Bed*. London: Macdonald & Company, Ltd., 1961. 251pp.

The daughter of the innkeeper of the White Boar in Leicester, where Richard III spent the night before Bosworth, becomes the friend, and then the wife, of the king's illegitimate son after Richard's death. The story of the king's camp bed, left at the inn, is found in John Heneage Jesse's *Memoirs of Richard III*, and figures prominently in this novel.

24. Barringer, Leslie. *The Rose in Splendour: A Story of the Wars of Lancaster and York*. Illus. by Alan Blyth. London: Phoenix House Ltd., 1952. 160pp.

Dickon Thorn, son of a sheepfarmer in Yorkshire, vows to avenge his father's murder by the Lancastrian Lord Dacre during the riots that followed the Duke of York's death at Wakefield. On his way to begin his apprenticeship in York, Dickon runs into the Yorkist army at Towton and meets an old friend of his father's. He finds and kills Dacre, and is rewarded by Edward IV. He finds further opportunities to help the king in York, and in the process destroys the enemies of his family.

25. Barrington, Michael. *A Mystery to This Day*. Illus. London: At the Press of Shield and Spring, 1949. 156pp.

Pierrequin Warbeck, the son of a Tournai merchant and his wife, is cruelly mistreated by his father. When he brings his mother's embroideries to the Duchess of Burgundy, sister of Edward IV, she is struck by his resemblance to the late king. The duchess discovers that Pierrequin's mother had had an affair with Edward during his exile, and the boy was the result. The duchess, who wants to replace Henry VII with a Plantagenet, convinces Pierrequin that he is Richard of York, and finances a rebellion against Tudor. When the rebellion fails, Warbeck realizes that he is not Richard, and he goes to his death willingly, never knowing that he is truly the son of Edward IV.

26. Belle, Pamela. *The Lodestar*. London: The Bodley Head Ltd., 1987. 534pp. New York: St. Martin's Press, 1987. 534pp.

Christie Heron, the son of an impoverished and uncultured Yorkshire landowner and his wife, the illegitimate sister of the Earl of Northumberland, offers his services to Richard of Gloucester. He rises rapidly, and when Richard becomes king he entrusts Christie and James Tyrell with spiriting Edward IV's sons, whom Buckingham had tried to poison, to safety. Christie is captured at Bosworth, and convinces Henry Tudor that both boys are dead.

27. Bennett, Mrs. [Mary]. *Jane Shore; or The Goldsmith's Wife*. London: Milner & Company, Ltd., n.d. 288pp.

The Jane Shore of this Victorian novel, in addition to being beautiful and merry, is a moralizing scold, who becomes the self-appointed conscience of Edward IV. After the king's death, she repents of her sinful life, and before she dies she is reconciled with her husband. He then goes on to support Henry Tudor's claim to the throne.

28. Bennetts, Pamela. *Bright Son of York*. London: Robert Hale and Company, 1971. 287 pp.

With the help of his cousin Richard Neville, Earl of Warwick, Edward Plantagenet seizes the crown from the weak-minded, pious Henry VI. Edward's secret marriage to Elizabeth Woodville alienates Warwick, who plots to restore Henry VI to the throne. Dominic Rocheford, a friend of Edward's, attempts to discover and foil Warwick's plans.

29. _____. *The Third Richard*. London: Robert Hale and Company, 1972. 288pp.

After the death of Edward IV, Giles Ravenbrook, one of the late king's friends living in Brittany, overhears a plot by agents of Henry Tudor to kill Edward's sons. He returns to London and foils an assassination attempt. When the boys disappear, Giles suspects in turn Tudor, Richard III, and Buckingham, but he becomes convinced of Richard's innocence, and fights for him at Bosworth.

30. Benson, Robert Hugh. *The History of Richard Raynal, Solitary*. London: Sir Isaac Pitman & Sons, Ltd., 1906. 257pp.

This novel purports to be a translation of a Latin version of an earlier English work written by a fifteenth century priest, which was found among the the papers of a religious order in Rome in 1904. Richard Raynal is a young solitary, or Quietist, who lives a life of contemplation dedicated to God. He is instructed in a vision to go to London to deliver a message to Henry VI. When he tells the king that he will suffer a Christ-like Passion, Henry falls into a catatonic state. Richard is attacked by an angry mob, beaten by servants of Cardinal Beaufort, who believes he has put an evil spell on the king, and thrown into prison, where he suffers physical, mental, and spiritual tortures. At Richard's deathbed, the temporarily recovered Henry convinces Beaufort that the solitary is a messenger from God. This work by a Roman Catholic cleric inspired Sophie Maude's *The Hermit and the King*. See entry 223.

31. Bentley, Elizabeth. *The York Quest*. London: Robert Hale Limited., 1980. 192pp.

When Margaret Stapleton goes to her old home of Midthorpe in Yorkshire, in response to a plea for help from her half-sister Katherine, she finds Katherine dead. Aided by Ralph Denys, Katherine's fiancé, she discovers that she was cheated of her inheritance by her late step-mother and half-brother. Katherine was murdered to prevent her from revealing the plot, and Margaret, too, is in danger. The time is August, 1485, just before Tudor's invasion, and like most Yorkshire-men, Margaret and Ralph are devoted to Richard III. After the king's death Margaret discovers that the sons of Edward IV are alive, and she and Ralph get them safely to Burgundy.

32. Bentley, Pauline. *Silk and Sword*. Richmond, Surrey: Mills & Boon, 1993. 254pp.

Eleanor Twyneham, the daughter of the cruel Yorkist lord of Highford, clashes with Conrad D'Arton, whose Lancastrian family had owned the estate until Edward IV awarded it to Twyneham. Conrad is determined to recover his birthright, and after Henry Tudor's victory at Bosworth, where Eleanor's father is killed, he claims it. Eleanor resents Conrad, but their mutual lust brings them together, and although she is betrothed to Sir Richard Norton, a man old enough to be her father, she is forced to marry Conrad. Eleanor's younger brother is mad, and when she learns that the madness runs in the family, she refuses to bear children. All ends well, however, for everyone in this novel, which is written in the cliché-ridden, overheated prose typical of the genre.

33. Bentley, Phyllis. *Sheep May Safely Graze*. Illus. by William Stobbs. London: Victor Gollancz Ltd., 1972. 159pp.

After the death of Lord Clifford, the murderer of the Earl of Rutland at Wakefield, the Yorkists swear to destroy his family. Young Henry de Clifford, his son, flees to the protection of shepherds in the Cumberlands, and after Henry VII seizes the throne and restores the Clifford estates, the young heir rewards the family who protected him from the Yorkists.

34. Bevan, Tom. *Held By Rebels*. Illus. by Percy Tarrant. London: Collins, 1906. 192pp.

Fifteen-year-old Arthur Cromer, the son of Sir Thomas Cromer and grandson of Lord Saye, two of Henry VI's most hated officials, is captured by Jack Cade. He is wounded during the encounter, but is cared for and well-treated by the rebels. Cade, believing he is helping both the youth and his own followers, turns Arthur over to his uncle, Sir Ralph, an evil, ambitious man, and his minion Father Anthony, who plan to kill him. The rebels have murdered Arthur's father and grandfather, and if he dies as well, Sir Ralph will inherit their vast estates. After Cade's defeat and death, Arthur is saved from his uncle's murderous plot by a faithful old

retainer, and all ends happily, as Sir Ralph and the evil priest meet their
deserved ends. This novel was written for young people.

35. Bibby, Violet. *The Mirrored Shield*. Illus. by Graham Humphries. Lon-
    don: Longman Young Books, 1970. 145pp.

    Thomas, an illegitimate orphan, is viewed with superstitious dread because
    he is left-handed. His left hand, however, is skilled in writing and carving,
    so he is apprenticed as a mason to the keeper of the palace. He carves the
    archbishop's shield 'mirrored' because of his left-handedness, and the
    carving of an angel resembles Margaret of Anjou. The likeness catches the
    eye of Henry VI, and Thomas is hired to help build the King's Chapel in
    Cambridge. The novel was written for young readers.

36. Blake, Margaret Glaiser. *A Sprig of Broom*. London: Robert Hale Limited,
    1979. 192pp.

    Spoiled, arrogant Yorkist heiress Cecily Hadfield is forced to marry
    Thomas Cadwalader, a Welsh supporter of Henry Tudor, in order to save
    her father's lands from confiscation. Their mutual loathing turns to love
    and survives many crises, including Cecily's arrest for treason for helping
    Richard III's illegitimate son escape to Burgundy. Thomas' unquestioned
    loyalty to Tudor saves Cecily from death, and the couple returns to Wales,
    determined to meddle in politics no more. Readers who enjoy well-written
    historical novels are advised to avoid this one.

37. Bolton, Ivy May. *A Loyal Foe; A Tale of the Rival Roses;* with an historical
    note by Cora L. Scofield. Illus. by Henry C. Pitz. London: Longmans,
    Green and Co., 1933. 200pp.

    Rex Damory, a young boy loyal to the cause of Lancaster, is imprisoned
    in the Tower during the reign of Richard III. He meets and befriends
    Edward V, the elder of the two sons of Edward IV. This work is written
    for young readers.

38. Bowden, Susan. *In the Shadow of the Crown*. Toronto and New York:
    Bantam Books, 1987. 424pp.

    Joisse Radcliffe, an orphaned Yorkshire heiress, is rescued from robbers
    by a retainer of Richard of Gloucester, and taken to Middleham Castle,
    where the duke makes her his ward. She becomes a lady-in-waiting to
    Elizabeth of York, and falls in love with Tom Thomson, a groom in
    Gloucester's service. After Bosworth, she marries Tom, relinquishing her

claim to her ancestral home, and they go to live at Jervaulx, where Tom
works as the horsemaster. The family finally recovers Radcliffe during the
reign of Henry VIII.

39. Bowen, Marjorie [Gabrielle Margaret Vere Campbell-Long]. *Dickon*. London: Hodder and Stoughton, Ltd., 1929. 343pp.

This is a novel about Richard III in which the author completely ignores
the central mystery of his reign, the fate of the Princes in the Tower. This
Richard is the perfect knight, handsome and upright, whose motive for all
his actions is to bring peace to England. After his death at Bosworth, one
of the nuns at Leicester who helps bury his naked and mutilated corpse,
describes him as "the best knight and a good king," whose "life and death
have been marvellous."

40. Brandewyne, Rebecca. *Rose of Rapture*. New York: Warner Books, 1984.
435pp.

Lady Isabelle Ashley, a Yorkist heiress, is married against her will to
Warwick, Earl of Hawkhurst, a favorite of Edward IV, and the two
eventually fall in love. Isabelle supports Richard III when he becomes
king, but Warwick joins Henry Tudor. When Tudor becomes king,
Isabelle is imprisoned in the Tower, but all ends well, with the lovers
reunited.

41. Bridge, S. R. *The Woodville*. London: Robert Hale Ltd., 1976. 202pp.

Elizabeth Woodville's Lancastrian husband dies at the Battle of St. Albans,
and when Elizabeth meets Edward IV to plead for the return of her late
husband's estates, the two fall madly in love, and she yields to his pleas to
marry him secretly. The marriage alienates the powerful Earl of Warwick,
and the rapid rise of the Woodvilles arouses the enmity of most of the old
nobility. Warwick captures the king, who escapes, but is forced to flee the
country. Elizabeth seeks sanctuary, where she gives birth to their first son.
Edward returns, Warwick is killed at Barnet, and the devoted royal couple
is reunited.

42. Britten, Frank Curzon. *Sir Roland Preederoy*: *A Tale of the Last Plantagenets*. Illus. by J. Jellicoe. London: The Religious Tract Society, 1909.
223 pp.

Roland Preederoy is the son of a loyal Lancastrian knight who has yielded
to Edward IV in order to retain his lands. His father sends him to France

with his Yorkist neighbor, Lord Thorndyke of Otterbourne, one of the king's diplomats. In France, Roland meets exiled Lancastrians Sir Roderic Marshall and his daughter Adela, and he secures permission for their return to England. Back in London, Roland saves the life of Richard of Gloucester, and although he is quite taken with the duke, he is pressured by Marshall into joining Buckingham's revolt. He, his father, and the Marshalls are captured, but Roland escapes and spends two years wandering with a troup of acrobats and clowns. He rescues Adela from her Yorkist captor, and joins Tudor's army on its way to Bosworth.

43. Brooks, Janice Young. *Forbidden Fires*. New York: Playboy Press Paperbacks, 1980. 303pp.

Margaret of Anjou's niece Mattie, the heroine of this historically inaccurate novel, and a devout Yorkist, marries Dickon, the Lancastrian son of her Yorkist stepfather, Sir Charles Seintleger. George of Clarence is plotting to kill Mattie's best friend Anne Neville, so that he can keep the entire Warwick inheritance. Anne escapes, Mattie finds her, and informs Richard of Gloucester, who rescues and marries her. Dickon deserts Mattie to join Henry Tudor, but Mattie thinks that he is killed when his boat explodes as he is escaping to France. Their son Britric becomes a companion to Edward IV's son Richard, whom he resembles. Dickon reappears and demands that she and their son return with him to France. Dickon and their son, who is mistaken for Prince Richard, are killed, and after Bosworth Margaret Beaufort, an old friend of Mattie's mother, saves Daffyd, Mattie's Welsh lover, and they and young Richard, now called Brithric, retire to Wales.

44. Buchan, John. *The Blanket of the Dark*. Boston and New York: Houghton Mifflin Company, 1931. 301pp.

Peter Pentecost, an Oxford scholar, discovers he is the grandson of the Duke of Buckingham, executed in 1483. He is used as a pawn to raise a rebellion against Henry VIII to restore the Plantagenets to the throne.

45. Bulwer-Lytton, Edward. *The Last of the Barons*. London: Saunders and Otley, 1843. 3 vols.

Warwick the Kingmaker is the hero of this anti-Yorkist novel, and Edward IV and Richard of Gloucester are the villains. Bulwer-Lytton viewed the Wars of the Roses as a struggle between the urban middle class and the feudal barons, and the Tudors as tyrants who used the middle class to destroy the feudal aristocracy, in order to establish an absolute monarchy.

46. Burgess, Mallory. *Passion Rose*. New York: Avon Books, 1987. 393pp.

Although she is in love with a man she mistakenly believes to be a Yorkist officer, Tallie, the plucky Welsh heroine, risks life and honor to put her childhood friend Henry Tudor on the throne. All ends happily, with the evil usurper Richard III dead, the rightful king Henry Tudor crowned, and the lovers reunited.

47. Burton, Edmund. *Under the Red Rose: A Tale of the Great Struggle Between the Rival Houses of York and Lancaster*. Illus. London: P. R. Gawthorn Ltd. [1946]. 152pp.

Cousins Harry and Stephen Mortimer, whose fathers were killed fighting on opposite sides at Barnet, have been brought up by their uncle, Sir Thomas Mortimer. When he dies, he leaves each youth half of an ivory marker, with instructions that his entire estate be given to the one who presents both halves to his executor. Harry, the Lancastrian, is willing to relinquish his half to Yorkist Stephen, but resents the latter's attempt to force him to do so. Harry joins Henry Tudor, determined to help defeat Richard III, and to claim the entire estate for himself. Stephen makes several attempts to kill Harry, including one at Bosworth, but all fail. Henry Tudor wins the crown, Harry gets the inheritance, and Richard III and Stephen get their just deserts. The novel is written for young people.

48. Campbell, Alexander. *Perkin Warbeck; or, The Court of James the Fourth of Scotland*. London: A.K. Newman and Co., 1830. 3 vols.

James IV of Scotland welcomes Perkin Warbeck to his court, convinced that the youth is the elder son of Edward IV, but Perkin is an imposter, the son of a Jew of Tournai, who is using his striking resemblance to the late king in an attempt to seize the throne from Henry VII. He is aided by Barnard Chudworth, a cut-throat, whom he tries to murder in order to protect his secret. James' cousin Catherine Gordon falls in love with Warbeck, and marries him, despite a warning that her union with the White Rose will prove disastrous. Catherine accompanies Perkin when they invade England, but the expected English support fails to materialize. Perkin is captured by soldiers under the command of his old enemy Chudworth, and taken to London. Catherine, aided by James, follows him to share his captivity, and the day before his execution he confesses that he is not Richard of York, but an illegitimate son of Edward IV.

49. Capes, Bernard. *Historical Vignettes*. London: Fisher Unwin, 1910. New York: Frederick A. Stokes Company, 1910. 319 pp.

This volume of short tales includes three about figures of the Wars of the Roses.

"Jane Shore." (pp. 117-128.) After Jane Shore performs her penance for her sinful life as the mistress of Edward IV, she follows a man who seems to be waiting for her, despite Richard III's stricture against anyone helping her. The strange man leads Jane to a nearby house, where she discovers that he is her husband Harry, the goldsmith. He tells her that, although he still loves her, he is leaving her, and she realizes that she is alone and friendless.

"The Chaplain of the Tower." (pp. 129-139.) The chaplain of the Tower is an evil Benedictine priest, who dreams of becoming Abbot of Westminster. To ingratiate himself with the king, Richard III, the chaplain tries to persuade Sir John (sic) Brackenbury to involve himself in the murder of the sons of Edward IV. Brackenbury, the Constable of the Tower, refuses, and so Tyrell, Dighton, and Forrest, hired murderers, do the deed, and the priest helps to bury the boys. He is later instructed to move the bodies to more hallowed ground, but is disappointed when he does not receive his expected reward. When his guilty conscience shows him a terrible vision, the priest falls down a flight of stairs, and dies on the very spot where he has buried the murdered princes.

"Margaret of Anjou." (pp. 249-260.) Margaret of Anjou and her son, escaping from the Yorkists after the defeat of the Lancastrian forces at Hexham, are captured by three ruffians, who plan to rape her, steal her jewels, and murder them. The robbers fall out and kill each other, and Margaret and her son escape and make their way to safety in France.

50. Carleton, Patrick [Patrick Railton]. *Under the Hog*. London: Rich & Cowan, Ltd., 1938. 514pp. New York: E. P. Dutton, 1938. 514pp.

The Richard III portrayed in this novel is neither saint nor monster, but a man who adheres rigidly to his own code of honor. The action takes place between 1470 and 1485, and shows Richard as the young warrior loyal to his brother the king, as Protector, and as the king who reluctantly orders the death of his nephews, in order to prevent their supporters from prolonging the bloody civil war. This is one of the best novels about the period.

51. Carr, Robyn. *The Everlasting Covenant*. Boston and Toronto: Little, Brown and Company, 1987. 393pp.

This novel covers a period of twenty-five years, during which the heroine, Anne Gifford, whose family plans to enter her in a convent, falls in love with Dylan deFrayn, the son of a rival family. The Wars of the Roses begin just as the couple plans to elope, and Dylan goes off to fight, unaware that Anne is pregnant. Edward IV's victory forces Dylan into exile in France, and Anne into marriage to save herself and her child. After years of Yorkist rule, Henry Tudor comes to save England, and the lovers are finally reunited.

52. Carsley, Anne. *This Ravished Rose*. New York: Pocket Books, 1980. 373pp.

There are sex, intrigue, and satanism, but little history in this 'historical romance' about Katherine Hartley, the daughter of an adherent of Edward IV who is accused of treason. Katherine is forced into marriage with a follower of Richard of Gloucester, in order to escape the clutches of an evil courtier, but finally learns to love her husband, as she discovers the secret of her father's fall.

53. Chesterman, Hugh. *A Maid in Armour*. London: Frederick Warne & Co., Ltd., 1936. 248pp.

A young girl leaves her farm with a Lancastrian survivor of the Battle of Barnet, to rescue her brother, wounded in the same battle. This charming novel, written for young people, presents the Lancastrian view of the conflict.

54. Church, Alfred J. *The Chantry Priest of Barnet: A Tale of the Wars of the Two Roses*. Illustrated. London: Seeley and Co. Ltd., n. d. [ca. 1908]. 301pp.

Written for young readers, this well-researched, historically accurate novel tells the history of the conflict of Lancaster and York, from the Wars of the Roses to the dissolution of the monasteries under Henry VIII, from a narrow monastic focus. The author was a prolific writer of historical novels for boys.

55. Clarke, Mrs. Henry. *A Trusty Rebel; or A Follower of Warbeck*. Illustrated. London, Edinburgh, and New York: Thomas Nelson and Sons, n.d. 340pp.

Christopher Cory, a Cornish youth brought up in Flanders, becomes the page and devoted adherent of Perkin Warbeck. When their invasion of Kent ends in disaster, Warbeck escapes, but Christopher is wounded, and saved by Sir Richard Kestell, an old friend of his father's. Christopher learns that his uncle, the evil Lord Bolsolver, has stolen his inheritance and plans to marry Kestell's daughter, whom Christopher loves. Despite this, he rejoins Warbeck, but when he learns that the man is a pretender, Christopher gains the pardon of Henry Tudor, and returns to Cornwall to claim his title and his bride.

56. Clynes, Michael [P. C. Doherty]. *The White Rose Murders*. London: Headline Book Publishing, 1991. New York: St. Martin's Press, 1993. 244pp.

Roger Shallot, 90 years old but with the mind of a prurient adolescent, is dictating his memoirs to his chaplain. He tells how he was befriended and employed by Benjamin Daunbey, a nephew of Cardinal Wolsey, who asked them to investigate Les Blancs Sangliers, a secret Yorkist group with ties to Queen Margaret of Scotland, who has fled to England seeking help from her brother, Henry VIII. Several locked room murders, at which a white rose is left near the corpse, puzzle the amateur detectives, but they finally solve the mystery, and find the solution to the puzzle of the death of the Scottish king at Flodden. Clynes, who also writes under his own name, P. C. Doherty, and Paul Harding and C. L. Grace, apparently intends this novel to be the first of a series.

57. Coates, Sheila. *A Crown Usurped*. London: Robert Hale Ltd., 1972. 160 pp.

In 1483, when she is sixteen, Eloise Flemyng, the daughter of a provincial wool and cloth merchant, falls in love with Dom Dalyon, the scion of a noble, but uncivilized, family. Eloise's father, aghast at the thought of her marrying into such a family, takes her to London and forces her to marry her cousin Tom. Dom marries, as well, and he and Eloise both have sons. In 1485, as Henry Tudor is getting ready to invade England, both Tom and Dom's wife die. Dom goes off to join Tudor's army, along with many other men of the district, who hate Richard III for killing his nephews. When Dom returns after Tudor's victory, he and Eloise decide to marry, confident that they and England have a bright future.

58. Cowper, Frank. *The Captain of the Wight: A Romance of Carisbrooke Castle in 1488*. Illus. by the author. London: Seeley and Co., Ltd., 1889. xi + 384pp.

Fifteen-year-old Ralph de Lisle of Hampshire is sent to learn the knightly arts in the household of Sir Edward Woodville, captain of Carisbrooke Castle and the Isle of Wight in 1487. Yorkist sympathizers are plotting the destruction of Woodville and Henry VII, whom they want to replace with

Perkin Warbeck, and Ralph becomes an object of their hatred. He accompanies Woodville to Brittany, where he is wounded, and Woodville is killed in battle. Ralph is rescued by his kinsman, the leader of the Yorkist plotters, who has regretted the error of his ways.

59. Cripps, Arthur Shearly. *Magic Casements.* New York: E. P. Dutton and Co., 1905. ix+185pp.

This work is a collection of stories about everyday life in England during the reigns of Henry VI and Edward IV. They are set in the midland and home counties.

60. Cummins, Mary. *The Glenorchan Ruby.* London: Robert Hale Limited, 1982. 191 pp.

When Edward IV invades Scotland in an attempt to regain Berwick, James III's nobles use the opportunity to destroy his favorites. Several are hanged, including Sir James Fielding, who had been given Glenorchan, the estate of his father-in-law, Sir Robert Boyd, after the latter had fallen from favor. Boyd's younger daughter Lindsay is forced to marry Sir Andrew Douglas, who had been granted Glenorchan after Fielding's death, and the young heroine becomes caught up in a possibly fraudulent marriage ceremony and the legend of the mysterious Glenororchan Ruby, which is believed to control the destiny of her family.

61. _____. *Fingala, Maid of Rathay.* London: Robert Hale Limited, 1983. 190 pp.

Fingala Montgomery promises her dying father that she will not marry Sir Kenneth Buchanan until her brother Patrick returns to Rathay with a wife. Patrick loves Katherine Gordon, who has been given in marriage to a young man calling himself Richard of York, the younger son of Edward IV, but many Scottish nobles believe him to be an imposter. They send for the princes' former tutor, Sir Andrew Heron, to identify him, but Heron and his daughter are attacked by bandits, and he is wounded and brought to Rathay. When Sir Kenneth realizes that Fingala is attracted to Heron, he forces her to honor their betrothal with an immediate marriage. Heron exposes Richard of York as an imposter, Patrick returns to Rathay disillusioned with Katherine Gordon, and Fingala realizes that she loves Kenneth. James IV abandons the imposter Warbeck, who is captured and executed by Henry Tudor, and the two kingdoms are united by the marriage of Tudor's daughter Margaret and James IV.

62. Daniel, Hawthorne. *The Honor of Dunmore*. Illus. by Henry Pitz. New York: The Macmillan Company, Publishers, 1927. 256pp.

In 1441, with England on the verge of civil war, Southwark, the castle of Edward Dunmore, Baron of Southwark, is attacked by Sir Richard Ower, an adherent of the Earl of Somerset, and the leader of a band of cut-throats who have been terrorizing the neighborhood. Dunmore's son Edward and a friend escape and bring reinforcements to save the castle, but the baron is killed by Ower. Several years later Edward, now Lord Dunmore, rescues Margaret Beaufort, Somerset's niece, from Ower, and after he is knighted by Henry VI, he joins other nobles opposed to Somerset, Suffolk, and Cardinal Beaufort.

63. _____. *The Red Rose of Dunmore*. Illustrated by William Blood. New York: The Macmillan Company, 1928. 212pp.

This sequel to *The Honor of Dunmore* (see entry 62) takes place in 1483, as Lord Dunmore, in exile in Brittany with Henry Tudor, sends his seventeen-year-old son Edward to England with secret messages concerning the proposed invasion during Buckingham's rebellion. The mission is betrayed by an agent in the pay of 'hunchbacked Dick O'Gloucester' and Lord Moreton, the Yorkist holder of the Dunmore estates. The invasion fails, but young Edward again serves Tudor, fighting at his side at Bosworth. Edward then destroys his enemies and wins the love of Lady Anne Montague, the Lancastrian ward of the evil Moreton.

64. Daniell, David Scott. *The Boy They Made King, a True Story*. Illus. by William Stobbs. New York: Duell, Sloan and Pearce, 1950. 151pp.

Lambert Simnel, the son of an Oxford shoemaker, is taken to be educated by Richard Symonds, a Yorkist priest. The boy, who must now answer to the name of Edward, is taught to behave like a gentleman, for he is to impersonate the Earl of Warwick, and will be crowned king when the rebel army, led by the Earl of Lincoln, defeats Henry VII. Lambert is crowned in Ireland, but the rebels are defeated at Stoke-on-Trent. Taken before Henry Tudor, who he had been told was a cruel tyrant, Lambert apologizes for his deception. Henry, who turns out to be a kindly man, forgives Lambert, and gives him a job as a scullery boy in the royal kitchen. The novel was written for young people.

65. Darby, Catherine [Maureen Peters]. *A Dream of Fair Serpents*. London: Robert Hale Limited, 1979. 254pp.

In this novel about Welsh magic and reincarnation, the lives of several people on the coast of Wales are traced throughout history, beginning in 61 A.D., and ending in the late 20th century. In one of their reincarnations, which takes place in the 15th century, Henry Tudor visits from Brittany, and Elinor, a young girl gifted with the ability to see the future, predicts that he will sit on England's throne, which brings joy to his Welsh supporters.

66. Davidson, Margaret. *My Lords Richard*. London: Cassell, Ltd., 1979. 277pp.

Anne Neville is the heroine of this novel, and the Lords Richard are her father, the Earl of Warwick, and her husband, Richard of Gloucester. The story, both personal and political, of the Wars of the Roses between 1464 and 1485, is told from Anne's point of view by the pro-Yorkist author.

67. Davies, Iris. *The Tudor Tapestry*. London: Robert Hale Limited, 1974. 222pp.

Catherine Valois is determined to marry Owen Tudor, a gentleman-at-arms, but she is thwarted by the family of her late husband Henry V. One brother-in-law, Humphrey of Gloucester, handsome and ambitious, is attracted to her, but Henry's other brother, the Duke of Bedford, wants to marry her to some foreign prince. Despite their opposition, and that of their uncle Cardinal Beaufort, Catherine marries Owen and bears him several children, but her weak young son, Henry VI, is taken from her to be raised by men not of her choosing.

68. _____. *Bride of the Thirteenth Summer*. London: Robert Hale Limited, 1975. 218pp.

Beautiful, kind, and loving Margaret Beaufort, the heiress of the Duke of Somerset, is sent to live at the court of Henry VI, where she and Edmund Tudor, the king's half-brother, meet and fall in love. Although St. Nicholas appears to her in a vision, and tells her that she will marry Edmund and have a son who will rule England, her wicked guardian, the Duke of Suffolk, forces her to marry his son John. After Suffolk's murder, the king has the marriage annulled, and Margaret marries Edmund. Through three marriages she clings to the belief that her son will be king, and on the night before Bosworth she rides to the battle site, watches the battle, and sees the prediction come true, as Henry is crowned on the field. This author takes great liberties with historical fact.

69. Deeping, Warwick. *Martin Valliant*. New York: R. M. McBride & Co., 1917. 318pp.

Martin Valliant, a young monk and the son of an old warrior, is hated by his fellow monks for his piety, and they plot to destroy him. He meets Mellis Dale, the daughter of a Lancastrian lord killed by Roger Bland, the cruel Yorkist lord who rules the area. Mellis and her brother have returned to England to raise the countryside for Henry Tudor, and when her brother is murdered, she and Martin, with the help of friends, defeat and destroy their enemies.

70. Dewar, Margaret. *Philippa*. London: Robert Hale Limited, 1982. 190pp.

In 1459, Lancastrian heiress Lady Philippa Mountford, lady-in-waiting to Margaret of Anjou, and widow of an elderly knight, meets Richard Rosslyn, a follower of Warwick's, who seems to be very interested in her past. When he forces her to marry him, she discovers that he has a claim on her estate. They fall in love, and Philippa becomes a loyal Yorkist.

71. _____. *The Loyalty Game*. London: Robert Hale Limited, 1984. 174 pp.

Not available for review.

72. Dexter, Susan. *The Wizard's Shadow*. New York: Del Rey/Ballantine Books, 1993. 277pp.

Crocken the peddler makes a reluctant bargain with the shadow of a murdered wizard. In return for 40 marks he will allow the shadow to attach itself to him, and will follow its orders until its task is completed. The wizard leads Crocken to Armyn, ruled by the Steward-Protector Risiart for his nephew Kieron. Risiart's loyalty to his brother, the late king, he now gives to his nephew, but Kieron is not what he seems. The Lady Ivy, the lady-in-waiting to Kieron's betrothed, enlists the aid of Crocken and the wizard to expose the evil Kieron, thus saving Risiart's life, and enabling him to take the crown.

73. Dinnes, Enid. *The Three Roses*. London: Sands and Company, 1926. 320pp.

Parkyn Pokeapart, a ploughman's son, is born on the same day as Henry VI, and at the age of ten he is hired to be the king's whipping boy, a job with little to do. He and Henry remain close, and both Cardinal Beaufort and Humphrey of Gloucester attempt to use Parkyn to spy on Henry and each other. When Henry marries Margaret of Anjou, open warfare breaks out between white rose and red, but Henry rejects both symbols, choosing instead to follow the golden rose of Christ. He dubs Parkyn a Knight of the Golden Rose, and the ploughman's son remains faithful to the saintly king for the rest of his life.

74. Doherty, P. C. *The Fate of Princes*. London: Robert Hale Limited, 1990. 192pp. New York: St. Martin's Press, 1991. 192pp.

Francis Lovell, loyal friend and councillor to Richard III, near death in his prison room at Minster Lovell, recounts how the king had asked him to investigate the disappearance of the Princes in the Tower. Lovell at first suspects that the king's charge is a ploy to disguise his guilt, but his investigation proves Richard's innocence and uncovers the identity of the true villains.

75. _____. *Dove Amongst the Hawks*. London: Robert Hale Limited, 1990. 160pp.

When Louis XI asks the pope to investigate the death of Henry VI, with an eye to beatifying him, the papal legate in England asks Edward IV to appoint a commission to look into the matter. Luke Chichele, the queen's physician, is asked to serve, along with retainers of both Clarence and Gloucester. As they go about their investigation, several of the commission members are murdered, and Luke knows he too is an intended victim. He finally learns the truth of both Henry's saintliness and the manner of his death, but discovers that neither the Yorkists nor Henry Tudor want the facts known. The novel is told through a series of letters from Luke to his brother, a monk at Aylesford.

76. Drake, Shannon [Heather Graham Pozzessere]. *Lie Down in Roses*. New York: Berkeley Publishing Group, Charter Books, 1988. 456pp.

Tristan, the second son of the Earl of Bedford Heath, serves Richard III, but demands to know the truth about the whereabouts of the two sons of Edward IV. When his entire family is murdered by the king's henchmen in response to his excessive interest in the princes, Tristan goes to Brittany to join Henry Tudor.

77. Durst, Paul. *The Florentine Table*. New York: Charles Scribner's Sons, 1980. 207pp.

American writer Ray Armacost goes to London for a year with his wife and two young sons, Edward and Richard. When they buy a 15th century Florentine table said to have belonged to Richard III, their lives become a nightmare. The boys are taken over by the spirits of the two murdered princes, the witch next door, and her priest companion. Two acquaintances named Dighton and Green, die mysterious and ghastly deaths, and another, Tyrell, barely escapes the same fate. The faces carved on the table change from demons to cherubs, and back again, until the 500 year old murders are avenged.

78. Dymoke, Juliet. *The Sun in Splendour*. London: Dennis Dobson Books Ltd., 1980. 204pp.

Bess Tilnew visits her old friends Elizabeth Woodville and her mother on her way to wed Sir Humphrey Bourchier, and learns that Elizabeth had married Edward IV that morning. Bess' fortunes are tied to those of the king and queen, and when her husband is killed at Barnet, her support of Richard of Gloucester's intention to marry Anne Neville earns her the enmity of Clarence. Bess later marries Thomas Howard; their son was the father of Catherine Howard, and their daughter the mother of Anne Boleyn.

79. _____. *The Lord of Greenwich*. London: Dobson Books Ltd., 1980. 224pp.

Humphrey of Gloucester, the youngest brother of Henry V, serves his brother loyally until the king's death in France. The new infant king, Henry VI, is put into the care of his uncles, Humphrey and John of Bedford, and his great-uncle, Henry Beaufort, Bishop of Winchester. Humphrey, despite his piety and love of learning, loves show and power, and he clashes with Beaufort over policy and the king's upbringing. Against his uncle's wishes, Humphrey marries the already married Jacqueline of Hainault, and takes an army to France to attempt to regain her lands. When the Duke of Burgundy takes Jacqueline prisoner, Humphrey abandons her for her lady-in-waiting Eleanor Cobham. They marry, but Eleanor's over-riding ambition to see her husband crowned king results in charges of sorcery against her, and brings her husband down.

80. Eckerson, Olive. *The Golden Yoke. A Novel of the War of the Roses*. New York: Coward-McCann, Inc., 1961. 415pp.

In this story of Richard of Gloucester from the age of seventeen to his death at Bosworth, Richard is depicted as a loyal brother, friend, and husband, betrayed by those whom he had every reason to trust. He believes, mistakenly, that friendship and loyalty will overcome greed and self-interest, and pays the price with his life.

81. Edmonston, C. M. and Hyde, M. L. F. *The Ragged Staff.* Illus. by Henry C. Pitz. New York and London: Longmans, Green and Co., 1932. 315pp.

Robin Fetyplace joins the household of the Earl of Warwick as a young boy, and follows his lord through all his reversals of fortune. He loves Anne, the earl's younger daughter, but the cruel, misshapen Richard of Gloucester is determined to marry her. Anne fears and despises Richard, and her father promises she will not have to marry him. She marries Edward of Lancaster, and after his death at Tewkesbury, Robin spirits her away to keep her from Gloucester's clutches, but the wicked duke finds her and forces her into marriage. During the wedding procession Robin attempts to stab Richard, but is himself slain.

82. Edwards, Rhoda. *Some Touch of Pity.* London: Hutchinson & Co. (Publishers) Ltd., 1986. 336 pp. Published in the United States as *The Broken Sword.* New York: Doubleday & Company, Inc., 1976. 296pp.

The story of the life of Richard III is told from several points of view: that of his wife Anne; Francis Lovell, his closest friend; his niece Elizabeth of York; and himself, as well as others who figured in his and his brother's reigns.

83. _____. *The Broken Sword.*

See entry 82.

84. _____. *Fortune's Wheel.* London: Hutchinson & Co. (Publishers) Ltd., 1978. 318pp.

This novel tells the story of Richard of Gloucester's life from 1468, when he was sixteen years old and caught up in the quarrel between his brother Edward IV and the Earl of Warwick, until, after many cruel disappointments and changes of fortune, he marries his childhood love Anne Neville.

85. Ellis, Beth. *A King of Vagabonds.* Edinburgh and London: William Blackwood and Sons, 1911. 375pp.

After Richard III seizes the throne Tyrell, Dighton, and Forrest steal into the Tower to murder the princes. The younger one miraculously escapes death, and is hidden by the warder and his wife. Years later, James Strangeways goes to Burgundy to offer his support to Richard, Duke of York, who is being trained by the Duchess of Burgundy to overthrow Henry Tudor. When they arrive in Scotland, where the king supports them, both Richard and Strangeways fall in love with Katherine Gordon. Strangeways learns, after Richard and Katherine marry, that Richard is an imposter, but supports him for Katherine's sake.

86. Elrington, H. *The Luck of Chervil*. Illus. by E. H. Shepard. London, Edinburgh, Dublin, and New York: Thomas Nelson and Sons, 1907. 190pp.

In the Yorkist town of Chervil in 1476, Martin, a poor carder, finds an abandoned child wrapped in a woolsack, and brings him home to join his family. Martin's sickly daughter recovers her health because of her interest in the strange child, and despite the opposition of his wealthy brother, Martin brings young Humphrey up as his son. The isolated town remains loyal to the Yorkists, despite rumors that Richard III has murdered his nephews, but a royal spy who works for Martin's brother, and hates Humphrey, accuses several townsmen of Lancastrian sympathies. Humphrey leaves home to seek safety in another town, and on his journey he meets his long-lost father, a supporter of Henry Tudor. After Bosworth Humphrey recovers his rightful inheritance.

87. Estrange, H. .O. M. *Mid Rival Roses*. London: Selwyn & Blount, Ltd., 1922. 492 pp.

Nigel Buckton learns, after his father's death, that he has been done out of his inheritance by the evil Abbot Hubert, who has also made improper advances to Margaret Elston. Nigel saves her from the abbot's assassins, marries her, and with the aid of Edward IV, regains his inheritance. The couple goes to court, where the handsome and charming Richard of Gloucester woos Margaret. When she resists his advances, he sends Nigel to fight the Scots. Richard murders Clarence, and after Edward's death, kills his nephews as well. He attempts to rape Margaret and arrests Nigel for treason, but after many hair-raising adventures, Nigel slays Richard at Bosworth, and the couple is reunited.

88. Evans, Jean. *The Divided Rose*. London: Robert Hale Ltd., 1972. 192pp.

Elizabeth Woodville, secretly married to Edward IV, schemes to raise her family to power, and divides both the old nobility and the king's own family. The novel ends with the defeat of the Lancastrians at Tewkesbury.

89. _____. *The Rose and Ragged Staff.* London: Robert Hale Ltd., 1974. 189 pp.

Not available for review.

90. _____. *The White Rose of York.* London: Robert Hale Ltd., 1972. 191pp.

After the death of Edward IV, Richard of Gloucester is persuaded by his advisors to have Hastings executed for treason, and to take the throne when Stillington reveals that Edward and Elizabeth Woodville were bigamously married. Buckingham orders the murder of the princes in the Tower, with Margaret Beaufort's encouragement, in the hope that he can take the crown himself, but his execution leaves the way open for Tudor. At Bosworth a discouraged and depressed Richard loses his life, which has become burdensome, and Elizabeth of York, who loved Richard, is forced to marry Henry Tudor.

91. Everett-Green, Evelyn. *In the Wars of the Roses: A Story for the Young.* Illus. London, Edinburgh, and New York: T. Nelson and Sons, 1899. 256pp.

Paul Stukely, the son of a Lancastrian knight, relies on his startling resemblance to Edward of Lancaster to save the young prince from kidnappers. Years later he is able to use a similar ruse to save Edward when he returns secretly from France at the time of his father's restoration to the throne. The prince has come to determine how much support exists for Lancaster, and he is able to win support for his cause by his charm and bravery. He returns to France when he learns that the Yorkists will stop at nothing to capture him. He and Paul fight side by side at Tewkesbury, where he is killed. Paul escapes, and lives to see the destruction of the House of York.

92. _____. *The Heir of Hascombe Hall: A Tale of the Days of the Early Tudors.* Illus. London, Edinburgh, and New York: Thomas Nelson and Sons, 1900. 447pp.

The Yorkist Lord Hascombe fights against Henry Tudor at the Battle of Stoke, and in fear of retribution, flees to Ireland and then Italy with his wife, leaving behind their newborn son Edgar in the care of the miller's wife. She passes Edgar off as the twin of her newborn son, but after a

long illness, she is unable to tell the two apart. Sixteen years later
Hascombe returns with his new Italian wife and children. Despite the
machinations of the wicked stepmother, the true heir of Hascombe is
discovered and recovers his birth-right.

93. _____. *White Wyvill and Red Ruthven. A Story of the Strife of the
Roses*. London: Ernest Nister, 1902. 296pp.

The Wyvills and Ruthvens are neighbors, distant relations, and bitter
enemies, the Wyvills being Yorkists and the Ruthvens Lancastrians. The
Ruthvens are at war with each other as well, since the baroness favors her
younger son Godfrey, and hates her elder son Rafe. Rafe saves the life of
Maud Wyvill, and the two fall in love. Kate Wyvill and her sisters
become friends with the two Ruthven sisters, and all deplore the enmity
between their elders. Rafe is wounded at Northampton and is hidden and
cared for by the Wyvills. Mervyn Wyvill falls in love with Joan Ruthven,
and despite the treachery of Baroness Ruthven and Godfrey, who attempt
to kill him, Rafe saves the lives of Mervyn and his father. When Edward
IV is crowned king, he is so impressed by Rafe's bravery and loyalty, that
he makes him Earl of Ruthven. All the villains are punished and all lovers
united, as England unites under the new king, who will bring peace to the
realm.

94. Eyre, Katherine Wigmore. *The Song of a Thrush*. Illus. by Stephani and
Edward Godwin. New York: Oxford University Press, 1952. 251pp.

In 1483, after the death of Edward IV, Margaret Plantagenet, daughter of
the Duke of Clarence, is sent to live with the royal children in Ludlow,
where she remains until 1485. She witnesses the capture of Edward V by
his uncle Gloucester, the arrest of Rivers and Grey, and the setting aside
and incarceration of the two princes. At Bosworth, the evil usurper gets
his due, despite Northumberland's attempt to save him.

95. Fairburn, Eleanor. *The Rose in Spring*. London: Robert Hale Limited,
1971. 192pp.

At age ten Cecily Neville, the youngest child of the Earl of Westmorland,
is betrothed to Richard, Duke of York, her father's ward and her childhood
friend. This first novel in a series about Cecily's life (see entries 96, 97,
98) tells of her marriage and her lonely life during the years of her
husband's involvement in the French wars. Her isolation leads her to a
friendship with John Blaeburn, a captain of archers, and they fall in love.
Although Cecily remains physically faithful to her husband, her love for

Blaeburn is noted by York's enemies. Cecily sends Blaeburn away, but scandal-mongers cast doubt on the paternity of her first child, Edward.

96. _____. *White Rose, Dark Summer.* London: Robert Hale Limited, 1972. 206pp.

The Duke of York and his family are sent to virtual exile in Ireland, where he will serve as the king's lieutenant. The imbecilic Henry VI is ruled by his arrogant and ambitious French queen, who fears York and his claim to the throne. Her mismanagement of the country finally forces the duke to advance his claim, thus putting his family and himself in jeopardy. Through all his difficulties, the duchess remains loyal and supportive to her beloved husband, and when he is killed by the queen's forces at Wakefield, the Yorkists vow to drive Henry from the throne. Cecily learns that her son Edward has secretly married Eleanor Talbot, who will bear his child. Edward, assured by his mother that he is the true son of the Duke of York and not the illegitimate son of the archer Blayburn, accepts the crown. This is the second novel in a series.. See entries 95, 97, 98.

97. _____. *The Rose at Harvest End.* London: Robert Hale Limited, 1974. 213pp.

Continuing the story of the life of Cecily Neville, (see entries 95, 96, 98) this novel opens with the coronation of her son Edward IV. As Edward falls under the spell of Elizabeth Woodville, whose mother uses witchcraft to help her seduce the king into marriage, Cecily reminds her son of his secret marriage to Eleanor Butler, who bore him a child. Edward becomes increasingly estranged from Cecily and Warwick as he yields to the ambitions of the Woodvilles. The novel ends with Edward's death in 1483, and Cecily's realization that Bishop Stillington intends to reveal the secret marriage, which will brand Edward's children as bastards.

98. _____. *Winter's Rose.* London: Robert Hale Limited, 1976. 190 pp.

In this last novel of the series about the life of Cecily Neville, (see entries 95, 96, 97) Richard of Gloucester, her youngest son, seizes the throne when he learns that his brother Edward's children are illegitimate. Edward, the elder of the princes, dies of natural causes, but Richard, the younger, is sent out of the country in order to protect him, and to prevent an uprising in his name. Richard fails to realize that Buckingham, whom he loves dearly, is devoured by jealousy, and believes that he can use Henry Tudor to gain the crown for himself. Agents of the duke and Tudor spread rumors that Richard has killed his nephews, Buckingham rebels and

is captured, and Tudor wins the crown. After Richard's death, Cecily
Neville shuts herself up in a convent, nursing a bitter hatred of Tudor, who
has destroyed her son's life and reputation.

99. Farrington, Robert. *The Killing of Richard the Third*. New York: Charles
Scribner's Sons, 1971. 287pp.

This is the first novel in a trilogy about the adventures of Henry Morane,
Privy Clerk to Richard III's secretary. (See entries 100, 101.) Morane
becomes the king's secret agent, and attempts to foil the schemes of Henry
Tudor and his adherents. The book ends with Richard's death and
Morane's capture at Bosworth Field.

100. _____. *Tudor Agent*. London: Chatto & Windus, 1974. 279pp.

This novel continues the adventures of Henry Morane (see entry 99), and
takes place during the first two years of the reign of Henry VII, ending
with the defeat of Lambert Simnel's uprising at Stoke-on-Trent in 1487.
Morane, still mourning the death of Richard III, survives as an agent of
Christopher Urswick, Tudor's spymaster, but he manages to avenge, in
part, the betrayal of his former master.

101. _____. *The Traitors of Bosworth*. London: Chatto & Windus, 1978.
251pp.

In this third novel of a trilogy (see entries 99, 100), Henry Morane
continues to take vengeance against the men who betrayed Richard III.
As Morane travels to York, Bristol, and Flanders in Henry Tudor's
service at the time of Warbeck's rebellion, he gives God a helping hand
to secure the deaths of Northumberland and Sir William Stanley, the two
men most responsible for Richard's death at Bosworth.

102. Few, Mary Dodgen. *Under the White Boar*. Atlanta, Ga.: Droke House/
Hallux, 1971. 219pp.

There are few heroes in this novel about the life and reign of Richard III,
and the sympathetically portrayed king and queen are surrounded by a
cast of villains. Edward IV, a boorish lout, is in love with Isobel
Neville, yet attempts to rape her. Clarence is a drunken, abusive, and
envious cad, and Hastings a self-serving conniver. The author offers an
unconventional solution to the mystery of the fate of the princes.

103. Ford, John M. *The Dragon Waiting*. New York: Simon and Schuster, 1983. 365pp.

The Byzantine Empire rules most of the fifteenth century world in this fantasy peopled by wizards, vampires, and sorcerers. Peredur, a Welsh wizard, attempts, with the aid of a strange group of adherents, to prevent the Byzantine conquest of England. His magic proves more powerful than that of the wizard employed by the Empire to help Henry Tydder, and Richard III wins the day at Bosworth.

104. Forster, R. H. *In Steel and Leather*. London: John Long, 1904. 314pp.

When sixteen-year-old Herbert Whittingham's father dies, the boy is sent to be educated at Alnwick Abbey, where his uncle is a canon. The defeat of the Lancastrians at Towton is a blow to Herbert, especially since his wardship and marriage have been sold to an ambitious Yorkist knight, Sir Thomas Tunstal, who plans to marry him off to the daughter of a man he hopes to impress. Herbert is sent to live at Bamburgh Castle, where he meets his guardian's Lancastrian brother and niece Dorothy. The three join in a plot with a priest to capture the castle for Margaret of Anjou, but their forces are destroyed by the quarreling of the leaders. Dorothy and Herbert are captured and taken to Edward IV, who so charms them, that they swear allegiance to him, and are rewarded with permission to marry.

105. Frazer, Margaret. *The Novice's Tale*. New York: Jove Books, 1992. 229pp.

The peace of the Priory of St. Frideswide is shattered by the murder of Lady Ermentrude Fenner, who has come to remove her great-niece Thomasine, the novice, from the priory. Thomasine is unwilling to leave, and when her aunt is murdered, suspicion falls on her. Dame Frevisse, the priory's hosteler, and niece of Thomas Chaucer, one of Henry VI's advisors, is charged with solving the murder. She must discover if Lady Ermentrude, who had left the service of Queen Katherine because of an impending scandal surrounding the queen, has been killed to keep her from revealing the queen's secret marriage to Owen Tudor, and the imminent birth of their first child, or for a secret closer to home. Dame Frevisse uses all her considerable intelligence to solve the mystery.

106. Frederic, Harold. "How Dickon Came By His Name: A Tale of Christmas in the Olden Times." *The Deserter and Other Stories*. Illus. by Merrill, Sandham, Gilbert Gaul, and George Foster Barnes. Boston: Lothrop

Publishing Company, 1898.   pp.239-316.

Dickon lives with his father, a smith, on the manor of Sir Watty Curdie, who favors the Lancastrians because his enemies, the Stanleys, are Yorkists. At Christmas time, Sir Watty gathers a band of cut-throats and attacks the estate of a baron believed to be a sorcerer. Dickon joins the mob, ignorant of their purpose, and when they murder the baron, Dickon rescues a young boy Andreas and his treasure, a printed book. Escaping into the woods, they are found by Richard of Gloucester, who takes Dickon into his service, and arranges for Andreas to work for Caxton. When Gloucester is killed at Bosworth, Dicken falls at his side, but recovers to live on into the reign of Henry Tudor.

107. _____. "Where Avon Into Severn Flows." *The Deserter and Other Stories*. (See entry 106.)   pp. 319-401.

Fifteen-year-old Hugh Overtown, an apprentice scribe in Tewkesbury Abbey, writes a letter to Sir Hereward for a Lancastrian noble. After the Yorkist victory at the Battle of Tewkesbury, the Duke of Gloucester sits in judgment on the Lancastrians who sought sanctuary in the Abbey, and discovers that the letter-writer was actually Lady Kate. The duke forgives the lovers, and is so impressed with Hugh's ability as a scribe, that he decides to take him to his castle of Baynard's.

108. Fullerton, Lady Georgianna. *A Stormy Life*. Illus. by Gaston Hay. London: R. Bentley, 1863. 3 vols. New York: D. Appleton & Company, 1868.   304pp.

The adventurous, but unhappy life of Marguerite of Anjou, who believes that she was born to be a queen, is told in part by her faithful lady-in-waiting Margaret de Roos, and in part through her own diary. Marguerite's arrogance, her savage treatment of the Yorkists, and her choice of favorites, make her unpopular in England, and when Henry is driven from the throne, she joins her enemy Warwick in an attempt to save her son's inheritance. The attempt fails, and Marguerite loses everyone and everything she loves.

109. Garabet, Marilyn. *Dearest of Princes*. London: Robert Hale Limited, 1981.   190pp.

When Tom Tunstall marries Alice Neville, niece of the Earl of Warwick and friend of Richard of Gloucester, he joins the young duke as his squire. He remains faithful to Richard, although not to Alice, and dies fighting alongside him at Bosworth.

110. Garrett, William. "The History of Jane Shore, Concubine to Viking [sic] Edward IV, giving an Account of her Birth, Parentage, her Marriage with Mr. Mathew Shore, a Goldsmith, in Lombard-Street, London. How she left her husband's bed to live with King Edward IV. And of the miserable end she made at her death." *A Right Pleasaunt and Famous Book of Histories.* Vol. VI, No.14. Newcastle: George Angus, Printer, 1818. 24pp.

This is probably another version of entries 144-152, 202, 225, 280, 302, 328.

111. Gaunt, William. *The Lady in the Castle.* London: W. H. Allen, 1956. 200pp.

Margaret Mauteby, the eponymous heroine, is the wife of John Paston of the Norfolk Pastons. The novel makes use of the Paston letters to portray the lives of a family of rural gentry during the Wars of the Roses, and shows the remarkable ability of Margaret Paston, as she copes with the problems of daily life and defends her home against powerful enemies during her husband's absence.

112. Gellis, Roberta. *The Dragon and the Rose.* Chicago: Playboy Press, 1977. 363pp.

Margaret Beaufort, a widowed thirteen-year-old, plans from the moment of his birth to place her son Henry Tudor on the throne of England. Brought up in exile by his uncle Jasper, the cold and crafty Henry finally realizes his mother's ambition, and his own, but he has to promise to marry Elizabeth of York, the daughter of his enemy Edward IV, in order to secure the aid of disaffected Yorkists. They marry and fall in love, but it is not until he learns to trust her that he allows her to be crowned.

113. Gerrare, Wirt [Greener, William Oliver]. *Men of Harlech: A Romance of the Wars of the Roses.* London: Ward & Downey, 1896. viii + 334 pp.

Not available for review.

114. Gleason, Edwin Putnam. *The Mystery of Boshingham Castle: A Tale Concerning the Wicked King Richard III and the Princes in the Tower.* Illus. New York: Pageant Press, 1967. 120 pp.

American student David Ludlum visits his classmate Ars Ardleigh, the son of an English diplomat, at the family home of Boshingham Castle. There the boys and Ars' sister search for the answer to the mystery of the ghosts that haunt the castle. They discover in an old crypt the diary of Elizabeth Brackenbury, the daughter of the Constable of the Tower in the reign of Richard III. Elizabeth had overheard the murderers, whom the evil king had hired, plotting to kill the princes in the Tower. The plotters see Elizabeth, but she is able to reveal the plot to her friend, Sir Arthur Adrleigh. With the help of others loyal to the rightful king, Edward V, they attempt to rescue the boys, but fail. Elizabeth and Ardleigh are both taken prisoner by the evil Lord Boshingham. Both escape, and Arthur joins the noble Henry Tudor in France. He later marries Elizabeth and is rewarded with the gift of Boshingham Castle, where their descendants still live. This novel, based largely on the traditional Tudor version of Richard III, is written, badly, for young people.

115. Grace, C. L. [P. C. Doherty]. *A Shrine of Murders*. New York: St. Martin's Press, 1933. 195pp.

Kathryn Swinbrooke, a physician and chemist in Canterbury, inherits her father's practice, and when several pilgrims to Becket's shrine are murdered, the city fathers hire her to assist Colum Murtagh, Edward IV's agent, in solving the crimes. Kathryn believes that the murderer is a physician familiar with Chaucer's *Canterbury Tales*, since the victims follow the trades of his pilgrims. Kathryn and Colum discover the murderer, but are unable to solve the mystery of the disappearance of her abusive husband, who she mistakenly believes was murdered by her father.

116. _____. *The Eye of God*. New York: St. Martin's Press, 1994. 208 pp.

Physician/apothecary Kathryn Swinbrooke and Irishman Colum Murtagh (see entry 115) are summoned by Edward IV and his sinister, misshapen brother Richard of Gloucester, to find the Eye of God, a priceless gold and sapphire pendant. Just before his death at Barnet, Warwick had entrusted the jewel to his squire, who was to take it to Canterbury. The squire is arrested, and dies of apparent gaol fever, and the pendant disappears. Many murders later, Kathryn and Colum discover both the whereabouts of the jewel and identities of the murderers.

117. Graham, Alice Walworth. *The Summer Queen*. New York: Doubleday & Co., Inc., 1973.   296pp.

England between 1460 and 1483 is seen through the eyes of Cecily Bonvile, the second wife of the Marquis of Dorset and lady-in-waiting to Elizabeth Woodville. Elizabeth, a lovely but ambitious and unprincipled schemer, whose marriage to Edward IV brings hatred to her family and renewed trouble to England, plots to marry her daughter Elizabeth to Henry Tudor after Edward's death.

118. Gretton, Mary Sturge. *Crumplin'*. London: Earnest Benn Limited, 1932. 288pp.

A group of loyal Yorkists, under the leadership of Francis Lovell, plots the overthrow of Henry VII and the crowning of the younger son of Edward IV as Richard IV. Well-drawn characters and ingenious plotting, by an author very much at home in the period, give freshness to this oft-told tale.

119. Grey, Belinda. *Proxy Wedding*. London: Mills & Boon Limited, 1982. 190pp.

Lady Gida Rune, the younger daughter of a Lancastrian knight who had been wounded at Tewkesbury, is coerced into marrying Sir Adam de Clancy, an adherent of Buckingham's, in order, she believes, to ensure her father's support for the Duke of Gloucester. She follows Adam to court, where they fall in love, and Gida is caught up in Buckingham's conspiracy against the king. She and Adam are powerless to help their beloved king and queen, although Adam fights at Richard's side at Bosworth.

120. Griffith, Kathryn Meyer. *The Heart of the Rose*. New York: Leisure Books, Dorchester Publishing Co., Inc., 1985.   477pp.

Bronwyn, a beautiful and virtuous peasant girl, is the object of desire and the victim of the rivalry between Edward IV and Warwick. This novel, by an author who is obviously unfamiliar with the period, is full of anachronisms and errors of fact.

121. Hamilton, Julia. *Son of York: A Novel of Edward IV*. London: Sphere Books Limited, 1973.   171pp.

The events of 1442 to 1485 are seen through the eyes of some of the leading figures of the time, including Edward IV, Margaret of Anjou, Elizabeth Woodville, and Jane Shore. Their accounts are interspersed with several chapters written in the third person from the Yorkist point of view.

122. Hammand, N. B. *Samaritana*. London: Robert Hale Limited, 1979. 191pp.

In 1459 Samaritana Mountry, a Cornish girl, is married against her will to the Lancastrian Earl of Crediton. His kindness and love win her over, and she joins him in exile after the accession of Edward IV. The characters are based on historical figures, and the author notes in an epilogue that the Earldom of Crediton, lost when the Yorkists came to power, was not restored by Henry Tudor, who the earl believed had less claim to the throne than Richard III.

123. Hammond, Jane. *The Red Queen*. London: Robert Hale Limited, 1976. 191pp.

Robin of Wakefield, angered at discovering his intended bride in the arms of Edward IV, joins Warwick's rebellion against the king. He escapes an attempted murder, plotted by Hastings, and at Warwick's house meets and falls in love with Margaret Wynford, the daughter of Margaret of Anjou. The queen has kept her daughter's existence secret because she fears, rightly, that the girl has inherited her father's madness. In France Robin and Margaret, who is married, become lovers, and after the Lancastrian defeat at Tewkesbury, Jasper Tudor, who is as mad as Margaret, has her secretly crowned. Robin, who realizes at last the extent of his beloved's madness, stabs her to death, and he and his first love are finally reunited. Almost every character in this historically innacurate, ungrammatical, and poorly written book is either mad or a monster.

124. Hardwick, Mollie. *I Remember Love*. London: Macdonald & Co., 1982. New York: St. Martin's Press, 1983.   335pp.

Divided into three sections, this novel follows the romance of two people through four hundred years and two reincarnations. The first part deals with the illegitmate daughter of John de Clifford, who is sent to live at Middleham as a companion to young Anne Neville. She falls in love with a retainer of Warwick's, but they are separated by his death at Barnet. The lovers are reunited sixty-five years later in the persons of a priest and the mistress of a merchant in Canterbury, but are separated

by her death. In 1865 they meet again as the daughter of a wealthy
London merchant and a pensioned Scottish soldier, and this time they live
out their lives together.

125. Hardy, Blanche. *Sanctuary*. London: Philip Allan, 1925. 249pp.

Based on "The Song of the Lady Bessie," (see entries 381, 387, 454,
462) this novel portrays an evil, scheming Richard of Gloucester, a
high-principled, if ambitious Henry Tudor, and a pure, noble, brave, and
ingenious Elizabeth of York, who takes an active part in the plot to
overthrow her uncle. Humphrey Brereton plays a significant role in the
plot, and in Elizabeth's life, as they help Henry Tudor to wrest the crown
from Richard III.

126. _____. *Dynasty*. London: Philip Allan, 1925. 250pp.

In this sequel to *Sanctuary* (see entry 125) Perkin Warbeck's rebellion
has thrown England into turmoil, and Henry Tudor's spies are
everywhere, seeking out traitors. Katherine, the queen's younger sister,
falls in love with William Courtenay, the son of the Earl of Devonshire,
but Henry's spies report that her secret lover is William de la Pole, her
cousin. Henry, who hates and distrusts all members of the House of
York, with the possible exception of his wife, throws Katherine into the
Tower. He finally allows her to marry Courtenay, but banishes them to
Devon. Warbeck is caught and imprisoned, but when Henry realizes that
his son will not be able to marry Katherine of Aragon until all the
Yorkist claimants are dead, he seduces Warbeck and Clarence's son into
a conspiracy and puts them to death. The Courtenays are allowed to
return to London, where they are spied upon, and William is accused of
conspiracy in the de la Pole plot, and thrown into the Tower.

127. Harnett, Cynthia. *The Load of Unicorn*. Illus. by the author. London:
Methuen Children's Books, 1959. 254pp. Published in the United
States as *Caxton's Challenge*. Cleveland and New York: The World
Publishing Company, 1960. 254pp. Published as *The Cargo of the
Madalena*. Minneapolis: Lerner Publications Company, 1984. 236pp.

In 1482 young Benedict Goodrich, the son of a scrivener, is apprenticed
to Caxton, who hopes to print the King Arthur stories, but is having
difficulty in finding enough paper. His order of unicorn paper, shipped
to England aboard the Madalena, has disappeared, and it is up to Bendy,
as the young Benedict is called, to solve the mystery.

128. _____. *Caxton's Challenge.*

See entry 127.

129. _____. *The Cargo of the Madalena.*

See entry 127.

130. _____. *The Writing on the Hearth.* Illus. by Gareth Floyd. London: Methuen's Children's Books, 1971.   300pp.

Stephen, the son of a soldier servant of the Earl of Suffolk killed in France after the seige of Orleans, lives with his sister and step-father, a ploughman. He is being schooled because of his father's service to the earl, and if he does well, he will be sent to Oxford. Out on the plains one day he finds shelter from a storm in the home of Meg, a reputed witch, and finds her with a well-dressed stranger. He notices the mysterious writings that Meg has drawn in the hearth ashes, and is drawn into events involving black magic and the plot of Eleanor Cobham and Duke Humphrey to destroy Henry VI.

131. Harraden, Beatrice. "How Master Caxton Showed Temper." *Untold Tales of the Past.* Illus. by H. R. Millar. New York: Dodd, Mead and Company, 1897.   pp. 97-113.

This tale for children tells the story of the printer William Caxton's attempt to persuade his neighbor not to lose her temper, and ends up losing his own.

132. Harrod-Eagles, Cynthia. *The Founding.* London: Futura Publications, Ltd., 1980.   494pp.

This is the first novel in a trilogy about the Morlands, a wealthy Yorkshire family founded in the early fifteenth century, when Eleanor Courteney, the ward of Edmund Beaufort, marries Robert Morland. Eleanor, who is in love with Richard, Duke of York, turns the family from their loyalty to their Lancastrian patrons to the Yorkists, and her sons and grandsons fight and die for Edward IV and Richard III. The novel ends with the accession of Henry VII who, in order to secure his claim to the throne, commissions James Tyrell to murder the sons of Edward IV.

133. Harwood, Alice. *Merchant of the Ruby*. Indianapolis and New York: The Bobbs-Merrill Company, Inc., 1950. 447pp.

Richard of Gloucester orders the murder of his nephews, but Richard, the younger boy, persuades the murderer to spare him. He is secretly conveyed to Flanders, where he grows up as Pierre Osbeck. With the aid of the Duchess of Burgundy, Pierre, now called Richard, raises an army and goes to Scotland, where he marries Lady Catherine Gordon. When he invades England with Scottish help, Richard is horrified by the reality of war, and he deserts his followers and surrenders to Henry Tudor. Although he recants his claim to be Richard of York, many in England believe he is the true king. Despite Catherine's pleas, Henry trumps up charges of treason against Richard and Clarence's half-wit son, and executes them, in order to destroy all Yorkist claimants, and ensure his son's marriage to Katherine of Aragon.

134. _____. *The Clandestine Queen*. London: Robert Hale Limited, 1979. 224pp.

Elizabeth Woodville, lady-in-waiting to Margaret of Anjou and wife of John Grey, watches in dismay as Henry VI's madness and the queen's ruthlessness destroy support for the Lancastrians. When Edward IV seizes the throne, the Woodvilles become loyal Yorkists, and Elizabeth seduces the king into marriage. Warwick, who has been negotiating for a French marriage for the king, is publicly humiliated, and rebels. Edward and Elizabeth decide to end the strife by marrying their oldest daughter to Edward of Lancaster, but they are too late. Warwick drives Edward from the country, and on her way to sanctuary, Elizabeth visits Henry VI, who tells her, in an obscure message, that her daughter will marry Henry Tudor and bring peace to England. There is much humor in this novel, all of it unintentional.

135. _____. *The Uncrowned Queen*. London: Robert Hale Limited, 1983. 220pp.

Margaret Beaufort grows up in the court of Henry VI, and at the age of twelve the king gives her the choice of marrying either Edmund Tudor or John de la Pole. She prays to St. Nicholas, who tells her in a vision that she must marry Edmund, who will be the father of her son. She obeys, but is widowed before her son Henry is born. She marries Henry Stafford, and after his death, Lord Thomas Stanley, and lives to see both her son and grandson on the throne. The author has little understanding of the period, and the characters and dialogue lack credibility.

136. Henley, Virginia. *The Raven and the Rose*. New York: Dell Publishing/ Bantam Doubleday Dell Publishing Group, Inc., 1987. 394pp.

Roseanna Castlemaine, the illegitimate daughter of Edward IV and Joanna, wife of Sir Neville Castlemaine, is betrothed to Roger Montford, Baron of Ravenspur, but she loves Sir Bryan Fitzhugh, a friend of her half-brother's and retainer of George of Clarence. She is forced to marry Ravenspur, a close friend of the king's. When she discovers that both her brother and Sir Bryan are agents of Warwick, who intends to overthrow the king, she realizes that she loves her husband, a loyal Yorkist.

137. Henty, G. A. *A Knight of the White Cross*. Illus. by Ralph Peacock. New York: Charles Scribner's Sons, 1906. 400pp.

Dedicated Lancastrians Sir Thomas Tresham and his wife flee into exile with Margaret of Anjou. When the queen becomes reconciled with Warwick, who promises to restore Henry VI to the throne if Edward of Lancaster will marry his daughter Anne, the Treshams return to England. The knight has promised to give his son Gervaise to the Order of the Knights of St. John, and when he is killed at Tewkesbury, his widow turns her son over to the order before she dies. Gervaise goes to Rhodes with the Knights to fight the Moors for many years, but finally asks to be relieved of his vows so he can marry. His bravery in defending Christendom so impresses Edward IV, that he restores the Tresham estates to Gervaise, and reverses the attainder against the family.

138. Heseltine, William. *The Last of the Plantagenets. An Historical Romance, illustrating some of the public events, and ecclesiastical manners of the fifteenth and sixteenth centuries*. London: Smith, Elder, 1829. xxiv+464pp. New York: J. & J. Harper, 1829. Two volumes in One.

This novel, based on Hull's *Richard Plantagenet*, (see entries 154, 238, 253, 432, 535) tells the story of Richard Plantagenet, who is brought up in the monastery of St. Mary in Ely. On the day before the Battle of Bosworth, he is brought to the tent of Richard III, who tells him he is his father, and that his mother, the king's betrothed, had died shortly after his birth. The king intends to name Richard as his heir, but urges him, if Tudor wins, to go into hiding and keep his identity secret. Young Richard is wounded while watching the battle, and rescued by Rabbi Israel, who nurses him back to health. After years of adventure and danger, during which he is aided by loyal Yorkists, he becomes a builder for Sir Thomas Moyle. He reveals his identity, and Moyle builds him a cottage on his estate, where he lives the rest of his life.

139. Hewlett, Maurice. "Brazenhead the Great." *Fond Adventures: Tales of the Youth of the World*. New York and London: Harper & Brothers Publishers, 1905. pp. 31-121. Reprinted as "The Captain of Kent." *Brazenhead the Great*. London: Smith, Elder & Co., 1911. xiii+333pp.

Captain Salomon Brazenhead, adventurer, rogue, and dedicated Yorkist, is on his way to Kent to join his old friend Jack Cade, who is marching to London to drive Henry VI from the throne and replace him with the Duke of York. Brazenhead recruits men along the way, but since they are all, himself included, illiterate, he persuades young Percival Perceforest to join them as scribe. Percival has been dismissed by his master because he and the master's daughter Mawdleyn have fallen in love. The adventurers join a pilgrimage bound for Canterbury, led by Mawdleyn's aunt, a prioress. Brazenhead convinces the prioress that he is of noble eastern blood, and that Percival is his nephew, but Jack Cade recognizes the youth as the nephew of the hated Earl Say. The comical adventure of the group ends well for everyone, except Lord Say, whom the rebels behead. Brazenhead realizes that Cade will fail, and abandons him, choosing to make his fortune with the help of his now wealthy protege.

140. _____. "The Captain of Kent."

See entry 139.

141. Hibbert, Eleanor. *The Goldsmith's Wife*. New York: Appleton-Century-Crofts, 1950. 325pp.

See entry 263.

142. Higgins, Paul. *Puzzlebone Wood*. Illus. by Alan Hepburn. London: Bachman & Turner Ltd., 1979. 129pp.

Three Yorkshire teenagers, twins Hattie and Tinker Brett and their friend Tich Armstrong, are transported back in time to 1461 and the Battle of Towton. Tich twice saves the life of nine-year-old Richard of Gloucester, who has escaped from the retainers taking him and his brother George to Flanders. Tinker saves the entire Yorkist army by finding the Duke of Norfolk and his men, who join the king and defeat the Lancastrians. In a note, the author of this novel for young readers gives a brief description of the battle and history of the Wars of the

Roses, adding that Henry Tudor joined the two factions by marrying Edward's daughter Catherine (sic), thus founding the great Tudor dynasty.

143. Hill, Pamela. *The King's Vixen*. New York: G. P. Putnam's Sons, 1954. 207pp.

Perkin Warbeck's rebellion forms the backdrop for this story of the scheming daughter of a Scottish nobleman, who forces her attentions on James IV of Scotland, and manages at last to become his mistress.

144. *The History of Jane Shore*. Samuel Croxall. *A Select Collection of Novels and Histories...The Second Edition, with Additions. Adorned with Cutts*. London: J. Watts, 1729. 6 Vols. vol. iii, pp. 167-200.

See entries 110, 145-152, 202, 225, 280, 328.

145. "The History of Jane Shore." Illus. Boston: Printed near Charles-river Bridge, 1801. 23pp.

See entries 110, 144, 146, 148-153, 202, 225, 280, 302, 328.

146. "The History of Jane Shore, and Fair Rosamond." Wilmington, Del.: Brynberg, 1796.

No copy has been located, but it is probably another version of entries 110, 144, 145, 147-152, 202, 225, 280, 328.

147. "The History of Jane Shore, Concubine to King Edward IVth." Keene, 1794? 16pp.

Jane Wainstead, the beautiful daughter of a prosperous and doting mercer, attracts the attention of Lord Hastings, who plans to abduct her, but fails. To ensure her safety, her father marries her to the goldsmith Shore, over her objections. Hastings tells the king of her beauty, and when Edward sees her he is smitten. Jane resists his advances at first, but finally yields, and becomes his mistress. Jane is popular with the people, but when Edward dies she is persecuted by the hunch-backed Richard of Gloucester, who deprives her and her family of all they own. Jane is forced to beg for her bread when a friend steals her remaining jewels. Before she dies, Jane repents of her sins. Numerous versions of this tale were printed in the late 18th and 19th centuries. See entries 110, 144-146, 148-152, 202, 225, 280, 302, 328.

148. "The History of Jane Shore, Concubine to King Edward VIth [sic] Containing an Account of her wit and beauty-Her marriage with Mr. Shore-The King's Visits to her-Her going to Court, and leaving her husband-Her great distress and misery after the King's death." Boston: Printed and Sold by Nathaniel Coverly, Jr., 1811. 19pp.

A later printing of entry 147. See also entries 110, 144-147, 149-152, 202, 225, 280, 302, 328.

149. *History of Jane Shore, concubine to King Edward IV: giving an account of her birth and parentage, her marriage with Mr. Matthew Shore, a goldsmith, in Lombard Street, London; how she left her husband to live with King Edward IV, and her great distress and misery after the King's death, with her deplorable end in a ditch; also, brief remarks on other unfortunate beauties who were royal favourites.* London: Printed by W. and T. Fordyce, 1820. 24 pp.

Another version of entry 147. See also entries 110, 144-148, 150-152, 202, 225, 280, 302, 328.

150. "The History of Jane Shore, Mistress to Edward IV. Shewing How she came to be Concubine to the King. With a frontispiece." London: [J. Richardson, Bookseller], 1809.

See entries 110, 144-147, 149, 151, 152, 202, 225, 280, 302, 328.

151. *The History of Jane Shore, Mistress to Edward IV, King of England, with an Account of her Untimely end.* Philadelphia: Freeman Scott, [1840]. 72pp.

Not available for review. See entries 110, 144-150, 152, 202, 225, 280, 302, 328.

152. *The History of Mrs. Jane Shore Concubine to K. Edward the Fourth, who was wife to one Matthew Shore, a goldsmith in London: wherein is declared her wanton life, with her miserable end, and the death of her husband.* Illus. London: Printed for J. Clark, W. Thackeray, & T. Passinger, 1688. 24 pp.

See entries 110, 144-151, 202, 225, 280, 302, 328.

153. Hocking, Mary. *He Who Plays the King.* London: Chatto & Windus, 1980. 232pp.

The lives of Richard of Gloucester and Henry Tudor, with their vastly different positions and prospects, are parallelled from early childhood until their meeting at Bosworth Field. The author gives a balanced portrait of both men.

154. Hodgetts, J. Frederick. *Richard IV., Plantagenet*. Illus. by Gordon Browne. London: Whiting and Co., 1888.   x + 375pp.

Richard III secretly marries Lady Alice Trevor after Anne's death, and their son, who should have been Richard IV, sees his father die at Bosworth. After many hair-raising escapes from his father's enemies, young Richard settles down to the anonymous life of a printer, and prints the first English Bible. The author writes in his introduction that he was inspired by a book he had read fifty years earlier, which professed to be the autobiography of a legitimate son of Richard III, but which named no author. It is apparent that Hodgetts was remembering Heseltine's *Last of the Plantagenets* (see entry 138), since except for some changes in names and the occupations of several characters, it follows the earlier novel closely. See also entries 253, 432, 535.

155. Hollis, Gertrude. *The King Who Was Never Crowned: A Tale of the Fifteenth Century*. Illus. by W. S. Stacey. London: Society for Promoting Christian Knowledge, [1904].   215pp.

A young kinsman of Sir Robert Brackenbury, Constable of the Tower, becomes a page to Edward V in April, 1483. This novel, which is based largely on More's *History of Richard III*, is written for young readers.

156. Holt, Emily Sarah. *At Ye Grene Griffin, or, Mrs. Treadwell's Cook; A Tale of the Fifteenth Century*. London: J. F. Shaw & Co. 1882. iv + 186 pp.

After her beloved husband Edward of Lancaster is killed at the battle of Tewkesbury, Anne Neville hides as a cook in the home of the Treadwells, a tailor and his wife, who live at the sign of the Grene Griffin. Anne fears that Richard of Gloucester will force her to marry him, a fate worse than death. He finally tracks her down, kidnaps her in the dead of night, and forces her to marry him in Westminster Abbey, despite her shrieks and screams for help, which continue throughout the secret midnight ceremony. This novel is a compendium of history lessons, recipes, and sermons, interspersed with Anne's story.

157. _____. *Red Rose and White: A Tale of the Wars of the Roses.*
London: J. F. Shaw & Co., 1882. vi+366pp.

Not available for review.

158. _____. *A Tangled Web: A Tale of the Fifteenth Century.* London: J.
F. Shaw & Co., 1885. 359pp.

Piers Osbeck, the godson of Edward IV and the son of converted Jews
from Tournai, becomes the tool of Margaret of Burgundy in her second
attempt to drive Henry Tudor from the throne. He is tutored in
Plantagenet family history and court manners, and accepted as Richard
of York, the younger son of Edward IV, by the kings of France and
Scotland. He marries Katherine Gordon, the daughter of the Earl of
Huntley, who had abandoned her as a baby. Katherine loves Piers, or
Perkin Warbeck, as he is called by the English, and when he is captured
after his failed attempt to gain the crown, she remains with him in
luxurious captivity. Perkin, a shallow, restless youth, attempts to escape,
and is placed in a dungeon in the Tower, where he continues to plot.
When the Spanish monarchs refuse to allow their daughter to marry
Prince Arthur as long as any possible Yorkist claimants remain alive,
both Perkin and the Earl of Warwick are executed. Katherine and her
new husband, Sir James Strangeways, go to Tournai to meet Piers'
family, and when she learns that he was a Jew, all remaining affection
for him vanishes, to be replaced by disgust.

159. Honeyman, Brenda. *Richard, By Grace of God.* London: Robert Hale
Limited, 1968. 255pp.

After he has seized the throne from his illegitimate nephew, Catesby and
Ratcliffe urge Richard III to kill both princes. His rejection of the
suggestion is not strong enough to convince the men that he really means
it, and they murder the boys and bury their bodies. Richard is horrified
by the deed for which he takes his share of the blame, and which he
knows will be laid at his door. Buckingham, who had helped him attain
the crown, is so distraught by the murders, that he turns against Richard
and throws his support to Henry Tudor. After the deaths of Richard's
son, wife, and cousin Buckingham, the king so loses heart, that he
becomes convinced that God is punishing him for his crimes, and he goes
to his death at Bosworth almost willingly.

160. _____. *The Kingmaker.* London: Robert Hale Limited, 1969. 208pp.

Richard Neville, Earl of Warwick, determined to rule England through Edward IV, whom he had placed on the throne, seriously misjudges both Edward and the English when he insists on a French marriage for the king. Angry and hurt by Edward's marriage to Elizabeth Woodville, and seduced by promises of land and titles by Louis of France, Warwick rebels and joins forces with Margaret of Anjou, in order to restore Henry VI to the throne. The earl plans to rule through Henry's son Edward and his bride, Anne Neville, but his other son-in-law Clarence returns to the king, Margaret delays too long in returning to England, Louis abandons him, and Warwick and his brother are both killed at Barnet.

161. _____. *Richmond and Elizabeth*. London: Robert Hale Limited, 1970. 224pp.

Elizabeth of York is deeply in love with her uncle Richard III, and hopes to marry him after the death of his wife. She is disappointed, but Henry Tudor is relieved, when Richard publicly disavows any such intention. Elizabeth's two young brothers are murdered by Catesby and Ratcliffe without the king's knowledge, but years later, when Henry Tudor's son Arthur dies, and he fears an uprising in the princes' names, he forces Tyrell to confess that he had them killed on Richard's orders.

162. _____. *Good Duke Humphrey*. London: Robert Hale Limited, 1973. 190pp.

Humphrey of Gloucester, the youngest brother of Henry V, opposes any policy favored by Cardinal Beaufort. The two are charged with governing England during Henry VI's minority, but their enmity leads to the brink of civil war. The cardinal chooses Margaret of Anjou as a wife for the weak young king, and Suffolk, who arranges the marriage, convinces Margaret that Humphrey is her enemy. Hoping to destroy Humphrey, the Beauforts charge his wife Eleanor with using sorcery to make her husband king, and Humphrey is arrested, and dies mysteriously. The commons, who loved him, are convinced that he was murdered by the queen and Suffolk, and they murder the hated duke. Somerset, the queen's new favorite, maintains Suffolk's policies, and the hostility between the factions leads to open warfare at St. Albans.

163. Hood, Evelyn. *The Kingmaker's Daughter*. London: Robert Hale Limited, 1974. 219pp.

Independent, rebellious Anne Neville falls madly in love with Peter Walton, one of her father's secretaries, but when Warwick rebels against

Edward IV, he forces Anne to marry Edward of Lancaster. Unaware that Peter has been killed by her father's henchmen, Anne reluctantly becomes betrothed to Edward. When Edward is killed at Tewkesbury, Anne is hidden by her brother-in-law Clarence. Rescued by Richard of Gloucester, she marries him and moves to Middleham. When her husband takes the crown after his brother's death and the revelation that the royal children are bastards, Anne is convinced by Buckingham that the princes in the Tower are a danger to Richard. With her cooperation he has the boys murdered, and a guilt-stricken Anne realizes that the duke was acting for Henry Tudor. When their son dies, Anne believes that she is being punished for her sin, and she dies soon after, hoping that Richard will not be blamed for the princes' deaths.

164. Horter, Pamela Jean. *Brief Candles*. New York: Vantage Press, 1983. 218pp.

Edward V, scholarly and mature beyond his years, is devastated by his father's death, but believes he can rule wisely with the help of his uncle Anthony Woodville. Edward IV had named Richard of Gloucester Protector, but the Woodville plot to destroy him leads to Rivers' downfall. Richard seizes the throne with the help and encouragement of the Duke of Buckingham, whose evil influence turns him from a kindly uncle into Edward's enemy. Richard puts Edward and his brother in the Tower to keep them safely out of the public eye, but Buckingham has them murdered, pretending to act on Richard's orders. Richard is distraught, but realizes that he must share the blame.

165. Hudson, Henry. *Wild Humphrey Kynaston: The Robber Troglodyte: A Romance of Robin Hood of Shropshire in the Reign of Henry VII*. Illus. London: Paul. Trench, Trubner, 1899. 375pp.

Not available for review.

166. Hueffer, Ford Maddox. *The Young Lovell*. London: Chatto & Windus, 1913. 310pp.

Fantasy and romance are blended in this Gothic novel by Ford Maddox Ford, written under his real name. Young Paris Lovell, a Yorkist lord living in Northumberland in 1486, is put under a spell. When he awakens three months later, he discovers that his father has died, his inheritance and betrothed have been stolen by his illegitimate half-brother, and he has been charged with sorcery. With the help of a young monk and the Bishop of Durham, a supporter of Richard III, Lovell recovers his patrimony, but chooses to live the remainder of his life sealed up in a hermit's cell.

167. Hughes, Beatrix. *Joan of St. Albans*. London: Heath, Cranton, 1926. 246pp.

In this novel of mistaken identity, which takes place in the vicinity of St. Albans and London, Richard of Gloucester mistakenly believes that the heroine, Joan, who is disguised as her twin brother, intends to kill him.

168. Hunt, Wray. *Satan's Daughter*. London: Robert Hale Limited, 1970. 240 pp.

Alys Hughes, the daughter of a drunken and abusive broom-maker in Dorset, sells her soul to the devil for wealth and power. Taught to read by a holy hermit, a former courtier of Edward IV, and educated by convent nuns, she repays them by burning down their church and causing the death of one of their members. She is taken in hand by a witch, Lady Jane Deane, the mother of Perkin Warbeck, who was fathered by Edward IV. Lady Jane plans to use Alys to wreak revenge on Henry Tudor, her son's murderer, but the plot is betrayed and Alys suffers the fate reserved for witches and traitors.

169. Irwin, Frances. *My Lady of Wycherly*. London: Robert Hale Ltd., 1971. 190 pp.

Orphaned heiress Katherine Seymour loves her handsome cousin Christopher, but she is forced by her uncle to marry the proud, stern widower Lord Jocelyn Vernon, one of Richard of Gloucester's knights. The marriage is plagued by disagreements and misunderstandings, but Katherine comes to love Jocelyn, although she has no opportunity to tell him so before he leaves to join Richard III at Bosworth. Their son is born before Jocelyn returns from the battle, where he has been wounded, and the couple finally express their love for each other, and go to Burgundy to start a new life.

170. _____. *The White Pawn*. London: Robert Hale Limited, 1972. 188pp.

Anne Neville and Richard of Gloucester become friends when he is sent to live at Middleham, but when Warwick, Anne's father, rebels against Edward IV and goes into exile, Anne falls in love with Francis Lovell, another of her Middleham friends, who has joined Warwick. Francis is married, however, and Anne is forced into a hateful marriage with Edward of Lancaster. After Edward's death at Tewkesbury, Anne's brother-in-law Clarence takes custody of her and plots to get rid of her so that he can seize her share of the Warwick estates. He hides her as a cookmaid in the house of a retainer, but she is rescued by Richard and agrees to marry him. After their wedding they return to their beloved Middleham.

171. _____. *The White Queen.* London: Robert Hale Limited, 1974. 190pp.

This sequel to *The White Pawn* (see entry 170) continues the story of the life of Anne Neville after her marriage to Richard of Gloucester, later Richard III. Although Anne is grateful to Richard for his many kindnesses, she does not love him. During their happy years together at Middleham, and the painful ones when he becomes king and they lose their frail, sickly son, Anne learns to love Richard, and to depend on his strength. Her health, never robust, fails after their son's death, and less than a year later she dies during an eclipse of the sun, leaving her grieving husband to face the threat of an invasion by Henry Tudor.

172. _____. *The Winter Killing.* London: Robert Hale Limited, 1977. 175pp.

Ralph Wentworth, squire to Edmund, Earl of Rutland, goes to Ireland with Edmund and his father, the Duke of York, after the king's forces defeat them at Ludlow. Ralph is disturbed by York's intention to seize the throne, but at Wakefield he fights at Edmund's side until the young duke is killed. Severely wounded himself, Ralph escapes and follows Margaret of Anjou's army to York, where he is horrified to see the heads of Edmund and other Yorkists mounted on the Micklegate Bar. Ralph is nursed back to health by Lady Elizabeth Mortimer, whom he loves, but who is engaged to marry his friend John Harrington. Ralph joins Edward of York at Mortimer's Cross, where Harington is killed, leaving Elizabeth free. Ralph, now a knight, looks forward to a Yorkist reign and marriage with the woman he loves.

173. James, G. P. R. *The Woodman; A Romance of the Times of Richard III.* London: T. C. Newby, Publisher, 1849. 3vols.

John Boyd, the head woodman of the Abbey of Atherston St. Clare, conspires with the abbess, her nieces Iola St. Leger and Lady Constance, and Lord Chartley, Lancastrians all, to save the life of Bishop Robert

(sic) Morton of Ely and convey him to Brittany, where he informs Henry
Tudor of the plot to kidnap him and deliver him to Richard III. Iola and
Chartley fall in love, but she has been contracted in marriage since
infancy to Lord Fulmer, a follower of the king's. Richard promises Iola
in marriage to both Fulmer and Chartley to ensure their loyalty, but she
escapes when her guardian attempts to force her to marry Fulmer.
Fulmer is killed at Bosworth, the true identities of the woodman and Iola
are revealed, and the lovers are united in marriage.

174. _____. "Perkin Warbeck: 1474-1499." *Dark Scenes of History*.
London: T. C. Newby, Publisher, 1849. 3 vols. New York: Harper,
1850. 419pp. pp.50-119.

Richard of York, the younger son of Edward IV, loves his uncle Richard
III, and when the king is killed at Bosworth, Elizabeth Woodville knows
that Henry Tudor is a threat to the boy's life. She tells her son to
remember everything about his life at court, so that he can reclaim the
crown for York, and then he is taken secretly abroad. When Richard is
grown, he convinces the kings of France and Scotland, and his aunt
Margaret of Burgundy, of his true identity, but all eventually abandon
him. He marries Catherine Gordon, a cousin of the king of Scotland,
and the Scots invade England, but the English, although they hate Henry,
are too afraid of him to rise in Richard's favor. Richard is captured and
imprisoned by Tudor, who then traps him and his cousin Warwick into
attempting to escape. Both are executed, thus ending the Yorkist threat.

175. Jarman, Rosemary Hawley. *We Speak No Treason*. Boston: Little, Brown
and Company, 1971. 565pp.

This novel tells Richard III's story through the eyes of three people who
knew and loved him: his young mistress, the mother of his illegitimate
daughter; the court fool; and the Man of Keen Sight, one of his knights.
This is the author's first novel, and set a high standard which she
excelled in her succeeding works. See entries 176-178.

176. _____. *The King's Grey Mare*. London: William Collins Sons & Co.,
Ltd., 1973. 448pp.

Elizabeth Woodville is the not entirely unsympathetic heroine of this
novel, which traces her life from her marriage to John Grey until her
immurement in a convent by Henry Tudor, her son-in-law, and the man
she had helped to seize the throne.

177. _____. *Crown in Candlelight*. Boston and Toronto: Little, Brown and Company, 1978. 416pp.

Katherine of Valois, daughter of a mad French king and his greedy and promiscuous wife, grows up in a poverty-stricken and unloving home. When Henry V invades and conquers France, he and Katherine fall in love, and they have a short, but happy marriage and a son. After Henry's death, Katherine falls in love with Owen Tudor, a minor Welsh squire in Henry's service. Their love survives, despite the antagonism of Henry's family, and she bears Owen three children. Their grandson Henry founded the Tudor dynasty.

178. _____. *The Courts of Illusion*. Boston: Little, Brown and Company, 1983. 370pp.

Nicholas Archer, the illegitimate son of the Man of Keen Sight, one of the narrators of *We Speak No Treason* (see entry 175), who was executed after Bosworth, takes up the cause of Richard IV, known as Perkin Warbeck. Through the good times, when the pretender has the support of the kings of France and Scotland and many of the Irish nobility, to the disasters and defeat that end the rebellion, Nicholas is his faithful servant and friend, though his loyalty costs him dearly.

179. Jefferis, Barbara. *Beloved Lady*. New York: W. Sloane Associates, 1955. 341 pp. London: J. M. Dent & Sons Ltd., 1956. 341pp.

John Paston the Eldest, the heir of Sir John Fastolfe, is forced to defend his newly inherited lands and manors from those who dispute his ownership, and the Lancastrian Pastons make their peace with the new king, Edward IV, hoping for his help. Their troubles are compounded when their daughter Margery falls in love with Richard Calle, their trusted and valued bailiff. Margery and Richard take a legally binding vow before God that they are man and wife, but her parents refuse to acknowledge it. Her mother beats her nearly to death, and then imprisons her in a dungeon, but Margery refuses to deny her love, or to marry a man favored by her parents. Richard and Margery endure many dangers, including a seige of Caister Castle by the Duke of Norfolk, before they finally achieve their hearts' desire. The author has captured the period very well, and her characters are well-developed and convincing. This is one of the best books written about the period.

180. Jones, Cherry Calvert. *Proud Cis*. London: Robert Hale Ltd., 1980. 174pp.

Edward IV marries Eleanor Butler in a secret ceremony performed by Stillington, a priest. Eleanor, who does not know that her husband is the king, bears him twins, Cicily and Richard. Edward, believing that Eleanor is dead, marries Elizabeth Woodville. Long after their mother's death in a convent, the twins, having figured out that they are related to the king, journey to London. They are acknowledged by the royal family as the king's legitimate children, but are sent to Middleham to protect them from the Woodvilles. After Edward's death, Hastings attempts to put young Richard on the throne, but is executed before he can carry out his plan. After the death of Richard III, Cicily helps the princes escape from the Tower, and then retires to a quiet life far from court. A rather far-fetched premise, unconvincingly executed.

181. Jones, Hannah Maria. *Jane Shore, or, The Goldsmith's Wife.* Illus. London: E.J. Brett, 1880, 1889? 362 pp.

Originally issued in twenty-nine parts, and published weekly in Princess's Novelettes Edition, this work has been attributed to Mrs. Mary Bennett. (See entry 27.)

182. Kettle, Jocelyn. *Memorial to the Duchess.* London: Herbert Jenkins Ltd., 1968. 251pp.

Alice Chaucer, grand-daughter of the poet, is married to the Earl of Salisbury, a proud, ambitious man, and after his death she marries the love of her life, William de la Pole, Earl of Suffolk, who is even prouder and more ambitious than Salisbury. After many years of marriage they have a son, and the couple, great favorites of Henry VI and Margaret of Anjou, are rewarded for their loyalty with lands, offices, and a dukedom. Suffolk, who secretly deeded English territory in France to secure the king's marriage, is accused of treason when the terms of the treaty are revealed, and becomes the most hated man in England. Sent into exile, he is murdered at sea by suspected Yorkists. York assures Alice that he had no part in her husband's death, and to save the family fortune she agrees to a marriage between her son and York's daughter. She remains loyal to her husband's memory, even while she and her son support Edward IV. This novel is well-researched and written.

183. Kilbourne, Janet. *Garland of the Realm.* London: Robert Hale Limited, 1972. 288pp.

Richard of Gloucester must guard himself against known enemies like Anthony Woodville, and those he believes to be his friends, like

Buckingham, Hastings, and Stanley. When Edward IV dies, Anthony Woodville plans to destroy Richard and make himself Protector, in order to control young Edward V. His plot fails, but Buckingham, who plans to make himself king, is a greater danger. Hastings, the Stanleys, and Morton are also planning Richard's death, so that Henry Tudor can seize the throne. Although Richard wins the love of the people, his inability to see the treachery all around him leads to his death at Bosworth.

184. _____. *Wither One Rose*. London: Robert Hale Limited, 1973. 256pp.

Henry Tudor watches with pleasure as Richard III is hacked to death at Bosworth, and his long-cherished dream of claiming the crown comes true. He marries Elizabeth of York, although the two despise each other. After years of marriage, they come to love each other, and despite Henry's pathological hatred of the Yorkists, his systematic murder of all surviving members of the house, including her brother Richard, and his deliberate blackening of Richard III's name, Elizabeth does not lift a hand to stop him. She, too, has become a Tudor, more interested in preserving her husband's and her positions, than in saving innocent members and adherents of her family.

185. King, Betty. *The Lady Margaret*. London: Herbert Jenkins Ltd., 1965. 224pp.

This is the story of the life of Margaret Beaufort from the age of three until the birth of her son Henry Tudor, told from the Lancastrian point of view. This Margaret, who is cheerful, affectionate, and passionately in love with her husband, the Earl of Richmond, is not at all the pious, dour, scholarly ascetic familiar to most readers of the history and literature of the period.

186. _____. *The Lord Jasper*. London: Herbert Jenkins Ltd., 1967. 256pp.

Edmund and Jasper Tudor, whose parents Katherine and Owen Tudor are cruelly persecuted by Humphrey of Gloucester, are finally acknowledged and brought to court by their half-brother Henry VI. Edmund marries Margaret Beaufort, the wealthy Lancastrian heiress, but dies before their son Henry is born. Jasper, who becomes the protector of his brother's family, falls madly in love with Margaret, and she with him, but they are prohibited by church law from marrying. Their pure, chaste love endures through Margaret's two succeeding marriages and years of exile for Jasper and Henry during the reigns of Edward IV and Richard III. When word reaches Jasper and Henry in Brittany of the unpopularity of the murderous, cruel Richard III, who has killed his nephews, Henry VI, Hastings, and Buckingham, they decide the time is ripe for Henry to invade and claim his rightful crown. Thousands flock to his cause, he defeats Richard, shows immediately that he will be a kind, just ruler, and rewards his uncle Jasper with the earldom of Bedford.

187. _____. *The King's Mother*. London: Robert Hale, Ltd., 1969. 224pp.

Margaret Beaufort, the heroine of this fictionalized biography, was the subject of several of the author's other books. See entries 185, 186, and 190.

188. _____. *The Rose Both Red and White*. London: Robert Hale Limited, 1970. 220 pp. Published in the United States as *The Rose, Red and White*. New York: Pinnacle Books, Inc., 1974. 224pp.

The life of Margaret Tudor, daughter of Elizabeth of York and Henry Tudor, from her marriage at age fourteen until her death in 1541, is the subject of this novel. Margaret is married to James IV of Scotland in order to cement peace between their countries, but after her husband's death at Flodden Field, she secretly marries the Earl of Angus, heir of the powerful Douglas family. The marriage proves a mistake, both personally and politically, and Margaret falls in love with the Duke of Albany, Regent of Scotland. Self-willed, selfish, spoiled Margaret shows very poor judgment in men, and lives an unhappy life in a country torn apart by factionalism.

189. _____. *The Rose, Red and White*.

See entry 188.

190. _____. *The Beaufort Secretary*. London: Robert Hale Ltd., 1970. 222pp.

William Elmer, a devout Lancastrian, goes to London to study law, but is hired as secretary to Margaret Beaufort. He becomes devoted to the kind, gentle, and loving woman, and pities the hopeless love she and Jasper Tudor bear each other. It is the last year of the reign of the evil, murderous usurper Richard III, and the whole country eagerly awaits the invasion of noble, kind, and generous Henry Tudor. In his second attempt, in August, 1485, Tudor seizes the crown, and proves himself a near-perfect monarch. William, meanwhile, has been in love with Perrot, an assistant governess to Jasper Tudor's stepchildren, and although she becomes his lover, she will not marry him, and William's unhappiness is made nearly insupportable by Perrot's promiscuity and involvement with witchcraft. When she gives birth to a still-born child, Margaret Beaufort nurses her, and then makes her a lady-in-waiting. William forgives Perrot, she realizes she loves him, and agrees to marry him.

191. _____. *Margaret of Anjou*. London: Robert Hale Limited, 1974. 255pp.

Margaret of Anjou is married to Henry VI, but before she sails for England she falls in love with Pierre de Brezé, a married emissary of the French king. She is disappointed in the monk-like Henry, but learns to love him as one would a child. Frustrated after eight years of childless marriage, and knowing she must produce an heir to protect herself against the hatred of the English, she becomes pregnant by her favorite, Somerset. When Henry is driven from the throne and Somerset is killed, she flees to France to beg aid from Louis XI. Pierre de Brezé pleads her cause and becomes her lover, and Louis agrees to help her if she will join her old enemy Warwick. Their plans to restore the Lancastrians fail when Warwick and Margaret's son are killed, and she is taken prisoner. She is ransomed by Louis XI, but Pierre is now dead and she lives in lonely poverty until her death.

192. _____. *Owen Tudor*. London: Robert Hale Ltd., 1977.   191pp.

This fictionalized biography of the Welsh squire who married Katherine of Valois, the widow of Henry V, tells of both their trials and triumphs as they attempt to keep their marriage secret from their enemies, Humphrey of Gloucester and Cardinal Beaufort. The eventual discovery of their secret leads to Owen's temporary imprisonment, and Katherine's death in a convent.

193. Kramer, Kathryn. *Desire's Masquerade*. New York: Dell Publishing Co., Inc., 1987.   397pp.

Stephen Valentine, an exile in Venice during the reign of Edward IV, returns to England early in the reign of Richard III, and meets and falls in love with Lady Madrigal. He rejects her and returns to Venice when he discovers that her father was his betrayer. Madrigal tries, but fails, to warn the king of Buckingham's plot against him, and knowing her life is in danger, she follows Stephen to Venice, wins back his love, and the two return to England just before the Battle of Bosworth.

194. Lamb, Hilda. *The Willing Heart*. London: Hodder & Stoughton, 1958. 314pp.

Stephen Hawes, the illegitimate son of Richard of Gloucester, is brought up by his mother and merchant step-father in Suffolk. After earning his degree at Oxford, where he is befriended by Thomas More, he enters his step-father's business. His mother, a former lady-in-waiting to Elizabeth Woodville, has connections at court, and Stephen meets Margaret Plantagenet, Clarence's daughter. He marries the daughter of a Suffolk neighbor, discovering too late that he loves Margaret, who has married Sir Richard Pole. Despite his devotion to the memory of his real father, Stephen becomes a courtier of Henry VII, who employs him on several secret missions.

195. Lawrence, Charles Edward. *The Gods Were Sleeping. A Romance of the Days of King Richard the Third*. London: John Murray, 1937.   317 pp.

Bart, a youth of uncertain parentage, goes to work in the Tower during the reign of the chivalrous, kind-hearted, enlightened Richard III, while the young sons of Edward IV are in residence.

196. Layton, Edith. *The Crimson Crown*. New York: Onyx/New American Library, a division of Penguin Books, 1990. 387pp.

Lucas Lovat, foster son of a wool merchant and one of Henry Tudor's many spies, returns from abroad, and is ordered to seduce Megan Baswell, lady-in-waiting to Katherine Gordon, Perkin Warbeck's wife, so that Henry can learn of any plots to free Warbeck. Megan is another of Henry's unwilling spies, but is protective of her mistress, and half in love with Warbeck herself, and she resists Lucas, an experienced seducer. Lucas has his own great secret, and feels endangered by a growing sympathy for Warbeck, and increasing attraction to Megan. The two fall in love, but Lucas' attempts to save Warbeck and Warwick place the lovers in danger. Few readers will anticipate the outcome of this novel.

197. Leary, Francis. *The Swan and the Rose*. New York: A. A. Wyn, 1953. iv + 304pp.

Arthur Adair, a London urchin, joins Lord Wenlock's company to fight for Lancaster at Barnet, and then journeys to Tewkesbury to join Queen Margaret's forces. All the while the evil, misshapen Duke of Gloucester is plotting the murder of Edward of Lancaster and the kidnapping of Anne Neville, Edward's loving wife. The Lancastrians are defeated, and Arthur watches as those who sought sanctuary are executed by the cruel Yorkists. He learns that Gloucester and Clarence had butchered the prince, and that Anne, who had been captured by one of Gloucester's agents, has been taken to London, where she will be forced to marry the duke. Gloucester then murders Henry VI in the Tower, thus securing the throne for York.

198. _____. *Fire and Morning*. New York: G. P. Putnam's Sons, 1957. 297pp.

Richard III is a hard and relentless, but just and efficient king who, though innocent of the murders of his nephews, is the victim of a nefarious plot by Henry Tudor and John Morton to place the blame for a crime committed by Buckingham on the king. The hero of the novel, a Lancastrian who attempts to unravel the mystery of the princes, realizes too late that he has betrayed a man of honor to villainous men.

199. Lewis, Hilda. *Wife to Henry V*. London: Jarrolds Publishers Limited, 1954. 418pp.

Catherine of Valois is determined to marry Henry V and become queen of France and England. Catherine is cold, ambitious, and greedy, but she has a romantic view of Henry as a knight in the old chivalric tradition. She discovers that he is an indifferent husband and a cold, vengeful conqueror. After his death she turns in her loneliness to her steward Owen Tudor, marries him secretly and against the council's orders, and bears him three children. Henry VI, her son by the late king, is mad and pious, but he loves his mother and vows to protect her Tudor children when she is sent to a convent and Owen is arrested. As the war in France drags on, Catherine's only fear is that her son's French crown will be lost, and she wastes little sympathy on her suffering countrymen.

200. Leyland, Eric. *The Silver Skein*. London: Hutchinson (Hutchinson Historical Series), 1946. 224pp.

At Christmas, 1944, Adrian Mortimer, his sister, and two cousins spend their school holidays at his home in Devon. With the help of their uncle Robert, they discover that the family's founder was Richard Mortimer,

the illegitimate son of Richard III. Richard is ignorant of his parentage
until he is taken prisoner by agents of Henry Tudor, who wants to
destroy all Yorkists with a claim to the throne. Richard is rescued by an
old retainer of his father's, who gives him a large ruby from the late
king's crown, and takes him abroad, where he lives for many years.
When he returns to England with his children, he settles in Devon.
Robert and the young Mortimers go through the family papers and trace
their history to the 19th century, when the ruby, known as the Luck of
the Mortimers, disappears. They unravel the mystery of its
disappearance, and the family's fortunes improve immediately upon its
recovery.

201. Lide, Mary. *Command of the King*. London: Grafton Books, 1990. New
York: St. Martin's Press, 1991.   287 pp.

Heiress Philippa de Verne, whose father had been executed for leading
a Yorkist rebellion against Henry VII, is now, in the reign of his son,
being cheated of her inheritance by her step-father, who wants her to
marry his elderly attorney. Philippa runs away, and is rescued by
Lancastrian Lord Richard Montacune, an admirer of her father's.
Philippa, advised to ask the king to pardon her father and restore her
lands, earns Henry's enmity when she spurns his advances. Richard
agains rescues her from both the king's plot to seduce her into treason,
and Wolsey's attempt to use her as a spy aginst Mary Tudor, and despite
the treachery of the Tudors and their minions, the story ends well for
Philippa and Richard.

202. *The Life and Transactions of Mrs. Jane Shore, Concubine to King Edward
IVth*. Glasgow: Printed for the Booksellers, 1800.   24 pp.

Another version of entries 110, 144-152, 225, 280, 302, 328.

203. Lindsay, Philip. *London Bridge is Falling*. London: I. Nicholson &
Watson, Ltd., 1934.   447pp. Boston: Little, Brown and Company,
1934.   xiv + 389pp.

In 1450, Andrew Picard returns from years of soldiering on the
Continent and in Ireland to his father's house on London Bridge.
Andrew, an adherent of the Duke of York, has come to enlist support for
Jack Cade's rebellion, designed to bring down the corrupt favorites of the
queen, and to reform the government. Andrew falls in love with Jane
Piel, the betrothed of his best friend Nicholas, who no longer wants to
marry her. Arthur, Nicholas' father's apprentice, also loves Jane, and

tries to kill Andrew. Their personal battle is played out against the battle on London Bridge between Cade's men and the citizens of London. The bridge and most of the shops and houses on it are destroyed by a fire set during the battle, and despite the king's promise of pardon, many of the rebels are hanged. Cade is hunted down and slain, and Nicholas, one of the few survivors, realizes that the rebellion has gained nothing.

204. _____. *The Duke is Served*. London: Ivor Nicholson and Watson Limited, 1936. 448pp.

Dionisia Alwyn, chamberer to Anne Neville at Middleham, is sent to London to serve Elizabeth Woodville after Warwick rebels against Edward IV. Dionisia is betrothed to Drew Purches, a king's archer, but she falls in love with Benedict Studly, a baker in the king's kitchen. The lecherous Benedict falls in love with Dionisia, whose great pride in her virginity is so novel to him that he respects, but cannot accept her intention to remain pure and to marry Drew, whom she hates. Dionisia has been entrusted by Anne to deliver a ring and assurances of her love to Richard of Gloucester, and realizing that the Duke has chosen loyalty to his brother over love for Anne, she vows to emulate him. The lovers and their friends join the queen in sanctuary when Edward flees the country, but after Benedict is wounded at Barnet, Dionisia realizes that pride, and not virtue, has kept them apart. After they marry they are able to reunite Richard and Anne, thus fulfilling Dionisia's fondest dreams.

205. _____. *The Merry Mistress*. London: Hutchinson & Co. (Publishers) Ltd., 1952. 304pp. New York: Roy Publishing Company, 1953. 304pp.

From her prison cell, in which she is confined after doing penance for her wicked life, Jane Shore, the merry mistress of the late king Edward IV, reminisces about her life. Her unloving parents sold her into marriage to a wealthy London mercer William Shore, who loved her but was dominated by his late wife's sister Agnes. Jane finds her life dull, and when she catches the eye of Lord Hastings, and then the king, she decides to leave her husband and the brutal Agnes, and go to court. As long as Edward lives she is protected from the intrigues of the court and the queen's hatred, but when the king dies she is seduced by Dorest and Hastings into plotting against Richard of Gloucester. He learns of the plot, punishes the plotters, and accedes to the church's demand that Jane do penance. She is rescued from prison by Thomas Lymon, Richard's solicitor general, and she marries him to escape a life of poverty.

206. _____. *They Have Their Dreams*. London: Hutchinson & Co. (Publishers) Ltd., 1956. 288pp. Published in the United States as *A Princely Knave*. New York: Sphere Books, 1971. 288pp.

Perkin Warbeck, his wife, and a small band of followers, land in Cornwall to wrest the throne from Henry Tudor. With a mob of unarmed and untrained Cornishmen, they attack Exeter, but are soundly beaten. Perkin and his three inept advisors are captured, and the pretender is imprisoned in the Tower. Katherine, his wife, does not believe he is the Duke of York, and feels only contempt for the man she considers a low-born coward. Only when she realizes that he will be hanged by the cruel, conniving Henry Tudor, does she admit that she loves her husband. She tries to persuade Perkin to admit his true identity, which is royal though illegitimate, so that Tudor will pardon him, but they are betrayed, and the king destroys the last living Yorkist claimants to the throne.

207. _____. *A Princely Knave.*

See entry 206.

208. Lofts, Nora. *The Town House*. New York: Doubleday & Company, Inc., 1959. 381pp.

Martin Reed, born a serf in 1381, rises to wealth during the first half of the 15th century. The novel portrays the lives of the merchant class during a period of great change and upheaval in England, with the Wars of the Roses as part of the background.

209. _____. *The Maude Reed Tale*. Illus. by Anne and Janet Grahame Johnstone. New York: Thomas Nelson, Inc., 1972. 174 pp.

Maude Reed, a descendant of Martin Reed (see entry 208) and grand-daughter of a wool merchant at Baildon, is sent to Beauclaire, the home of distant wealthy relatives, to be educated. Maude wants to take over the family business, but that will go to her twin brother Walter. After more than a year at Beauclaire, Walter visits her to tell her he has chosen the life of an itinerant lute player, and signs over his rights in Baildon to her. She returns home to find the house in disarray, her mother and grandfather ill, and the business taken over by Walter's former tutor. Maude sets things to rights and wins her grandfather's approval to learn the business, as she awaits the return from the war of Henry Rancon, a friend from Beauclaire whom she had promised to marry. The Wars of the Roses are going on, but they affect only the powerful families like the owners of Beauclaire, and the Reeds continue their peaceful lives undisturbed.

210. _____. *Knight's Acre*. London: Hodder and Stoughton, 1975. 256pp

This novel, which covers the period between 1451 and 1460, tells of the founding of Knight's Acre, an estate in Suffolk, by Sir Godfrey Tallboys and his wife Sybilla. Part of the action takes place in England during the early stages of the Wars of the Roses, but a large part is devoted to the hero's adventures during a crusade against the Moors.

211. _____. *The Homecoming*. New York: Doubleday & Company, Inc., 1976. 282pp.

In this sequel to *Knight's Acre* (see entry 210), Sir Godfrey Tallboys, after an absence of eight years, returns from Spain to his wife and family, bringing with him the young woman who had saved his life and will bear his child. He arrives just before the Battle of Wakefield, and loyal Yorkist that he is, he leaves to join the Duke of York's forces, but falls ill and misses the battle. The Wars of the Roses form part of the background of the novel, which deals with the lives of the northern gentry in the latter half of the 15th century.

212. _____. *The Lonely Furrow*. New York: Doubleday & Company, 1976. 308 pp.

This third novel in a trilogy (see entries 210, 211) tells of the fortunes and misfortunes of Henry Tallboys after the Battle of Tewkesbury. Although they are Yorkists, Henry, his wife and son, and Joanna, the daughter of Henry's father's mistress, have not prospered, in part because Henry will not use Joanna's fortune. Joanna is in love with Henry, and when his wife dies, she agrees to his plan to send her away to be educated as a lady, only if he promises to marry her when she returns. She flees her hosts' manor when they try to force her to marry an old man, although Henry, in order to spare her, has told her guardian, the bishop, that they are betrothed. When Edward IV is persuaded by his advisors to take control of the wardships of all wealthy, unattached orphans, Joanna comes to his notice, and she is informed that she must enter a convent. Henry saves her again by going through a formal betrothal, although he has learned that they can never marry because they had the same father. Joanna is satisfied with the situation as long as they can live in safety at Knight's Acre, even as brother and sister.

213. Long, Freda M. *The Coveted Crown*. London: Robert Hale Ltd., 1966.
     240pp.

Weak, pious Henry VI marries strong-willed Margaret of Anjou, but he
has taken a vow of chastity. Margaret rules the country, but she is
unpopular and knows she must produce an heir to secure the succession.
She seduces Henry into doing his marital duty, and a son is born, but the
English do not believe the king is the father. When Henry is driven from
the throne by Edward IV, Margaret goes to France. She reluctantly
agrees to join forces with her old enemy Warwick, and mad Henry is
briefly restored to the throne. After delaying her return too long,
Margaret lands in England to learn that Warwick has been killed in
battle, and her dreams are shattered when her son is captured at
Tewkesbury, beaten by Clarence and Gloucester, and brutally murdered
by Edward. The three evil York brothers then sneak into the Tower and
murder Henry VI at his prayers.

214. _____. *Requiem for Richard*. London: Robert Hale & Company,
     1975.   190pp.

The novel opens with the coronation of Richard III and Anne Neville,
and then flashes back to 1470, after the marriage of Clarence and Isabel
Neville. After Warwick's death, Richard and Clarence quarrel over his
inheritance, but Richard marries Anne despite Clarence's objections.
Elizabeth Woodville, fearful that Clarence will reveal Edward's pre-
contract with Eleanor Butler, persuades the king to kill Clarence, but the
drunken duke saves them the trouble by drowning himself accidentally in
a butt of Malmsey. After Edward's death, Richard is saved from a
similar decision to murder his nephew, when Buckingham gets them
drunk and smothers them. The book ends with the death of the king who
had lost all he loved, and yielding to the lure of power, betrayed his
loyalty to his brother.

215. Lynn, Escott. *Under the Red Rose: A Tale of the Wars of the Roses*. Illus.
     by Christopher Clark. London: Cassell & Co. Ltd., 1910.   x+351pp.

Brave, impetuous, loyal Guy Talbot is an esquire to Anthony Rivers at
Ludlow when Edward IV dies and Rivers' ward becomes Edward V. On
the way to London for the coronation, Guy attempts to rescue his master
from the evil Richard of Gloucester. Unsuccessful, he goes to London
to warn Elizabeth Woodville, but Gloucester has seen him, and he is a
marked man. This unimportant retainer manages to be in all the right
places, at the right times. At the meeting in the Tower when Hastings

is executed, he saves Stanley's life. After an unsuccessful attempt to rescue the princes from the Tower, he is sent as a prisoner to Brecon with Morton, and helps the bishop escape. When Henry Tudor attempts to land in England during Buckingham's rebellion, Guy and his friends warn him off and save his life. Tudor escapes to Brittany, where Guy almost singlehandedly holds off the villains who want to capture him. At Bosworth, Guy gets in a blow at the evil Richard, thus helping to defeat him. All these good deeds do not go unrewarded, for Guy learns that his mysterious father is of noble blood, he himself is knighted, and marries the beautiful, virtuous girl who adores him.

216. McChesney, Dora Greenwell. *The Confession of Richard Plantagenet*. London: Smith, Elder, 1913. 319pp.

Richard of Gloucester is a man doomed from birth to pay for the sins of the House of York, and he commits a few of his own on the way to the throne. McChesney portrays Richard as a saintly, conscientious man, who was innocent of the murders of his nephews, and whose other crimes were the result of necessity. The author died before completing the book, and a friend tied it together and published it, with the omission of a few unfinished chapters.

217. McDonald, Eva. *Cry Treason Thrice*. London: Robert Hale and Company, Ltd., 1977. 204pp.

Edmund Sallis, Richard of Gloucster's tilting master at Middleham, is devoted to his young charge. Edmund falls in love with Cecily Scrope, an arrogant heiress who spurns his proposal of marriage. When she learns, however, that she is her father's illegitimate daughter, and thus must forfeit her position and wealth, she agrees to marry Edmund. Cecily becomes a lady-in-waiting to Anne Neville, conquers her pride, and falls in love with her husband. Edmund performs many services for Richard, as Duke of Gloucester and king, travelling to the continent several times to spy on Henry Tudor, an evil, greedy adventurer. When Tudor defeats Richard at Bosworth, he murders both princes to safeguard his title, and accuses Richard of the crime. Edmund, recognizing the danger to all loyal Yorkists under the new king, escapes to Italy with his family.

218. Maiden, Cecil. *The Borrowed Crown*. Illus. by L. F. Cary. New York: The Viking Press, Inc., 1968. 222pp.

Twelve-year-old Lambert Simnel, the son of an Oxford organ builder and his wife, who have just died of the plague, is taken under the wing of Richard Symonds, a dedicated Yorkist priest. With the aid of the Earl of Lincoln and Elizabeth Woodville, young Lambert is groomed to impersonate Edward of Warwick, Clarence's son. They gather an army of mercenaries, intending to drive Henry Tudor from the throne, but the rebellion fails, and Tudor puts Lambert to work in the royal kitchens.

219. Makepeace, Joanna [Margaret E. York]. *Pawns of Power*. London: Hurst and Blackett, 1972. 185pp.

Marian Hurst, daughter of a Lancastrian and widow of an elderly merchant, falls in love with Sir Ralf Compton, a friend of Edward IV. When he proposes marriage, she accepts, but overhears Richard of Gloucester telling Anne Neville that the king has ordered Ralf to marry her in order to keep her wealth in Yorkist hands. Marian learns that Ralf truly loves her, but the two are separated when Warwick rebels and Giles Crosby, her father's man, attempts to poison the king. Although Ralf drinks the poison, Marian is arrested for complicity, but she is kidnapped by men loyal to her father and taken to France, where she is reunited with her old friend Anne Neville. Anne loves Richard of Gloucester, but is forced to marry Edward of Lancaster. After the Battle of Tewkesbury, the two young women, the pawns in their fathers' games of power, find happiness at last when they are reunited with the men they love.

220. _____. *My Lord Enemy*. London and Sydney: Macdonald and Co., 1984. 271pp.

At the betrothal ceremony of Elinor Beckwith, the daughter of an adherent of Warwick, and Lord Gerard Cranley, a follower of Edward IV, the young couple fall in love. Her father plans to use the occasion to capture Gerard and Richard of Gloucester, but the plot fails and Gerard takes Eleanor and her father hostage. Gerard forces Elinor to marry him, and after releasing her father, the newlyweds join the king in exile in Burgundy. Gerard, who is insanely jealous, beats Elinor when he discovers that she has tried to communicate with her beloved cousin Reginald, who has joined Margaret of Anjou in France. After many misunderstandings, separations, and escapes from danger and death, the two are finally reconciled. Eleanor learns that her father and Reginald care nothing for her except as a pawn in their bid for power, and that it is her husband who is on the side of the angels.

221. _____. *Battlefield of Hearts*. London: Mills and Boon Limited, 1991. 253 pp.

Orphaned Yorkist heiress Aleyne Risby flees her home before the Battle of Tewkesbury to escape a hateful marriage to her step-mother's cousin, Sir Thomas Stoodely. On her way to Gloucester, where she plans to seek safety with her cousin Ellis, an adherent of Warwick's, and his mother, she is attacked by Lancastrian soldiers, and rescued by Sir Dominick Allard, one of Richard of Gloucester's men. As a reward for his loyal service, Gloucester gives Aleyne in marriage to Dominick. Despite their mutual distrust, the two fall in love, but when Aleyne discovers that Ellis has been imprisoned by the Yorkists for spying, she arranges to set him free. He later repays the favor by rescuing her from the clutches of the evil Sir Thomas, who has conspired with Clarence to murder Anne Neville. After Anne's rescue, the grateful Gloucester takes Aleyne and Dominick to Middleham to serve in his household.

222. _____. *Reluctant Rebel*. London: Mills & Boon Limited, 1993. London: Masquerade Books, 1993.   252 pp.

Isabel Hatfield, whose father was wounded and betrothed killed at Bosworth fighting for Richard III, wants to forget the quarrels of the past. She is attracted to James Tarvin, the son of their Lancastrian neighbor, but their fathers oppose the match. When her father's old comrade Sir Adam Westlake arrives with the wounded Francis Lovell, she resents him for involving her father in the Lambert Simnel rebellion. In her attempt to protect her father, she accidentally kills James' father. After her father dies of wounds suffered at Stoke, Isabel and Adam are betrothed and flee to the protection of Margaret of Burgundy. There Isabel meets Richard of York, the younger son of Edward IV, and her doubts about the character of Richard III are laid to rest.

223. _____. *Crown Hostage*. London: Mills & Boon Limited, 1994.   284 pp.

Sir John Rushton breaks his daughter's betrothal to Guy Jarvis because the young man has lost his fortune. Eight years later, Margaret Rushton's betrothal to Bennet Hartwell is posponed by the death of Edward IV and her father's decision to go to the aid of the Woodvilles. Margaret is taken hostage by Richard of Gloucester and placed in the charge of his friend Guy Jarvis. Despite their mutual hostility, the two are attracted to each other, and Margaret learns too late to save her father's life that his loyalty was misplaced. The book is written to standard historical-romance formula, but the author knows the history of the period.

224. Malvern, Gladys. *The Queen's Lady*. Philadelphia: Macrae Smith Company, 1963.   189pp.

On her way home from work one rainy night, fourteen-year-old servant-girl Joanna rescues a young woman from the clutches of Yorkist soldiers, and takes her to the room she shares with her friend Cicely. She discovers that the woman is Anne Neville, who has run away to escape the evil hunchbacked Richard of Gloucester, who is determined to marry her. Anne is mourning the death of her beloved husband Edward of Lancaster, and Joanna finds her work in the great house where she is employed. Cicily betrays Anne, and Gloucester forces her to marry him, though he knows she despises him, and Joanna becomes her maid.

225. Maude, Sophie. *The Hermit and the King. A Fulfilment of Monsignor R. Hugh Benson's Prophesy of Richard Raynal*. (See entry 30.) London: R. & T. Washbourne Limited and St. Louis, Mo., B. Herder, 1916.   260pp.

Written for Catholic young people, this novel tells the story of Harry, the infant son of the Earl of Avon, who is kidnapped by his father's enemies. His cruel Yorkist stepmother refuses to ransom him, because she wants her son to inherit the title. Harry is taken to France for several years, and when he returns, a kind peddler takes him to King Henry VI. The saintly monarch believes the boy's tale and places him in Eton, and from thenceforth young Harry fights for the Lancastrian king against his Yorkist enemies, following him into exile, and losing his life attempting to save Henry's, when Edward IV regains the throne.

226. Melady, John. *The Little Princes*. Richmond Hill, Ontario: Scholastic-TAB, 1899.   135pp.

This novel about the Princes in the Tower, written for children, is not available for review.

227. *Memoirs of the Lives of King Edward IV. and Jane Shore*. London: Printed for E. Curll, 1714.   28 pp.

Another version of entries 110, 144-152, 202, 225, 280, 328.

228. Miall, Wendy. *John of Gloucester*. London: Robert Hale Ltd., 1968. 189pp.

John of Gloucester, the bastard son of Richard III, is in love with his cousin Margaret, Clarence's daughter, but she is betrothed to the future

Earl of Salisbury. The king sends John to visit the Stirlings, where he meets Elizabeth, whom he decides to marry, and her sinister brother Edward, who is secretly working with Morton and Henry Tudor. When rumors circulate that the king has murdered his two nephews, Richard asks John to spirit the two boys to safety in the north, fearing that if Tudor defeats him in battle, he will have them killed. John takes them to his mother, now the wife of a farmer, but Edward, the elder, sickens and dies. After Bosworth, Henry uses Edward Stirling to attempt to discover the boys' whereabouts, but although Edward keeps John under constant surveillance, he is unable to learn the truth. Henry trumps up charges implicating John in the Lambert Simnel rebellion, and has him executed, but his final words destroy the king's hopes for setting the question to rest. He will never know if the princes are alive to threaten his throne, and Edward, who has failed to learn the answer, loses Henry's favor.

229. _____. *The Playing Card Queen.* London: Robert Hale Ltd., 1970.
   207pp.

Elizabeth of York is required to marry Henry Tudor, and although she remains a devoted Yorkist, she is determined to be a loyal wife. She is bitterly disappointed, however, in her cold, unfeeling, and frequently cruel husband, who obviously hates her and cares for his sons only because they will secure the throne for the Tudor line. Henry trusts no one, least of all Elizabeth and her family, and he sets spies to watch them. When Perkin Warbeck makes his bid for the throne, Elizabeth thinks he may be her brother Richard, but she decides in favor of her sons, and refuses to recognize Perkin. This is a much more successful portrayal of the period than the author's earlier work. (See entry 228.)

230. Morgan, Denise. *Second Son.* London: Robert Hale Limited, 1980.
   208pp.

Ralph de Giret, reprobate son of Sir Harold and his second wife, a socially inferior Frenchwoman, returns from Calais to his father's house, steals his half-brother's intended bride, and becomes a spy for Richard Neville, Earl of Warwick. The murder of Sir Harold and his elder son make Ralph the heir to the estate, and Warwick's help in having murder charges against him dismissed bind Ralph to the earl's service.

231. _____. *Kingmaker's Knight.* London: Robert Hale Limited, 1981.
   208pp.

The is the second novel in a trilogy about Ralph de Giret, a retainer of the Earl of Warwick, who had saved him from hanging for the murder of his father and brother. (See entry 230.) Ralph encourages a friendship between his wife Isabella and her godfather's young wife Ursula, and when both Isabella and Ursula's husband die, Ralph and Ursula marry. Ursula then finds herself caught up in Warwick's attempt to place Edward Plantagenet on the throne.

232. _____ . *Sons and Roses*. London: Robert Hale Limited, 1981. 222pp.

This third novel in a trilogy (see entries 230, 231) about Ralph de Giret, begins in 1464 when Warwick goes to France to negotiate a marriage for Edward IV. Ursula, Ralph's French wife, has been made a lady-in-waiting to the Countess of Warwick, so that she can be the earl's informant about the king and his proposed new wife. The marriage plans fail, but Ralph decides that his son, also named Ralph, will join the earl's household. When Warwick rebels against the king, however, young Ralph leaves his service to join Edward, and persuades his father to do likewise, with unfortunate results.

233. Muddock, J. E. *Jane Shore*. London: John Long, 1905. 312 pp.

Jane Shore, a kind and generous young woman, meets Edward IV when she goes to plead with him for her Lancastrian husband's life. She becomes the king's mistress, but after his death she is forgiven by her husband, the goldsmith Shore.

234. Musgrave, Agnes. *Cecily, or the Rose of Raby. An Historical Novel*. London: Printed for W. Lane, 1795. 4 vols.

Not available for review.

235. Neele, Henry. *The Romance of History*. London: E. Bull, 1828. 3 vols. Philadelphia: Carey, Lea & Carey, 1828. 2 vols.

This is a collection of stories about historical figures and events, including several about the Wars of the Roses.
"The Witch of Eye." Eleanor Cobham employs Margaret Jourdmain and two priests to cast a wax figure of Henry VI, which they use in satanic rites to destroy him, so that her husband, Humphrey of Gloucester, can take the throne. The Duke of York learns of the plot and arrests Eleanor, who is then banished to the Isle of Man.
"The Prophesy." The Duke of Suffolk, imprisoned in the Tower for

treason, is told that he will live if he escapes the dangers of the Tower. He escapes, but on his way to France he is captured and executed by the captain of the ship "The Tower."

"The Wooing at Grafton." Elizabeth Woodville, the widow of a Lancastrian, waits in the forest to beg Edward IV for the return of her confiscated estates. She is attacked by the evil, deformed Richard of Gloucester, and rescued by a handsome young man named Edward March. They fall in love, but when he returns to London she is told that the king has killed him. Elizabeth joins her mother at court to plead with the king for her inheritance, and is amazed to learn that he is Edward March. He takes her immediately to Westminster Abbey, where they are married.

"Richmond's Three Perils." Henry VI prophesies that Henry Tudor will be king of England, but the young man is forced into exile by Edward IV. In Brittany, Henry sees a picture of Edward's daughter Elizabeth, and falls madly in love with her. He sends her his picture, and she falls madly in love with him. After Henry escapes the clutches first of Edward IV and then Richard III, he returns to England, defeats Richard at Bosworth, and marries Elizabeth.

"The White Rose of England." Beautiful Katherine Gordon, a kinswoman of the King of Scotland, is visiting her friend Margaret of Burgundy, when she is saved from drowning by a handsome young man, Perkin Warbeck. They fall in love, to the great chagrin of Margaret's friend Eleanor Lyndsay, who also loves Perkin. The Duchess of Burgundy is obsessed with the desire to drive Henry Tudor from the throne of England, because he has destroyed her family and mistreats her niece, Elizabeth of York. Margaret persuades Perkin to impersonate her late nephew, Richard, Duke of York, by promising that he can marry Katherine. The lovers go to Scotland and marry, but Eleanor exacts her revenge by informing her admirer Lord Clifford of Warbeck's true identity. Clifford betrays Perkin's invasion plans to Tudor, Warbeck is captured and executed, and Katherine dies of a broken heart.

236. Nichols, Wallace B. *A Wonder for Wise Men*. London and Melbourne: Ward, Lock & Co., Ltd., 1930. 320pp.

On his way to Bosworth, Richard III and his hostage Lord Strange stop at Basset Flamel, the home of Edmund Northiam, whose father had died fighting for the Yorkists years before. The estate is in ruins, the family impoverished, and Edmund, a pacifist scholar, cannot equip himself to fight for the king, and lectures Richard on the benefits of peace. After the battle, the wounded Sir John Spane, an old friend of Edmund's father, seeks sanctuary. When Henry Tudor, who has been told of the youth's pacifism, arrives, he engages him to work for Bishop Morton, and to bring Spane as his prisoner to London. There he meets Averill Spane, lady-in-waiting to Elizabeth of York, and falls in love with her. Edmund becomes Tudor's man because of the king's policy of peace, but the two fall out, and Edmund loses everything. He and Averill then leave for Bristol, where they join John Cabot on his voyage of discovery.

237. _____. *King Perkin's Knight*. Illus. by H. J. White. London: Sir Isaac Pitman & Sons, 1938. 218pp.

Clemsy Polgrene, the son of a Cornish fisherman, saves Perkin Warbeck from drowning when the pretender, calling himself Richard IV, lands near their village. Perkin knights Clemsy, and the boy and his sister join Perkin's band. They are left at St. Michael's Mount with Warbeck's wife Katherine, who discovers that her husband is not Richard of York, as he believes, but is being used by the Duchess of Burgundy in an attempt to place her real nephew, the Earl of Warwick, on the throne. The children go to Perkin to tell him to stop the rebellion, but it is too late. All are captured and sent to the Tower, Perkin as prisoner, and the children as his attendants. Henry Tudor lures Warbeck and Warwick into an attempted escape, both are executed, and the children return to Cornwall with many exciting adventures to relate. This book was written for young people.

238. _____. *The Secret Son*. Leicester: Norman Wolsey Limited, 1944. 256pp.

Inspired by Hull's *Richard Plantagenet* (see entries 138, 154, 253, 432, 535), this novel tells the story of Diccon Dicconson, brought up by a priest under the protection of Sir William Lovell, Francis' brother, who learns the day before Bosworth that he is the son of Richard III and a woman to whom he was contracted in marriage before he married Anne Neville. The king intends, should he survive the battle, to make Diccon his heir. For two years after the king's death the Lovells train and protect Diccon, planning to use Lambert Simnel as a stalking horse in a rebellion designed to place Diccon on the throne. When both Lovells are killed at Stoke, Diccon is forced to protect himself against agents of Henry Tudor. He is saved by a giant bricklayer, who teaches him his craft. Diccon decides not to reveal his true identity, even when Perkin Warbeck attempts to seize the throne. As an old man, living on the estate of Sir Thomas Moyle, he reveals his secret, and Moyle builds him a house on his property, where he lives out his life.

239. _____. *Turn the Hour-glass*. London and Melbourne: Ward, Lock & Co., 1938.   319 pp.

Elizabeth Woodville swears revenge on the Earl of Warwick for causing the death of her first husband, and for the earl's hostility to her family, but her plot is foiled by the wily Richard of Gloucester.

240. Nicholson, Joan. *Cuckoo Summer*. London: Hurst & Blackett, 1962. 184pp.

Twelve year old Roselys de Mowbray is betrothed to Simon de Havilland, the son of her father's closest friend, just before their fathers go off to join Jack Cade's rebellion. Mowbray reluctantly signs over Roselys' guardianship to his cousin Ralph Bulstrode, and when he is killed in battle the evil Bulstrode takes over the manor and forces Roselys' mother to marry him. Roselys becomes his prisoner, and when she refuses to marry his bastard son, he shuts her up in a nunnery. When Simon finally returns, and the Lancastrians are defeated, he and Roselys evict Bulstrode from her property, and marry.

241. Nickell, Leslie J. *The White Queen*. London: The Bodley Head Ltd., 1978.   349pp. New York: St. Martin's Press, 1978.   349pp.

Anne Neville, afraid of everything and everyone around her, is befriended by young Richard of Gloucester when he comes to live in her father's household. When Warwick turns against Edward IV to embrace the Lancastrian cause, Anne is forced to marry Edward of Lancaster, a cold youth who is completely dominated by his mother. Rejected and ignored by the Lancastrians, and cruelly mistreated by her brother-in-law Clarence, Anne suffers silently, but both her health and mind are damaged. She finally finds happiness with her old love Richard, until the death of her son once more threatens to destroy her tenuous grip on life.

242. Oakeshott, Ronald. *The Merchant at Arms*. New York: Longmans, Green and Co., 1920.   248pp.

Twelve-year-old George Nuttman, son of a Yorkist London merchant, joins the household of the Duke of Norfolk, where he is befriended by the duke's favorite, Sir Walter, who makes George his page. After Bosworth, where Sir Walter is badly wounded, George helps him escape to the Low Countries. There George becomes an apprentice merchant, and meets and falls in love with Richard Ratcliffe's daughter Marion. He saves Marion from the clutches of her evil cousin and guardian Nicholas, who is attempting to involve Walter and George in the Simnel and Warbeck rebellions. All ends well when Nicholas is killed and Walter and George are pardoned by Henry Tudor.

243. Oldfield, Pamela. *The Rich Earth*. Vol. 1 of *The Heron Saga*. London: Macdonald Futura Publishers Ltd., 1980. 461pp.

In 1468, Elizabeth Sheldyke, on her way from Yorkshire to Devon to marry elderly Daniel Heron, meets John Kendal, who is going to London to learn the goldsmith's trade. Twelve years later, when both are widowed, they meet again, marry, and return to Devon, where Elizabeth has become wealthy from tin mining. Although Kendal is a Yorkist who loses three brothers and several other relatives to the cause, the Wars of the Roses have little impact on the lives of the family, except for the Battle of Bosworth and the rebellion of the miners of Cornwall and Devon in support of Perkin Warbeck.

244. Oman, Carola [Lenanton]. *King Heart*. London: Fisher, Unwin, 1926. 319pp.

James IV of Scotland marries his great love Margaret Drummond, but she is poisoned and dies before he can acknowledge her as his wife. He then marries Janet Kennedy, an 'evil genius,' and after her death, for political reasons, he marries Margaret, the irritating daughter of Henry VII. The novel covers the Perkin Warbeck rebellion, and ends at Flodden Field, where James is killed.

245. _____. *Crouchback*. London: Hodder & Stoughton, 1929. 359pp.

The title notwithstanding, this is really Anne Neville's story, by an author who views Richard III as cold, brave, and probably a murderer, at least of the princes in the Tower. Anne's relationships with other members of her family, and her unhappy marriage to the man she believes killed his nephews, are the focus of the novel.

246. Onions, Oliver [George Oliver]. *Poor Man's Tapestry*. London: Michael Joseph, 1946. 303pp.

Journeyman goldsmith Wilson Middlemiss comes to Yorkshire to present a locket to Hannah Thurlow, and is falsely accused of her father's murder. He flees to Wales, and comes to the Castle of Gwlad, the stronghold of a Yorkist lord. Willie is given work by Sir William, the cruel, devious treasurer, who has learned that the youth knows where there are gold deposits in the nearby mountains. Willie falls in love with Joslin, the wife of a sickly fourteen-year-old knight. Meanwhile Hannah has set off on a pilgrimage with her grandmother, whose death leaves her alone and friendless. She is taken under the wing of Gandelyn, a Yorkist spy who travels the country entertaining at fairs. After the Yorkists' defeat at Ludlow, all the characters meet at Gwlad, where Gandelyn saves Willie from Sir William's murderous intentions.

247. Orford, Margaret. *That Beloved Esquire*. Swansea, Wales: Christopher Davies (Publishers) Ltd., 1980.   156pp.

Welshman Owen Tudor, who claims descent from the kings of Wales, saves the life of Henry V at Agincourt, becomes the king's Esquire, and later Clerk of the Wardrobe to Queen Catherine. Owen falls in love with Catherine, and after Henry's death she turns to him for comfort. Her late husband's cruel, ambitious uncles, Humphrey of Gloucester and Cardinal Beaufort, take her son, Henry VI, away from her and refuse her permission to remarry, and she takes Owen for her lover. When she becomes pregnant, they marry in secret, but several years and four children later, the marriage is discovered by the vengeful Humphrey and his wife Eleanor Cobham. Owen and Catherine are separated and their children taken from them. Catherine dies in a covent, and Owen is imprisoned. He escapes to Wales, where he remains a dedicated Lancastrian, fighting and dying for Henry at Mortimer's Cross.

248. Paget, Guy. *The Rose of London: 1471-1483*.   London: Collins, 1934.   279 pp.

Beautiful, brilliant Jane Wainstead, the daughter of a London merchant, becomes infatuated with Lord Hastings, a married man, and to protect her honor her father forces her to marry elderly goldsmith Will Shore. When Edward IV, disguised as a Flemish merchant, pays court to her, she falls in love with him and deserts her husband. When she learns her lover's true identity, the king persuades her to continue their relationship. Jane soon becomes the king's conscience, encouraging him to do his duty, and suggesting many wise policies. After Edward's death, she plots with Hastings and Dorset to murder Richard of Gloucester, in order to protect the late king's sons. The plot is discovered, and Hastings is tried and executed, but Jane's only punishment is the penance exacted by the church. Thomas Lymon, the king's solicitor, comes to her aid, and she marries him out of gratitude, and lives on into the reign of Henry VIII.

249. _____. *The Rose of Raby*. London: Collins, 1937. 355pp.

This fictional biography of Cecily Neville, daughter of the Earl of
Westmoreland and wife of Richard, Duke of York, tells the story of her
life and times from the day in 1415 when her three year old future
husband is brought to Raby Castle to be brought up as her father's ward,
until his death at Wakefield in 1460. Their marriage, a political union,
is shaky at first, since they are frequently apart, but it grows into one of
mutual love and respect. The madness of Henry VI, and the arrogance
and hostility of the queen, push York into the position of having to fight
for his life, and then for the crown. Cecily, a descendant of John of
Gaunt, supports her husband completely, and at his death she retreats to
the convent of Berkhampstead.

250. _____. *The Rose of Rouen: 1460-1471*. London: Collins, 1940.
301pp.

The third in a trilogy about the Wars of the Roses (see entries 248-249),
this is the story of Edward IV, called the Rose of Rouen from the place
of his birth. When his father, the Duke of York, is killed, Edward
defeats the Lancastrians with the help of his cousin Warwick. Edward
is shallow, pleasure-loving, and rather stupid, and he alienates Warwick
when he secretly marries Elizabeth Woodville, a Lancastrian widow with
a large, greedy family. Edward's mother tries but fails to heal the
breach with Warwick, who defects to Margaret of Anjou. He drives
Edward from the country and puts Henry VI back on the throne.
Edward returns, defeats and kills Warwick at Barnet, and then destroys
the Lancastrian army at Tewkesbury, where Margaret's son is killed.
When the victorious Yorkists return to London, Edward's advisors urge
him to kill Henry, but he refuses. When Henry dies in the Tower,
Richard of Gloucester urges his brother to defend himself against the
charge that he was responsible. A drunken Clarence tells Richard that
if anyone asks questions, they will be told that he, Richard, was guilty.

251. Palmer, Marian. *The White Boar*. New York: Doubleday and Company,
Inc., 1968. 373pp.

Richard III is seen through the eyes of Frances Lovell, his close friend,
and Phillip Lovell, Francis' cousin. Richard is portrayed as a good, but
driven man, who is forced by circumstances to take harsh measures in
order to secure his life and the kingdom. Although he is absolved of the
murder of the princes, his actions lead to their deaths, and some of the
blame attaches to him.

252. _____. *The Wrong Plantagenet.* New York: Doubleday and Company, Inc., 1972. 311pp.

Simon de Brezy, the stepson of Phillip Lovell (see entry 251), exiled in Burgundy since Bosworth, learns that he is actually Phillip's illegitimate son, conceived when his mother was still married to de Brezy. Simon leaves home to join Warbeck's ill-fated adventure, and after the pretender's capture, he learns that Sir James Tyrell had indeed murdered the two young sons of Edward IV, on Buckingham's orders. Tyrell is the villain of the novel, and his hatred of Phillip determines the course of his life, and eventually the lives of Simon and Phillip.

253. *The Parallel: or, A Collection of Extraordinary Cases Relating to Concealed Births, and Disputed Successions. Containing 1. The History of Richard Plantagenet, Son to Richard III.* London: J. Roberts, 1744. 56 pp.

This work contains five cases of concealed births, including the supposed life and career of an illegitimate son of Richard III, whose existence was concealed both before and after Bosworth, in order to protect him from the king's enemies. In this version, he becomes a bricklayer, but it is undoubtedly based on Hull's *Richard Planatagenet.* (See entries 138, 154, 238, 432, 535.) The author of this work professes to believe Hull's tale, citing as evidence of its truth, the fact the Sir Thomas Moyle believed the old bricklayer's tale, and that a grey-haired old man who was nearing death, would not die with a lie in his mouth. Indeed, Richard did not make his confession voluntarily, only admitting his true identity when pressed by Moyle, and with no intent to profit from his story. He was, declares the author, given an honorable burial, either in the church or churchyard of the parish church of Eastwell, when he died at the age of 81.

254. Peard, Frances Mary. *The Blue Dragon.* Illus. by C. J. Staniland. London: National Society's Depository, n.d. [ca. 1890]. 296pp.

In Chester, ten years after Bosworth, Meg Morecombe, the granddaughter of the proprietess of the Blue Dragon inn, and her cousin Jack, who lives with her and her grandmother, find a starving Flemish youth and help him escape capture, since the king has banished all foreigners. With the help of a kindly friend and a mysterious friar, she helps the youth escape, and learns that the friar is her father, long believed killed fighting for Richard III at Bosworth. Meg becomes a heroine by helping the victims of the plague, including her father, and learns that he is involved in a Yorkist plot. She protects him, and all ends well when the ban on foreigners is lifted, and the young Fleming returns to claim Meg as his bride.

255. Peck, William Henry. *Siballa the Sorceress; or the Flower Girl of London. A Tale of the Days of Richard III.* Illus. New York: Street & Smith, Publishers, 1890. 256 pp. The Sea and Shore Series-No. 16. Issued monthly.

Sir Roger Vagram, who has acquired the title of Earl of Montford through fraud and murder, joins a plot by supporters of Henry Tudor, in order to report their plans to the evil Richard III. The noble Sir Mortimer de Clair, one of the plotters, is searching both for clues to the identity of his long-lost father, and the whereabouts of his fiancée Lauretta, who disappeared without a trace. Mortimer discovers Lauretta in London, where she is forced to work as a flower girl by her kidnapper, the murderous Siballa, the Sorceress. Fellow conspirators Lord and Lady Tempest have also lost their two daughters to the kidnapper Siballa, but after after many murderous attacks on Tudor's supporters, all ends happily, as people long believed dead return from the grave, children and parents are reunited, true identities revealed, and villains punished. The usurper Richard III is killed at Bosworth, and Mortimer recovers his birthright and marries Lauretta.

256. Penman, Sharon Kay. *The Sunne in Splendour.* New York: Holt, Rinehart and Winston, 1892. 936pp.

Possibly the longest novel about the Wars of the Roses ever written, this work chronicles the life and times of Richard III from his capture by Margaret of Anjou's forces at Ludlow in 1459, until his death in 1485, and the growth of the lies and legends that followed.

257. Peters, Elizabeth. *The Murders of Richard III.* New York: Dodd, Mead & Company, 1974. 244pp.

Members of a splinter group of the Richard III Society gather at an English country house to see the letter in which Elizabeth of York confessed her love for her uncle, Richard III. Each of the guests is dressed as an important character of the period, and one by one someone attempts to murder them in the ways the originals were supposed to have been killed by Richard III.

258. Peters, Maureen. *Elizabeth the Beloved*. London: Robert Hale Ltd.,
1965. 222pp.

Elizabeth of York and her siblings are declared illegitimate after their
father's death. She is in love with her uncle Richard, now king, and
hopes to marry him after the death of his queen. Frustrated in that
ambition when he disavows his intention to marry her, she turns to Henry
Tudor, but even after years of marriage and motherhood, she remembers
Richard with love.

259. _____. *The Woodville Wench*. London: Robert Hale & Company,
1972. 176pp. Published in the United States as *The Queen Who Never
Was*. New York: Pinnacle Books, 1972. 187pp.

This novel tells the story of the life of Elizabeth Woodville from the age
of thirteen, through her marriages to Sir John Grey and Edward IV, until
the marriage of her eldest daughter Elizabeth to Henry Tudor. With the
exception of Anne Neville, all the female, and most of the male characters are portrayed as proud, greedy, and coldly ambitious.

260. _____. *The Queen Who Never Was*.

See entry 259.

261. _____. *Beggarmaid Queen*. London: Robert Hale Limited, 1980.
191pp.

The story of the life of Anne Neville from the age of five until her death
is the subject of this novel. Used as a pawn by her beloved father in his
bid for power, she finds happiness at last as the wife of Richard of
Gloucester.

262. Pierce, Glenn. *King's Ransom*. Los Angeles, Calif.: Medallion Books,
Inc., 1986. 333 pp.

Two archeologists, one English and one American, and an English civil
servant, excavate the tomb of Godfrey of Westminster, a Cistercian lay
brother who was the squire, friend, and confidant of Richard of
Gloucester, later Richard III. In the coffin is a manuscript written by
Godfrey, in which he tells, most sympathetically, the story of Richard's
life. Hawgood, the civil servant, who is a devotee of Richard's, wants
to rebury the manuscript with the coffin, fearing it will reveal the king
in an unfavorable light. The archeologists refuse, make copies of the

manuscript, and give the original to Hawgood, with the intention of eventually depositing it in a museum or library. Hawgood, however, claims that the manuscript was stolen, but the archeologists publish their findings in scholarly journals, despite the loss of the original work.

263. Plaidy, Jean [Eleanor Hibbert]. *The Goldsmith's Wife*. New York: Appleton, 1950. 325pp. London: Robert Hale Ltd., 1950. 319 pp. New York: G. P. Putnam's Sons, 1974. 318pp. Also published as *The King's Mistress*. New York: Pyramid Books, 1960. 319pp. (See also entry 141.)

Jane Shore, daughter of a tradesman and wife of a goldsmith, rises to become the mistress of Edward IV. After Edward's death, Dorset tries, but fails to lure her into treason against Richard of Gloucester. When Henry Tudor defeats Richard at Bosworth, he sends Dighton, Slaughter, and Green to murder the princes in their beds. Jane Shore lives into the reign of Henry VIII, but by then she has been reduced to beggary by the Tudors.

264. _____. *The King's Mistress*.

See entry 263.

265. _____. *Epitaph for Three Women*. London: Robert Hale Ltd, 1981. New York: G.P. Putnam's Sons, 1983. 333pp.

Katherine of Valois, Joan of Arc, and Eleanor Cobham are the three women of the title, and although all lived at the same time, and were concerned in affairs of state, their lives did not really intersect, and they had little in common. Henry V was not yet in his grave when his widow Katherine, daughter of the mad king Charles of France, fastened her eyes on the late king's young Welsh squire Owen Tudor. She makes him a part of her household, and pursues him relentlessly until he succumbs. They become lovers, and when she becomes pregnant, she coerces a priest into performing a marriage ceremony.
Ignorant, pious Jeannette d'Arc, a peasant girl from Doremy, hears voices directing her to drive the English out of France, and to crown the Dauphin. Her early successes are followed by failure in battle, and she is captured and sold to the English, who burn her as a witch. Her power lives on, however, and misfortune follows the English in the death of Bedford, the alliance of Burgundy and France, and the eventual loss of English territory in France.
Eleanor Cobham, lady-in-waiting to the Duchess of Gloucester, becomes

the mistress of Duke Humphrey. Using witchcraft, she ensnares him into marriage, and encourages his enmity to Cardinal Beaufort and Bedford, hoping that the sickly Henry VI will die, and that her husband will become king. She conspires with the Witch of Eye and others to bring about the king's death by sorcery, and she is forced to undergo penance and imprisonment for life.

266. _____. *The Sun in Splendour*. London: Robert Hale Ltd., 1982. New York: G. P. Putnam's Sons, 1983. 365pp.

Edward of York seizes the throne with the help of his cousin Warwick, but the two become enemies when Edward marries Elizabeth Woodville, the daughter and widow of Lancastrians, as Warwick is negotiating a French marriage for the king. Warwick defects to the Lancastrians, but his plans to restore Henry VI fail, and the earl is killed at Barnet. The queen and her greedy family alienate the old nobility, and after Edward's death they find they have no support for her son. Her children are declared illegitimate, and Richard of Gloucester takes the throne. When he is killed at Bosworth, Henry Tudor and a new dynasty come to the English throne.

267. _____. *Red Rose of Anjou*. London: Robert Hale Ltd, 1982. New York: G. P. Putnam's Sons, 1983. 348pp.

Domineering Margaret of Anjou marries weak, mentally deficient Henry VI, but is opposed by the Duke of York and the Earl of Warwick, the most powerful men in the country. Margaret's vindictiveness alienates the country, and her husband is driven from the throne, to be restored briefly with Warwick's help. Her son is killed at Tewkesbury, her husband dies in the Tower, and she is kept confined by Edward IV. Ransomed by the French king, Margaret realizes that Henry lacked the qualities necessary to a king, qualities which Edward had in abundance.

268. _____. *Uneasy Lies the Head*. London: Robert Hale Ltd., 1982. 345pp. New York: G. P. Putnam's Sons, 1984. 345pp.

Henry Tudor is plagued by rebellions to restore the Plantagenets to the throne. The author implies that it was he, and not Richard III, who had the sons of Edward IV killed, in order to keep the crown, but he got little joy from his prize. To the end of his life he remained suspicious and paranoid, ever fearful that he would lose it to some Yorkist pretender.

269. _____. *The Queen's Secret*. London: Templeton, Charles, Severn House, 1988.   379 pp.   London: Robert Hale Limited, 1989.   303 pp. New York: G. P. Putnam's Sons, 1990.   307 pp.

Katherine of Valois, on her deathbed, tells the story of her life. Married to Henry V as part of the price of her country's defeat, she soon realizes that war is more important to him than she is. After his death, she settles in England, hoping to rear her son peacefully, but he is the king, and his training becomes the concern of the powerful men of the council. Katherine is pushed aside, and in her loneliness she turns to her clerk of the wardrobe, Owen Tudor. They fall madly in love, become lovers, and decide to marry when Katherine becomes pregnant. To protect themselves from Humphrey of Gloucester, they keep the marriage secret, but they are discovered and Owen is arrested, Katherine is sent to a convent, and their children taken from them. Katherine's son, Henry VI, refuses to help her, and she dies broken-hearted.

270. _____. *The Reluctant Queen*. London: Robert Hale Ltd., 1990. 299pp. New York: G. P. Putnam's Sons, 1991.   294pp.

On her deathbed, Anne Neville recalls her life as the daughter of the powerful Earl of Warwick, and the wife of Richard of Gloucester. With childlike simplicity she tells of a life full of sorrow and danger, as her father, once the pillar of the Yorkist crown, turns against Edward IV and joins the Lancastrians, forcing Anne to marry Edward of Lancaster. After her father's death, and despite the bitter opposition of Clarence, she is finally permitted to marry Richard, her life-long love. The death of their sickly son devastates them both, and Ann dies convinced that she has lost Richard's love because she failed to give him healthy heirs.

271. Pollard, Eliza Frances. *For the Red Rose*. Frontispiece by James Durden. London and Glasgow: Blackie and Son Ltd., 1902.   240pp.

Sylvester, a Gypsy, discovers Maggie, with the body of her nurse, after the battle of Towton, and takes her to live with his tribe, adopting her as his daughter. They later rescue Harry, the grandson of a shepherd, and the two young people become friends. When Margaret of Anjou is shipwrecked near their home, Maggie becomes devoted to the unfortunate queen and her son, and the gypsies, aided by Sir John Conyers and his son William, who becomes the rebel Robin of Redesdale, rescue the Lancastrians. Maggie accompanies them to France, where Margaret reluctantly joins forces with Warwick, and allows her son to marry his daughter. When Warwick is killed, the Lancastrian cause is lost, but when Henry Tudor comes to the throne, Maggie, who has married Robin of Redesdale, and young Harry discover their true noble identities.

272. Potter, Jeremy. *A Trail of Blood*. London: Constable and Company Limited, 1970. 282pp. New York: The McCall Publishing Co., 1971. 281pp.

During the uprising known as the Pilgrimage of Grace, a protest against the suppression of the monasteries in the reign of Henry VIII, Robert Aske, the leader, and a chancellor of the Bishop of Lincoln come to Croyland Abbey to search the records to find a Plantagenet who will defend the old faith and save the monasteries. They discover that the sons of Edward IV had escaped an attempted assassination by Buckingham's agents, but that Edward, the elder, had drowned during the flight. Aske discovers Richard, the younger prince, but he refuses to lead a rebellion to recover the crown, and the plan fails. This is one of the better novels about the period.

273. Powers, Anne. *The Royal Consorts*. Los Angeles, Calif.: Pinnacle Books, Inc., 1978. 276pp. Also published as *Queen's Ransom*. New York: Leisure Books, 1978. 394pp.

Margaret of Anjou, Elizabeth Woodville, Anne Neville, and Elizabeth of York are the eponymous heroines of this novel, which tells the story of the Wars of the Roses from both the Lancastrian and Yorkist points of view. The author makes an attempt at historical accuracy, but the superficial characterizations and over-heated prose are typical of the historical romance genre.

274. _____. *Queen's Ransom*.

See entry 273.

275. Price, Eleanor O. *The Queen's Man: A Romance of the Wars of the Roses*. London: Constable & Company Ltd., 1905. 319pp.

Lord Marlowe, a follower of Margaret of Anjou, falls in love with the grand-daughter of Sir William Roden. Her two other suitors, unscrupulous knaves, do their utmost to undermine Marlowe's suit, and one of them is aided in his plans by Marlowe's own step-mother, a secret Yorkist sympathizer.

276. Rabinowitz, Ann. *Knight on Horseback*. New York: Macmillan Publishing Company, 1987. 197 pp.

Eddy Newby, a young American boy on vacation with his family in England, acquires a small wooden statue of a knight on horseback, and is pursued by the ghost of Richard III, who appears to be intimately acquainted with him. Eddy finds himself drawn into the world of the 15th century at Middleham Castle, as he becomes attached to, and dependent on the spirit of the long-dead king. This is one of the better books about the period written for young people.

277. Ragosta, Millie J. *Gerait's Daughter*. Garden City, N.Y.: Doubleday & Company, Inc., 1981. 179pp.

Margaret Fitzgerald, the daughter of loyal Yorkist Irish clan leader Gerait More, who had supported Lambert Simnel, is forced to marry Sir Piers Butler, the heir of the leader of a hated rival clan loyal to Henry Tudor. When Perkin Warbeck arrives to seek her father's aid, she is attracted to him, although she does not believe he is the son of Edward IV. She marries Piers to save her father from the accusation of treason, they fall in love, and together they battle Black James, Piers' evil cousin, and convince Tudor that he can rely on Gerait's loyalty in future.

278. _____. *The Winter Rose*. Garden City, N.Y.: Doubleday & Company, Inc., 1982. 179pp.

Anne de Syon, the daughter of Edward IV and Eleanor Butler, is brought up in a convent, ignorant of her parentage. She is brought to court by Sir John Howard, and presented as his ward. Anne falls in love with Sir Adam Booth, Howard's squire, but attracts the lustful attention of the evil Duke of Buckingham. Edward IV dies, Richard of Gloucester seizes the throne, and Buckingham's rebellion collapses. Anne and Adam escape to France, where they plan to join Henry Tudor, believing he would be a better king than the infanticide Richard III.

279. Reddicliffe, Sheila. *The Cornish Serjeant*. London: William Kimber and Company Limited, 1984. 255pp.

The lives of three young men in Cornwall are joined by friendship and marriage, and affected by politics, from late in the reign of Henry V, through the early years of that of Edward IV. One of them, Nicholas Ayssheton, becomes a Serjeant at Law in the reign of Henry VI, a time when law and order had broken down, and his duties keep him in

London much of the time. His friends John Fursdon and Richard Chyket remain in Cornwall, an area plagued by dissension and lawlessness.

280. Rede, Lucy Leman. *The Monarch's Mistress, or, The History of Jane Shore, the Concubine of Edward IV: Containing an account of her early life, her marriage, the love and stratagem of King Edward to obtain her, her elopement, and conduct when mistress to the King of England...the fate of her husband, her reverse of fortune, sufferings, and miserable death.* Illus. London: Dean and Munday, 1828. 24 pp.

See entries 110, 144-152, 202, 225, 302, 328.

281. Reed, Margaret Baines. *Sir Adam's Orchard: A Story of York and Lancaster.* Illus. by the author. London: Arnold, 1926. 176 pp.

Roger and Cecily, the children of a loyal Yorkist, Sir William Frankland, are kidnapped by their Lancastrian neighbor, the evil Sir Adam La Roche, who wants to get possession of a paper which the king has given to Sir William, allowing him to raise men. Sir Adam plans to use the paper to raise forces to help Margaret of Anjou. Roger, drugged and abandoned by Sir Adam, is rescued by the Earl of Warwick, and Cecily escapes, only to be captured by gypsies. Roger saves Warwick from a Lancastrian trap laid by Sir Adam, and rescues Cecily from the gypsies. After Sir Adam is murdered by his servant, Roger and Cecily are reunited with their father.

282. Rhodes, T. D. *The Crest of the Little Wolf.* Cincinnati: Robert Clarke, 1904. 181pp.

Francis Lovell, the friend of both Edward IV and Richard of Gloucester, and whose family crest is the little wolf, is in love with Anne Fitzhugh, a kinswoman of Warwick, who is in rebellion against the king. She loves him in return, but she is also being courted by Sir Guy Nevil, another of Warwick's relations. When Edward IV is forced to flee to Burgundy, Francis works in his behalf both at home and abroad. Anne's brother, a Lancastrian, is wounded at Barnet, but Francis saves his life, and then rescues Anne, now his betrothed, from the clutches of the evil Sir Guy. The happy couple marry, with the blessing of the king and Gloucester, and retire to Minster Lovell, unaware that their future holds the destruction of the Yorkist cause and the house of Lovell.

283. *Richard of York; or "The White Rose of England."* New York: Wallis & Newell, Publishers, 1835. 272 pp.

The evil Franciscan Father Lawrence, who had been spurned by Elizabeth Woodville in favor of Edward IV, vows to destroy all Yorkists. As Henry Tudor's confessor, he easily persuades the king to support his plans, and Edward V, a prisoner in the Tower, is poisoned. When Edward's brother Richard, who has married Catherine Gordon, lays claim to the crown, supported by James IV of Scotland, Father Lawrence must destroy him as well. Richard's friend and supporter, Sir Edward Stanley, the imprisoned Sir William's son, is in love with Anthony Woodville's daughter Agnes, and they too are pursued by the Franciscan. The evil monk succeeds in destroying Richard, whom Tudor declares to be an imposter named Perkin Warbeck, and Catherine, whose son dies at birth, goes mad with grief. Stanley escapes the clutches of Father Lawrence, who is stabbed to death by one of his intended victims, and the young knight and Agnes are married, but forced to live under assumed names for many years. The unknown author, in an introductory first chapter, acknowledges his/her debt to Walpole's *Historic Doubts*, but Richard III is nevertheless portrayed as a usurping villain, as is Henry Tudor.

284. Richings, Emily. *White Roseleaves: A Story of the Yorkist Court*. London: Henry J. Drane, 1912.   345pp.

This novel about Elizabeth Woodville is unavailable for review.

285. Ridge, Antonia. *The 13th Child*. London: Faber & Faber, 1962.   199pp.

Katherine of Valois, the thirteenth child of the mad King Charles VI of France, is married to Henry V of England, and bears him a son, the future Henry VI, who inherits his grandfather's madness. After her husband's death, Katherine falls in love with Owen Tudor, a minor Welsh gentleman, and they are secretly married. The couple has three sons, but they are separated by the evil, ambitious Duke Humphrey of Gloucester. Katherine dies in childbirth, but she leaves her mark on England through her mad son Henry VI and her grandson Henry VII.

286. Rosenthal, Evelyn B. *Presumed Guilty*. New York: Vantage Press, 1982. 256pp.

This novel describes the reign of Richard III from the standpoint of five people who knew him. The first section is narrated by Buckingham just before his execution. He had helped Richard seize the throne as part of his plan to use the king and Henry Tudor to destroy each other, so that he could seize the throne for himself. The second part is told by

Elizabeth of York, now the wife of Henry Tudor. She wonders if the tale spread by her husband about her uncle Richard murdering her brothers could possibly be true, since it was so out of character. Although she does not love the cold, distant Henry, she supports him, knowing that the pretenders are not really her brothers. Francis Lovell and Margaret of Burgundy, both loyal to Richard III, narrate the next two sections. Archbishop Morton is the narrator of the final section, and he confesses that he lured Buckingham into treason, letting him believe that he would be crowned. Morton hints to Buckingham that the princes are a danger, and leads him to plot their murder and then blame Richard. Morton then deserts Buckingham and joins Tudor in France.

287. Ross, Barnaby. *The Passionate Queen.* New York: Pocket Books, Inc., 1966. 152pp.

Margaret of Anjou, married to the weak and frequently mad Henry VI, tries to protect him, their son, and herself from the intrigues of the court and the men who would like to seize the throne. Her efforts are futile, and her husband loses his throne and his life, their son is killed, and she is made prisoner, only to be ransomed by the wily, stingy Louis XI of France.

288. Ross Williamson, Hugh. *The Butt of Malmsey.* London: Michael Joseph Ltd., 1967. 253pp.

Brave, loyal, scholarly George of Clarence adores his older brother Edward, and supports him even when he learns that the king is the son of Cecily of York and an archer named Blackburn, and that he himself, as the oldest legitimate son of York, is the rightful king. When Edward marries Elizabeth Woodville, and her greedy, ambitious family rises over the old nobility, George joins Warwick, his father-in-law, in rebellion. When he realizes, however, that Warwick does not intend to make him king, he returns to Edward. When his wife Isabel and their infant son die suddenly, George is convinced that Elizabeth Woodville is responsible, and he hints to her that he knows that her marriage is bigamous. This ensures his downfall, but before his death his mother admits to him that he is the true king of England.

289. _____. *The Marriage Made in Blood.* London: Michael Joseph Ltd., 1968. 221pp.

Margaret Plantagenet, Clarence's daughter, loses all of her beloved family, for Henry Tudor is determined that no claimant with Yorkist blood will survive to threaten his crown. He suggests to Morton that the sons of Edward IV be done away with. Morton takes care of the matter, writes a report of the incident in Latin, and later gives it to his protégé Thomas More to translate. Henry imprisons Margaret's brother in the Tower, hoping he will lose his mind. When the king, eager for a Spanish marriage for his son Arthur, realizes that Spain will not send the Princess Catherine to England so long as any Yorkist claimants remain, Henry executes both Edward of Warwick and Perkin Warbeck. The marriage made in blood can then take place. Henry allows Margaret to marry Richard Pole, a kindly Lancastrian, and Henry VIII restores Margaret's title of Countess of Salisbury and her father's confiscated estates.

290. Rowling, Marjorie. *Shadow of the Dragon*. London: Faber and Faber, 1965. 214pp.

The novel begins in 1485 with Henry Tudor's victory over Richard III at Bosworth, and follows the ill fortunes of those who remained loyal to the late king. The young hero, fifteen-year-old Mark Harrington, joins Francis Lovell and the Earl of Lincoln to find his father, who had disappeared after Bosworth. After the final defeat of the Yorkists, Mark escapes to Ireland.

291. Rush, Philip. *My Brother Lambert*. Illus. by David Walsh. London: Phoenix House, Ltd., 1957. 143pp.

Vain young Lambert Simnel, the son of a London baker, is used as a tool by the Yorkists, who plan to pass him off as Clarence's son, the Earl of Warwick, and seize the throne in his name. Lambert's sister, who fears he will die a traitor's death, reveals the plot to Henry VII, who defeats the rebels at Stoke. The book is written for young readers.

292. St. James, Scotney [Varner, Lynda and Hoy, Charlotte]. *By Honor Bound*. New York: Avon Books, 1989. 391pp.

Marganna Tudor, the illegitimate niece of Margaret Beaufort, is ordered by her aunt to spy on Richard III, to find out where he has hidden the sons of Edward IV. Caught in the act, she is sent to Yorkshire as a prisoner of the king's friend, Lord Rathburn. Despite opposing loyalties they fall in love and marry, and Marganna comes to realize that Richard is not the monster her aunt had claimed. Margaret's plot to kill the princes is foiled, and after Bosworth, in accordance with Richard's plan, they are sent to safety in Burgundy. Henry Tudor pardons Rathburn for supporting Richard, and he and Marganna return to Yorkshire.

293. Saunders, Susan. *The Tower of London*. #19 in *Choose Your Own Adventure*. Illus. by Lorna Tomei. Toronto and New York: Bantam Books, Inc., 1984. 53pp.

A young American boy and his English friend visit the Tower of London in the hope of meeting some of the ghosts reputed to haunt the place. The young reader is invited to write his own story by choosing different pages which lead to different conclusions of the adventure. The boys meet the ghost of Anne Boleyn, and are attacked by the ghost of the evil Richard III, but are saved by those of his two murdered nephews, the Princes in the Tower.

294. Schoonover, Lawrence. *The Spider King: A Biographical Novel of Louis XI of France*. New York: The Macmillan Company, 1954. 403pp.

Slightly misshapen, plain, epileptic, despised and feared by his father, who tried to have him set aside as heir to the throne, Louis XI learns early to deal with court intrigue, and when he becomes king he destroys the power of his vassals, and works to unite France. He supports Warwick's attempt to place Henry VI back on the English throne, because he fears that his enemy, Charles of Burgundy, will join Edward IV in an invasion of France. When Edward invades in 1475, he receives little help from Burgundy, and Louis is able to buy him off. In 1483, as Louis lays dying, he rejoices to learn that Edward has died, leaving his young son to rule. He becomes concerned, however, when he discovers that Richard of Gloucester has murdered Edward V and his brother, and seized the throne. When Louis dies, it is France, not England, which is left to be ruled by a child.

295. Schuster, Rose. *The Triple Crown*. London: Chapman & Hall, Ltd., 1912. 331pp.

This novel relates the life of Henry VI from the Lancastrian viewpoint, covering the period between 1437 and 1460. The early influence of Cardinal Beaufort, Henry's marriage to the proud and beautiful Margaret of Anjou, Cade's rebellion, and the Battles of St. Albans and Wakefield are detailed. An epilogue describes Henry's death in 1471.

296. Scott, Amanda. *The Rose at Twilight*. New York: Dell Publishing, 1993. 390pp.

Lady Alys Wolveston, a kinsman and lady-in-waiting to Anne Neville and a loyal Yorkist, is claimed as a ward of Henry Tudor after Bosworth, and given in marriage to his friend Nicholas Meriod, a fellow Welshman. Although the couple fall in love, each remains faithful to his/her allegiance. Alys has evidence that Edward, the elder son of Edward IV, has died of the plague, but that Richard, the younger, has been saved by Tyrrell. She lends her support to Francis Lovell in his rebellion to place Richard on the throne, but comes to terms with Henry Tudor after the rebels' defeat at Stoke-on-Trent.

297. Scott, John Reed. *Beatrix of Clare*. Illus. by Clarence F. Underwood. Philadelphia and London: J. B. Lippincott Company, 1907. 365pp.

Love blossoms between Sir Aymer de Lacy, a retainer of Richard of Gloucester, and Beatrix de Beaumont, Countess of Clare, the greatest heiress in the country and a lady-in-waiting to Anne Neville. They meet shortly after the death of Edward IV, and soon after Richard becomes king, he gives them permission to marry. Beatrix is kidnapped by Lord Darby and the Abbot of Kirkstall, who are both involved in Buckingham's rebellion, and who attempt to force Beatrix to marry the traitorous lord. Buckingham is captured, but before his execution he reveals Darby's plans, and tells de Lacy where to find Beatrix. All ends well, with the villains killed and the lovers reunited.

298. Scott, Sir Walter. *Quentin Durward*. Edinburgh: A. Constable and Co., 1823. 3 vols.

Young Quentin Durward, orphaned by the murder of his family by rival Scottish noblemen, escapes to France, where he joins the elite Scottish archers in the employ of Louis XI. He is commissioned by the king to conduct the young Countess of Croye, the runaway ward of Charles of Burgundy, to the protection of the Bishop of Liege. The young couple becomes involved in the rebellion of the Liegeois against their lord, the Duke of Burgundy, and in the bitter quarrel between the duke and his lord the king of France. All ends happily, however, when Quentin wins the beautiful countess' hand in marriage. Although Edward IV and events in England are mentioned several times throughout the book, it is concerned mainly with the hostility between France and Burgundy, which was of the greatest interest to England.

299. _____. *Anne of Geierstein or the Maiden of the Mist*. Edinburgh: Cadell & Co., 1829. 3 vols.

After the battle of Tewkesbury, the exiled Lancastrian Earl of Oxford and his son Arthur, travelling as merchants under the name of Philipson, journey to Dijon to seek the aid of Charles of Burgundy for the Lancastrian cause. In the Swiss mountains, Arthur is saved from certain death by Anne of Geierstein, the niece of a local rustic nobleman and daughter of the Count of Geierstein. The two Englishmen become involved in the quarrel between the Swiss and Burgundy, and after many hair-raising adventures, during which both are saved many times by Anne, they reach the court of King René, father of Margaret of Anjou. Margaret is willing to give what is left of her father's lands in exchange for Charles' aid, but the latter's defeat by the Swiss destroys her hopes, and she dies a broken woman. After Burgundy's death, Arthur and Anne marry, and returning to Engand after Bosworth, live happily ever after.

300. Sedley, Kate. *Death and the Chapman.* London: The Crime Club/Harper Collins Publishers, 1991. New York: St. Martin's Press, 1992. 190pp.

Roger Carverson, later surnamed Chapman, leaves Glastonbury Abbey, where he has served as a novice, to take to the road as a chapman, or peddler. In Bristol, he meets Alderman Weaver, whose son Clement has disappeared with a great deal of money from the Crossed Hands Inn in London. It is just before the Battle of Tewkesbury, and the country is in turmoil, but Roger promises to investigate the mystery when he gets to London. In Canterbury, he learns of another strange disappearance from the same inn. He discovers that Anne Neville is being held at the inn, whose owner has connections with Clarence, and reports the fact to Richard of Gloucester, thus earning the duke's friendship. Roger solves the mystery of the disappearances, and implies that this was only the first of his successful attempts at crime solving, and that more of his adventures will be published.

301. _____. *The Plymouth Cloak.* New York: St. Martin's Press, 1992. 192pp.

Roger Chapman, the itinerant peddlar hero of *Death and the Chapman* (see entry 300), is given another commission by the Duke of Gloucester. He is to serve as bodyguard to Philip Underdown, a man who has made his living selling dwarfs to the noble houses of Europe and England, and is now setting out to carry a letter from Edward IV to Francis of Brittany, requesting that he not aid Henry Tudor. Gloucester fears that agents of Tudor, Elizabeth Woodville, or Clarence, who all have reason to fear Underdown, will attempt to murder him before he boards the ship to Brittany. Roger, armed with his Plymouth Cloak, a stout cudgel, goes along to protect Philip, but they are followed, and despite Roger's care, Philip is murdered. It is up to Roger to unravel the mystery and learn the identity of the killer.

302. Seibert, Elizabeth. *White Rose and Ragged Staff*. Illus. by Ray Cruz. Indianapolis: Bobbs-Merrill, 1968. 222pp.

Hugh Brere, a squire to Richard of Gloucester, and Cicely Assenhurst, a lady-in-waiting to Anne Neville, find their romance endangered by the quarrel between Edward IV and Warwick in the period between 1469 and 1471. All ends happily when Edward IV regains his throne.

303. Sewell, George. *The Life and Character of Jane Shore*. Illus. London; J. Brown and W. Mears, et al., 1714. 46 pp.

See entries 110, 144-153, 202, 225, 280, 325.

304. Seymour, Arabella. *Maid of Destiny*. London: Robert Hale Ltd., 1971. 256pp.

Jane Beaufort is the daughter of the Duke of Somerset, a cousin of Henry VII, who believes his claim to the throne is stronger than the king's. Henry seems to agree, for he arrests Somerset, his two elder sons, and several of his friends on trumped-up charges of treason. Although her father has never shown her any affection, the thirteen-year-old Jane defends him, defying the king, Archbishop Morton, and the Star Chamber, and refusing to save herself by accusing her father. The duke, his sons, and several companions are executed, but Jane later finds brief happiness in her marriage to Edward L'Isle. This author's style can best be described as Egregious Gothic.

305. Shelley, Mary Wollstonecraft (Godwin). *The Fortunes of Perkin Warbeck, a Romance*. London: H. Colburn and R. Bentley, 1830. 3 vols. in 1. Philadelphia: Carey, Lea & Blanchard, 1834. 2 vols.

After the death by natural causes of Edward V, his brother Richard is taken from the Tower by order of Richard III, who causes a rumor to be spread that the boys have died. Young Richard is hidden in the house of Jahn Warbeck, a Flemish merchant, where he is discovered after Bosworth by Francis Lovell and Edmund Plantagenet, Richard III's illegitimate son, who had helped to smuggle the boy to safety. Henry Tudor spreads the story of the murder of the princes to further his own aims. Edmund, who loved his father, believes he treated his nephews badly, and so he devotes his life to restoring the young prince to the throne in order to expiate his father's sin.

306. Simonds, Paula. *Daughter of Violence*. London: Robert Hale Limited, 1981. 224pp.

The story of Anne Neville's life, from the time of her father's defection to the Lancastrians until her marriage to Richard of Gloucester, is told in this improbable novel. Margaret of Anjou tries to murder Anne, and Thomas Mallory is responsible for her rescue when she is hidden in a cookshop by Clarence. Anachronisms, including vulgar modern slang, abound.

307. Sisson, Rosemary Anne. *The Queen and the Welshman*. London: W. H. Allen, 1979. 232pp.

Katherine de Valois, the widow of Henry V, is separated from her young son, Henry VI, and banished to a rural castle by her late husband's quarrelsome, ambitious brothers, Humphrey of Gloucester and John of Bedford, and their uncle, Cardinal Beaufort. Lonely, isolated, and surrounded by spies, Katherine falls in love with Owen Tudor, her Clerk of the Wardrobe. They wed secretly, in defiance of the council's orders, and they and their children live happily, until their marriage is discovered. Their children are taken from them, Katherine is sent to a convent, where she dies, and Owen is imprisoned. After his release he returns to Wales, where he remains loyal to Henry VI. This beautifully written novel has the same subject and title of an earlier play by the author. See entry 558.

308. Small, Bertrice. *The Spitfire*. New York: Ballantine Books, 1990. 490pp.

In 1483, spirited beauty Lady Arabella Grey, a cousin of Richard III, is betrothed to Sir Jasper Keane, an evil but handsome man who is protector of her ancestral home on the Scottish border. She is kidnapped at her wedding by Tavis Stewart, Earl of Dunmor, in revenge for Keane's murder of his fiancee. Dunmor forces Arabella to marry him, and she learns to love him despite their differences. While she is in Scotland, Jasper Keane gains control of her old home, and Richard III dies at Bosworth. Arabella sues to Henry Tudor for the return of her lands, and she becomes his agent as part of the agreement.

309. Stanier, Hilda Brookman. *The Kingmaker's Daughter*. London: Robert Hale Limited, 1978. 207pp.

The novel is narrated by Anne Neville, Francis Lovell, who tells of
Buckingham's rebellion, and Anne's lady-in-waiting, who describes
Anne's death. Anne and Richard of Gloucester have loved each other
since they were children at Middleham, and their enforced separation,
caused by the rift between Warwick and Edward IV, does not diminish
their affection. After Warwick's death, Clarence attempts to prevent the
marriage of his brother and sister-in-law by hiding Anne as a serving
girl, but Richard finds her, marries her, and takes her to live at
Middleham. When Edward dies, Richard takes the throne because his
brother's children are illegitimate. The death of his son and Anne's fatal
illness destroy his happiness, and his own death at Bosworth comes
almost as a relief.

310. _____. *Plantagenet Princess.* London: Robert Hale Limited, 1981.
188pp.

This novel tells of the life of Elizabeth of York from her childhood
through her marriage to Henry Tudor, and her death in 1503. As a
young girl she falls deeply in love with her uncle, Richard of Gloucester,
and hopes to marry him when Anne dies. Richard, however, is grief-
stricken at Anne's death, and denies the story, spread by Elizabeth
Woodville, that he intends to marry her daughter. He sends the heart-
broken young Elizabeth to Sheriff Hutton, and when he is killed at
Bosworth, she is forced to marry Henry Tudor. Although Henry is cold
and reserved, and completely dominated by his clever, ambitious mother,
he and Elizabeth develop mutual respect and affection. When she dies
in childbirth at the age of 35, her moderating influence dies with her, and
Henry becomes more grasping and greedy than ever.

311. Stephens, Peter John. *Battle for Destiny.* New York: Atheneum, 1967.
300pp.

Young Ithel ap Meredith and his father flee to Brittany when their manor
in Wales is seized by a supporter of Richard III. The ship carrying them
sinks and Ithel, the only survivor, is cast ashore. Several years and
many hair-raising adventures later, he joins forces with Henry Tudor,
who sends him as a messenger to Rhys ap Thomas. Ithel recaptures his
manor, secures the support of Rhys, and joins Henry at Bosworth. This
novel is written for young readers.

312. Stevenson, Robert Louis. *The Black Arrow.* London and New York:
Cassell & Co., 1888. viii+324pp. New York: Charles Scribner's Sons,
1888. 322pp.

Young Dick Shelton learns that his guardian, the Lancastrian Sir Daniel Brackley, is responsible for his father's murder. In fear for his own life, Dick flees his guardian's house with his companion Jack, who turns out to be Joanna, his intended bride. In the course of his adventures, Dick saves the life of the evil Duke of Gloucester, and reluctantly accepts a knighthood as a reward.

313. Stewart, A. J. *Falcon. The Autobiography of His Grace James the 4 King of Scots.* London: Peter Davies Ltd., 1970. New York: Delacorte Press, 1970. 247 pp.

This novel purports to be the memoirs of James IV of Scotland, written by his reincarnation, A. J. Stewart, some 450 years after the king's death. As a fifteen-year-old monarch, James attempted to unify his poor country and deal with the hated English, led by the usurper Henry VII. James had admired Richard III for his kindness and ability, and when Perkin Warbeck claims to be the younger son of Edward IV, the Scots welcome and support him. When he is captured and executed by Henry, James sees it as proof that he was a Plantagenet, or Henry would not have feared him. James is pressured into marrying Henry's spoiled, shallow daughter Margaret, who is very different from his beloved Margaret Drummond, whom his nobles would not accept as his queen. After the death of the wily Henry VII, James has even more difficulties with his son, Henry VIII, who is determined to subjugate Scotland. In 1513 James invades England, and is killed in battle at Flodden Field.

314. Stoker, M. Brooke. *Prince Perkin.* London: Robert Hale Limited, 1966. 192pp.

Perkin Warbeck claims to be the younger son of Edward IV, saved from death in the Tower and sent to Tournai to be raised as a commoner. Margaret of Burgundy, Edward's sister, recognizes Perkin as her nephew, he is crowned Richard IV in Ireland, and goes to Scotland where the king gives him Catherine Gordon, his kinswoman, for a wife. Warbeck's invasion of England to claim his throne is a failure, and he is captured and imprisoned by Henry VII, who has him executed, along with Clarence's son, in order to secure the marriage of Prince Arthur and Catherine of Aragon.

315. Strang, Herbert and Lawrence, George. *For the White Rose.* London: Henry Frowde and Hodder and Stoughton, 1912. 160pp.

After the murder of the Lancastrian Sir Gibert Raglan by his Yorkist

cousin, Ralph Ormond, Raglan's four-year-old son Hugh is given into the
keeping of Simon Payton, a London merchant. He raises the boy as his
nephew, and tries to keep him from the notice of Ormond and his
henchman Wolf. Hugh becomes a page in the household of Edward IV,
and during the king's exile he befriends and aids the queen in sanctuary.
After the king's return, Hugh joins his army, and regains his manor and
lands from Ormond, who is slain in battle. This novel for young people
contains an informative summary of the events and personalities of the
Wars of the Roses at the end of the book.

316. Strickland, Agnes. *The Royal Sisters. An Historical Romance of the
      Middle Ages.* Boston: Saxton, Peirce, & Co., 1845. 139pp.

This is a fictional account of the lives of Cecily, Anne, and Catherine
Plantagenet, three of the younger daughters of Edward IV, by the
historian best noted for her exhaustive work, *The Lives of the Queens of
England.*

317. _____. "The Royal Brothers. A Story of the Times of Richard the
      Third." *Historical Tales of Illustrious Children.* Illus. Boston: Munroe
      and Francis, 184? pp. 45-125. *Stories From English History.*
      Philadelphia: Porter & Coates, n.d. pp. 45-125.

Written for young people by the author of *Lives of the Queens of
England*, this is the tale of Edward V and Richard, Duke of York, the
Princes in the Tower, cruelly murdered by their wicked uncle.

318. Stubbs, Jean. *An Unknown Welshman.* New York: Stein and Day, 1972.
      319pp.

This novel tells the story of the life of Henry Tudor, from his birth in
1457 until his victory at Bosworth and his marriage to Elizabeth of York.
Although the author is a Lancastrian sympathizer, and admires Henry,
she acknowledges his faults, and more surprisingly, the virtues of
Richard III and others of the House of York.

319. Sudworth, Gwynedd. *The King of Destiny.* London: Robert Hale Limited,
      1973. 238pp.

Henry Tudor is brought up to believe that he is the rightful heir to the
crown, and after years of danger and exile, he finally achieves his goal.
He becomes cold, grasping, and distrustful, but when he falls in love
with Elizabeth of York, whom he married reluctantly, she softens him

somewhat. Henry is obsessed by the need to have many sons, but when Elizabeth dies, worn out by her many pregnancies, she has borne only two boys, one of whom, Arthur, has pre-deceased her. Henry decides to marry again so that he can father more sons. His proposals, first to Arthur's widow, Catherine of Aragon, and then to her sister Mad Juana, are rejected, as are those to other European princesses, who are repulsed by his age and appearance. When he dies, only his mother mourns him.

320. _____. *Dragon's Whelp*. London: Robert Hale Limited, 1973. 224pp.

Owen Tudor, the son of the murderer Meredydd Tudor, who has fled from Beaumaris, is brought up by his kinsman Owain Glyndwr. The boy grows to love Owain, who is more a father to him than his weak sire, who soon abandons him. When Owain is defeated in battle by Henry IV and his son, he sends Owen to the English court to serve as Prince Henry's squire. When the prince becomes Henry V and invades France, Owen goes with him, and falls in love with Katherine, the king's bride. After the king's death, Owen joins the queen's household, but the late king's brothers, who intend to control the kingdom, send her from the court. Owen accompanies her, and the two secretly marry and have several children. Humphrey of Gloucester discovers their secret, and sends Katherine to a convent and Owen to prison. Katherine dies and Owen is released to return to Wales. When the Yorkists claim his stepson Henry's throne, Owen and his son Jasper fight for Henry, and at Mortimer's Cross, Owen is captured and beheaded.

321. _____. *The Game of Power*. London: Robert Hale Limited, 1975. 220pp.

Richard Neville, who becomes Earl of Warick when he marries Anne Beauchamp, is the real power and brains of the opposition to Margaret of Anjou. Richard is attracted to the queen, but when she attempts to seduce him, he rejects her and earns her enmity. Although he supports the king, he becomes convinced that the Yorkists' only safety lies in replacing him with the Duke of York. York's poor leadership leads to his and Richard's father's and brother's deaths at Wakefield, and so Warwick throws his support to York's son Edward. With his help Edward is proclaimed king, and Warwick retires to Middleham so that he will not overshadow the young man with his popularity.

322. _____. *The Game of Kings*. London: Robert Hale Limited, 1977. 188pp.

Proud, ambitious Richard Neville, Earl of Warwick, expects to rule England through a puppet Edward IV. He is disappointed and humiliated by Edward's marriage to Elizabeth Woodville, the rise of her family, and the king's refusal to ally with France, rather than Burgundy. The frustration of his plans leads Warwick to scheme against the king, and finally to break with him and join forces with Margaret of Anjou, who seduces him with the intention of killing him. She fails, and they decide to work together, she for the restoration of Henry VI, and Warwick with the secret intention of ruling the country. Edward is forced to flee, but returns in triumph, as Warwick, realizing that his popularity and power are gone, goes to defeat and death at Barnet, on the day that Margaret's forces land in England, too late to save him or Henry's crown.

323. Symonds, Rev. W. S. *Malvern Chase. An Episode of the Wars of the Roses and the Battle of Tewkesbury. An Autobiography.* Tewkesbury: William North, 1881. viii + 336pp.

This novel purports to be the autobiography of Hildebrande de Brute, of a Lollard family in Malvern Chase in Gloucestershire. The family supports the Yorkists, believing that Edward of March will grant religious freedom, and father and son fight for Edward at Mortimer's Cross. Hildebrande loves his neighbor, Rosamund Berew, but her Lancastrian uncle takes her into exile with Margaret of Anjou. Hildebrande is knighted by Edward IV, but becomes disenchanted by the loose morals of the court, and he realizes that Edward has no interest in helping the Lollards. He remains loyal to Edward, but is disillusioned by the king's cruel murder of Lancastrians at Tewkesbury. He rescues Rosamund, who has returned to England with Margaret, and the king gives the couple permission to return to Malvern Chase.

324. Tey, Josephine [Mackintosh, Elizabeth]. *The Daughter of Time.* New York: The Macmillan Company, 1951. 180pp.

Scotland Yard detective Alan Grant, flat on his back in hospital, becomes fascinated by a portrait of Richard III, and with the help of a young American, searches out the truth of the legend surrounding him. His discoveries lead him to the conclusion that Shakespeare and Thomas More were unreliable at best, and probably time-servers with no regard for the truth. This novel has probably been the most effective counter to the so-called Tudor Myth about the life and character of Richard III.

325. Thompson, C. J. S. *The Witchery of Jane Shore.* London: Grayson & Grayson, 1933. 288pp.

This romantic view of Jane Shore purports to be non-fiction, but with little or no evidence to support him, the author has supplied Jane with a detailed background and history. This Jane is a great beauty, who bewitches every man who sees her. After Richard III seizes the throne, he takes her possessions, throws her in prison, and forces her to do public penance, because years before he had conceived a great passion for her, and she had discouraged the advances of this misshapen, evil, and sinister suitor. Part two of the book covers Jane Shore in poetry and drama, and lists all known portraits of her. Several of them are reproduced in the book, all showing her bare-breasted. There is an index.

326. Townsend, Guy M. *To Prove a Villain*. Menlo Park, Calif.: Perseverance Press, 1985. 190pp.

Marian James-Tyrell, an attractive but promiscuous college professor, is smothered to death in her bed, and her colleague John Miles Forest, an arrogant, self-righteous professor of English history, tries to help the police solve the murder. Forest's class in a survey of English history is studying the Wars of the Roses, and when a student, using Josephine Tye's novel as his source (see entry 324), challenges his view of Richard III as a murdering tyrant, the professor assigns the other students the traditional anti-Ricardian (or Richardist, as the author unaccountably terms it) sources to prove his thesis. When the police inform Forest that an elderly mailman named John Dighton has also been smothered in his bed, and that he will probably be the next victim, he solves the case, confronts the murderer, and is nearly murdered himself.

327. Tranter, Nigel. *Chain of Destiny*. London: Hodder and Stoughton, 1964. 445pp.

Seventeen-year-old James IV of Scotland comes to the throne when his father is murdered by rebellious nobles, who have used the boy as a figurehead. He must bring his nobles under control, and protect himself from Henry VII, who covets Scotland. To weaken Henry, James supports Perkin Warbeck, calling himself Duke of York, and together they invade England. When the expected support of the English for his cause fails to materialize, partly because of the cruel depredations of the Scots, Warbeck returns to Scotland. Humiliated by his defeat at the hands of the English, James vows revenge, and during the reign of Henry VIII he invades England. Outwitted by the Earl of Surrey, James and most of his army are killed at Flodden Field.

328. Trevan, Ruth. *Loyalty Binds Me*. London: Robert Hale Limited, 1966.
253pp.

Richard of Gloucester remains loyal to his brother Edward IV, and
before the king's death he promises to protect his son and the kingdom.
When Richard learns, however, that Edward's children are illegitimate,
he takes the throne with the help of his cousin Buckingham. When
Buckingham hints that he has killed the princes, Richard realizes that he
will be blamed. Within a few months, Buckingham rebels and dies a
traitor's death, and Richard's son, and then his wife, die. Richard feels
that he has been cursed for violating Edward's trust, and he goes to his
death at Bosworth knowing that, except for a loyal few like Lovell and
Norfolk, the nobility and commons have turned against him.

329. *The Unfortunate Concubine: or, History of Jane Shore, Mistress to Edward
IV, King of England; showing how she came to be concubine to the King;
with an account of her untimely end*. Illus. New York: S. King, 1828.
24 pp.

See entries 110, 144-152, 202, 225, 280, 302.

330. Vance, Marguerite. *Song for a Lute*. New York: E. P. Dutton, 1958.
160pp.

This novel for young readers is an often inaccurate account of the
boyhood and reign of Richard III, concentrating on his romance with
Anne Neville.

331. Viney, Jayne. *The White Rose Dying*. London: Robert Hale Limited,
1973. 256pp.

Richard of Gloucester remains loyal to his brother Edward IV, despite
his dismay at the king's cruelty and coarseness, which he blames on the
Woodvilles' influence. Edward orders Richard to kill Henry VI after
Tewkesbury, and equivocates when Richard wants to marry Anne
Neville. After Edward's death, Richard intends to serve the new king,
but when he learns that Edward's marriage was invalid, and his children
illegitimate, he takes the crown. His conscience is troubled, but he
knows that a boy king controlled by the Woodvilles means danger to the
realm. When Richard's son and wife die, he believes he is being
punished, but he can't believe that any one would listen to the false
rumors that he has murdered his wife and nephews, and intends to marry
his niece. He is mistaken, and he loses his life and crown to Henry

Tudor, who then orders Bishop Morton to eliminate the princes.

332. _____. *King Richard's Friend*. London: Robert Hale Limited, 1975.
206pp.

Francis Lovell is sent to Middleham, where he is befriended by the
King's brother Richard, and falls in love with Anne Neville.   At
fourteen, Francis is married to Warwick's relation Anne Fitzhugh.   He
dislikes her at first meeting, the marriage is unhappy and childless, and
Francis later takes a mistress, by whom he has three children.   When
Warwick breaks with the king, Francis, his ward, goes with him into
exile in France, where Anne Neville is forced to marry Edward of
Lancaster.   After the Lancastrian defeat at Tewkesbury, Francis joins
Richard, and is rewarded with titles and honors.   He remains a loyal
Yorkist, leading the Simnel rebellion against Henry Tudor.   The rebels
are defeated at Stoke, and Francis escapes to Minster Lovell, only to die
of starvation, when he is unable to leave his hiding place.

333. Welch, Ronald. *Sun of York*. Illus. by Doreen Roberts.   Oxford: Oxford
University Press, 1970.   212pp.

Owen Lloyd, the son of a Welsh Yorkist gentleman, fights alongside his
father at the battle of Edgecote, and then joins Edward IV in exile in
Burgundy after his father's murder by Lancastrian neighbors.   Owen
becomes squire to Richard of Gloucester, distinguishes himself at Barnet
and Tewkesbury, and is rewarded with vast estates and high offices.
This novel, written for young people, gives a good account of life during
the Wars of the Roses, including its harshness and the brutality of
powerful men on both sides of the conflict.

334. Wensby-Scott, Carol. *Lion of Alnwick*. Illus. London: Michael Joseph
Ltd., 1980.   416 pp.

This novel, which covers the period between 1357 and 1409, is the first
of a trilogy about the Percy family, Earls of Northumberland.   See
entries 335, 336.

335. _____. *Lion Dormant*. London: Michael Joseph Ltd., 1983.   373pp.

In this second novel of a trilogy about the Percies of Northumberland
(see entries 334, 336), Hal Percy, imprisoned after the deaths of his
grandfather and Harry Hotspur, his father, by the duke of Albany in
Scotland, secures his freedom after ten years, and pledges his support to

the House of Lancaster. He marries Alianore Neville, the daughter of his family's bitter enemy, Ralph Neville, and the two families fight on different sides for the next half century. The novel ends with the deaths of all the male Percies except young Harry, the heir, and the loss of the Northumberland title. Although the author is strongly anti-Yorkist, there are no real heroes in this tale of a cruel and lawless age.

336. _____. *Lion Invincible*. London: Michael Joseph Ltd., 1984. 330pp.

In this third novel of a trilogy about the Percies of Northumberland (see entries 334-335), Henry Percy is released from a long imprisonment by Edward IV, and restored to his earldom of Northumberland. His rivalry with Richard of Gloucester, whose power in the north equals his, grows into love and friendship when they realize that they share a dream of a strong and prosperous north. Northumberland continues to support Richard after he seizes the throne, but when he becomes convinced that the king has murdered his nephews, he stands by with his army at Bosworth, and allows Henry Tudor to gain the victory.

337. Westcott, Jan. *The Hepburn*. New York: Crown Publishers, 1950. 278pp.

James IV of Scotland seizes the throne from his father in a bloody coup, with the help of Patrick Hepburn, a powerful border lord. When Perkin Warbeck is offered to him, he decides to make the young 'Duke of York' the centerpiece of his foreign policy. He gives him his cousin Mary (sic) Gordon in marriage, and forces her sister Jane to marry Hepburn. After Warbeck's defeat, Mary is reunited with her true love, Matthew Craddock, an English spy in the pay of Henry VII, and England and Scotland agree to a treaty. James IV agrees to marry Henry's daughter Margaret, Jane and Hepburn realize that they love each other, and everyone lives happily ever after.

338. _____. *The White Rose*. New York: G. P. Putnam's Sons, 1969. 480pp.

This novel tells the love story of Edward IV and Elizabeth Woodville. The Woodvilles, especially Elizabeth and her brother Anthony, are the heroes, and the views of Edward IV and Richard III are those of the Tudor chroniclers, presented in slightly more sophisticated terms. See also entry 339.

339. _____. *The Lion's Share*. London: Robert Hale Limited, 1969.
317pp.

This is an abridged English version of *The White Rose*. See entry 338.

340. _____. *Set Her on a Throne*. Boston: Little, Brown and Company,
1972.   233pp.

Anne Neville is forced by her father to marry Edward of Lancaster after
Warwick's reconciliation with Margaret of Anjou. The newlyweds fall
madly in love, and after Edward's death at Tewkesbury, Anne discovers
she is pregnant.   In order to escape the attentions of Richard of
Gloucester, she goes into hiding, but after the loss of her baby she agrees
to marry the duke, her childhood friend. The marriage is happy until
Richard seizes the throne, and their sickly young son dies. Anne follows
him to the grave the following year.   The author romanticizes the
Lancastrians, but is generally sympathetic to the Yorkists, including
Richard, who she does not believe murdered the princes.

341. Whittle, Tyler. *The Last Plantagenet: A Study of Richard the Third King
of England, France and Ireland*. London: William Heinemann Ltd.,
1968.   275pp.

This is a fictional treatment of the life of Richard III from the age of
seven, when he was captured with his mother and brother George at
Ludlow, until his death at Bosworth in 1485. He is portrayed, in this
sympathetic novel, as neither monster nor saint, but as a man of honor
and courage, doing his duty as best he can.

342. Whitton, Dorothy. *Halo of Dreams*. Macdonald & Co., Ltd., 1948.
224pp.

Joan Mountford, the devoutly religious daughter of a Lancastrian knight
slain at St. Albans, is inspired by the story of Joan of Arc and a vision
of St. Michael and St. George, to go to London to rescue Henry VI from
the Tower. She sets off with her cousins, Michael and Lawrence, the
sons of her guardian.   They are befriended on the way by Sir Giles
Cordale, a cynical Yorkist turncoat, who decides to use the pious Joan
for his own ends when he realizes that many of the ignorant peasants
believe she is a saint. When Joan meets the mad Henry VI, however, she
is disillusioned, and returns home, hoping to marry Lawrence. Her uncle
insists that she marry Michael, and it is not until after Warwick's defeat
at Barnet that she achieves her heart's desire.

343. Wiat, Philippa. *The Master of Blandeston Hall*. London: Robert Hale
     Limited, 1973.   207 pp.

Henry Wyatt, a Yorkshire friend of Henry Tudor, incurs the enmity of
his villainous neighbor, Giles Athelstane, when he refuses to allow the
latter to marry his sister Elena. Giles seduces Elena's friend Catherine
into marriage, and forces her to reveal that Wyatt had sheltered Tudor.
The remorseful Catherine hangs herself, but Giles informs Richard III,
who has Wyatt arrested and tortured. He is rescued by Tudor on his way
to Bosworth, and after the battle the friends return to Blandeston Hall,
only to discover that the evil Giles has taken possession, murdered
Wyatt's wife and son, and raped Elena. Giles is suitably punished for his
crimes by the loyal, sensitive Henry Tudor. This novel is typical of this
author's rather strange, convoluted tales.

344. _____. *Prince of the White Rose*. London: Robert Hale Limited,
     1984.   368pp.

When Edward IV dies, Richard of Gloucester seizes his two sons, puts
them in the Tower, and spreads the rumor that that they are illegitimate.
Both boys are at the meeting in the Tower where Hastings is executed
without trial and their other supporters arrested. Gloucester orders the
murder of the boys, but Richard, the younger, is spared and sent to
Tournai to live with Catherine Osbeck, who bore Edward IV a son at the
time of Richard's birth. He takes the place of the Osbecks' dead son
Perkin, until he can claim the throne. Henry Tudor defeats and kills the
evil hunchbacked Richard III, seduces Elizabeth of York, gets her
pregnant, and marries her. When Perkin/Richard is captured, Elizabeth
refuses to see him, although she believes him to be an imposter. Finally
convinced by Jane Shore that Richard is her brother, an act that costs
Jane her life, it is too late. Richard's wife, Katherine, discovers that she
is pregnant, but Henry Tudor rapes her, both for lust, and so that he can
claim the child as his. Tudor tries to convince his wife that the doomed
Perkin is not her brother, but she has come to believe that he is, and she
dies consumed by guilt because she feared Henry and loved her children
enough to deny her brother.

345. _____. *The Kingmaker's Daughter*. London: Robert Hale Limited,
     1989.   311 pp.

Although their marriage was part of a political arrangement between their
parents, Anne Neville and Edward of Lancaster are madly in love. She
mourns his death at Tewkesbury at the hands of Richard of Gloucester,

her childhood friend, and Clarence, Hastings, and Dorset. Richard, who
also kills Henry VI, wants to marry Anne, but Clarence, who doesn't
want to share the Warwick inheritance, hides her as a scullery maid in
his London home, where she is brutally mistreated. Richard rescues her,
and she agrees to marry him to protect her mother and her inheritance.
She learns to love Richard, although she knows his ruthless ambition
leads him to eliminate anyone who stands in his way, and his victims
include, in addition to Edward of Lancaster and Henry VI, Clarence and
the elder of the princes in the Tower. After their son's death, Ann's
physical and emotional health are broken, and she dies, leaving a
grieving husband, who loved her deeply.

346. _____. *The Child Bride*. London: Robert Hale Ltd., 1990. 215pp.

Eight-year-old Anne Mowbray is married to five-year-old Richard, Duke
of York, the younger of Edward IV's two sons. She then goes home to
Framlingham Hall in Suffolk with her mother, the dowager Duchess of
Suffolk. Her mother engages as her companion Joan Halidon, the
illegitimate daughter of the late duke, and soon the girls are mirror
images of each other, and Joan learns the truth of her parentage. The
family moves to Westminster, where both girls fall in love with Prince
Edward. He returns Joan's love, but after the king's death Richard of
Gloucester seizes the throne and imprisons Edward and his brother. Joan
sneaks into the Tower, where she and Edward consummate their love.
During a second visit she sees Edward's corpse, and she too is killed by
the murderers, who mistake her for Anne. It is her body that is buried
as Anne's, and when the real Anne dies of the plague, her body is
secretly interred, as her husband, who has escaped the murderers,
watches in disguise.

347. Willard, Barbara. *The Lark and the Laurel*. Illus. by Gareth Floyd.
London: Longman Group Limited, 1970. 170pp. New York: Harcourt,
Brace & World, 1970. 207pp.

Sixteen-year-old Cecily Jolland is sent to Mantlemass, her aunt Dame
Elizabeth's estate, after Bosworth, when her Lancastrian turned Yorkist
father flees to France. There the spoiled young heiress learns to live the
life of a country woman, and meets and falls in love with Lewis Mallory,
the highborn cousin of a neighbor. Lewis has been disowned by his
Lancastrian father, and the secret of the pasts of both young people
threatens to destroy their happiness. Their love and courage enable them
to overcome their difficulties.

348. _____. *The Sprig of Broom*. Illus. by Paul Shardlow. London: Longman Group Limited, 1971. 185pp.

The sequel to *The Lark and the Laurel* (see entry 347), this novel relates the story of fourteen-year-old Medley Plashet, who lives in Sussex with his parents, Anis and Richard. When Richard disappears, Medley discovers that his parents had never married. When Anis dies, their neighbors, the Mallorys, take the boy in and educate him, but differences in class prohibit the mariage between him and Catherine Mallory, whose father owns the estate on which Medley and his parents lived. Medley goes in search of his father, and discovers that Richard is the illegitimate son of Richard III, and that ambitious men are attempting to use him to raise a rebellion against Henry Tudor. All ends well, however, and Medley and Catherine are able to marry.

349. Williams, Bert. *Master of Ravenspur*. Study materials by Jennifer Harvey. London and Toronto: Thomas Nelson and Sons, 1970. 156pp.

Twelve-year-old Dickon, the son of a servant of Sir Reginald de Cherche, Lord of Ravenspur, continues to serve his master after his mother's death, since he has never known his father, and has nowhere else to go. Kindly retainers teach him to read and and handle weapons, and when Sir Reginald is murdered by the treacherous Lancastrian Duke Percival d'Abernon, Dickon joins the Duke of Gloucester. He goes into exile with him when Warwick drives Edward IV from the country, and returns to fight at Gloucester's side, saving his life at Barnet. As a reward, he is given the castle of Ravenspur, and learns his true, and noble, identity. This novel was written as a text to be used in middle schools.

350. Williamson, Joanne S. *To Dream Upon a Crown*. Illus. by Jacob Landay. New York: Alfred A. Knopf, 1967. 184pp.

Shakespeare's *Henry VI*, parts I, II, and III, are recast in the form of a novel for young readers, using Shakespeare's words for the dialogue. The author fills in the tale with background about the period and characters in the plays, faithfully following Shakespeare's portrayal of Richard of Gloucester, Henry VI, and Edward IV.

351. Willman, Marianne. *Rose Red, Rose White*. Toronto and New York: Harlequin Books, 1989. 301 pp.

Welsh heiress Morgana Hartley is twice forced by Edward IV to marry his retainers.   On the day of the execution of her first husband for treason, she is joined in marriage to Ranulph the Dane, a Yorkist from Orkney.   When they arrive at her castle in Wales, they discover it is under siege by her Lancastrian neighbor and would-be husband.   Ranulph defeats the besieger, and after many misunderstandings and reconciliations, he and Morgana discover that they are made for each other, and they live happily ever after.

352. Wilson, Sandra. *Less Fortunate Than Fair*. New York: St. Martin's Press, Inc., 1973. 223pp.

This novel is the first of a trilogy about Cecily Plantagenet, the younger sister of Elizabeth of York.   At the death of her father Edward IV, Cecily and all of her siblings had been declared illegitimate because their parents were bigamously married.   When Richard III, their uncle, takes the throne, Cecily meets and falls in love with Richard's illegitimate son, John of Gloucester.   After Richard's death at Bosworth, John is taken prisoner by Henry Tudor, and Cecily realizes that they will never be able to marry.

353. _____. *The Queen's Sister*. New York: St. Martin's Press, Inc., 1974. 189pp.

In this second novel of a trilogy (see entries 352, 354), Cecily, the second daughter of Edward IV, is in love with John of Gloucester, the illegitimate son of Richard III.   After Bosworth, Henry Tudor forces her to marry his uncle, John Welles, the half-brother of Margaret Beaufort. Despite her hatred for the evil Henry, and her continued loyalty to the memory of Richard III and John of Gloucester, she eventually falls in love with the kind and gentle Vicount Welles.

354. _____. *The Lady Cecily*. New York: St. Martin's Press, Inc., 1974. 190pp.

In this third novel of a trilogy about Cecily, the younger sister of Elizabeth of York (see entries 352,353), Cecily promises her husband Lord Welles, Henry Tudor's uncle, that she will not become involved in Perkin Warbeck's rebellion.   She discovers, however, that Warbeck is really her younger brother Richard, who she knew had not been murdered by her uncle Richard III.   Cecily is unable to save him, and he is put to death by Henry Tudor.

355. _____. *Wife to the Kingmaker*. New York: St. Martin's Press, 1974. 238pp.

Anne Beauchamp, heiress of the Earl of Warwick, is married as a young child to Richard Neville, son of the Earl of Salisbury. Her contempt for him turns to love as he becomes the most powerful and popular man in England, throwing his support to the Duke of York, and then to York's son Edward. After a brief affair with her husband's brother John, Anne again becomes a dutiful and loving wife, and supports her husband throughout his turbulent career.

356. _____. *The Penrich Dragon*. London: Robert Hale Ltd., 1977. 192pp.

Elaine Stanhope is brought up in a priory on the Welsh border, ignorant of her background and parentage. She is taken to Penrich Castle by Sir Ralph Gifford, the Lancastrian widower of her aunt Joanna, to take the place of his recently deceased wife, to whom she bears a remarkable likeness. Once there, she falls in love with Ralph, only to discover that he is under the spell of his mistress, an evil witch named Alianor. They are searching for the Penrich Dragon, the source of great riches, which they plan to bring to Henry Tudor to finance his invasion of England. Elaine and the treasure are saved in the nick of time by Sir Roger Stanhope, a Yorkist neighbor, and Joanna's cousin. Roger and Elaine fall in love, the villains are punished, and Edward IV's throne is saved.

357. Winter, L. F. *Castle Harcourt or, The Days of King Richard the Third. A Tale of 1483*. London: A. K. Newman Co., 1834.   3 vols.

Not available for review.

358. Wynne, May [Knowles, Mabel Winifred]. *The Gipsy Count*. Frontispiece. New York: The John McBride Co., 1909.   322pp.

This romance-adventure tale is set in Brittany in 1483, and concerns the evil doings of Pierre Landais, the chancellor and favorite of Duke Francis.   Landais, the so-called Tailor of Vetre, in reference to his former occupation, abuses his position to destroy his enemies and make himself all-powerful.   He was the official who attempted to capture Henry Tudor and sell him to Richard III, but although Tudor is mentioned several times in the novel, it is only peripherally concerned with events in England.   See entry 359.

359. _____. *Red Rose of Lancaster*. London: Holden & Hardingham, 1922. 252pp.

In 1483 Hugh Conway, who is carrying a message to Henry Tudor from his mother, meets Guy Standon, a fellow Englishman, in the forest in Brittany. They fight, but soon become friends and rescue the Chatelaine of Querrien, a noble damsel in distress. The three join together to foil a plot by Pierre Landois to betray Henry to Richard III. (See entry 358.) Henry escapes Landois' clutches, invades England, and defeats Richard III at Bosworth Field.

360. Yonge, Charlotte M. *Grisly Grisell or The Laidly Lady of Whitburn; A Tale of the Wars of the Roses*. London: Macmillan and Co., 1883. 2 vols.

Ten-year-old Grisell Dacre, the daughter of a Yorkist lord from the north, is sent to live in the household of the Earl of Salisbury. She is disfigured in an accident caused by her intended bridegroom, Leonard Copeland, the son of a Lancastrian lord, and nursed back to health, but not beauty, by her dear friend, Margaret of York. Grisell then goes to live for several years in a convent, where she learns the value of patience and kindness. Returning to her home, and her neglectful parents, she is forced to marry Leonard, whom her father has captured in battle. The return of Henry VI to the throne forces her Yorkist family into exile, and Grizell is forced as well to endure accusations of witchcraft, because her loving nature wins love despite her ruined face. Eventually, she wins Leonard's love, and they return to live at her childhood home.

361. _____. *Two Penniless Princesses*. London: Macmillan and Co., Ltd., 1890. 2 vols.

The eponymous princesses are the two younger sisters of James III of Scotland, who sends them to France to the protection of another sister, the wife of the future Louis XI, in order to get them away from the danger posed by his warring nobles. On the way, they visit and are charmed by the Duke and Duchess of York and their two young sons Edward and Edmund. Their Lancastrian uncle, the Bishop of Winchester, places them in a convent until they can leave for France, in order to get them away from the Yorkist party. Once in France, they discover that the French court offers no protection, when they are kidnapped by Alsation nobles, with the connivance of their brother-in-law. Their sister dies of a broken heart caused by her husband's mistreatment, but the two princesses are rescued by their future husbands, and they live happily ever after.

362. _____. *The Herd Boy and His Hermit*. London: National Society's Depository, n.d. 261pp.

This is a sentimental tale of young Harry Clifford, the son of the Lord Clifford who slew Edmund, Earl of Rutland, at Wakefield. After his father's death, young Harry is sent to live with a herdsman, to protect him from the vengeance of the Yorkists. He meets a holy hermit in the woods, who turns out to be the exiled Henry VI. After Henry's restoration to the throne, Harry joins the Lancastrian army, and is wounded at Barnet. When he recovers, he marries his Lancastrian sweetheart, and despite the Yorkists' return to power, we are led to believe they will live happily ever after.

363. York, Elizabeth. *The Heir of Berkwell*. London: Robert Hale Limited, 1977. 204 pp.

Not available for review.

364. Young, D[orothy] V[alerie]. *The White Boar*. London: Robert Hale Ltd., 1963. 191pp.

This novel, which begins in 1459 at Fotheringhay, is narrated by Sir Gervaise a Penn, knight and Gentleman at Arms, and son of a Cornish knight, who is sent to live in the household of the Duke of York. There he meets Richard of Gloucester, to whom he remains faithful for the rest of his life. At Middleham, Gervaise falls in love with Joletta Barham, Warwick's ward, but her evil brother, a follower of Henry Tudor, sends her to a convent so that he can steal her inheritance. Richard, however, pays off her brother, and she agrees to marry Gervaise. When Richard becomes king and discovers that the princes have been killed, both he and Gervaise realize that Buckingham was responsible for their deaths. Gervaise survives Bosworth and goes into exile to Bruges, refusing to accept Henry Tudor as king.

❖

Verse

365. "Advice to the Court, I." (Cotton Rolls ii. 23) *Historical Poems of the XIV and XV Centuries.* (See entry 430.) p. 203.

This one stanza poem of fifteen lines is an attack on Suffolk and his friends on the council, written in 1450, at the height of their power. The writer warns the king's advisors not to lose the love of the commons or to listen to false friends, be they dukes, judges, or archbishops. Let those accused of crimes be punished with the loss of their titles, positions, and wealth, he counsels.

366. "Advice to the Court, II." (Cotton Rolls, ii, 23) *Historical Poems of the XIV and XV Centuries.* (See entry 430.) pp. 203-205.

This ten stanza verse, of six lines each, is a companion piece to "Advice to the Court, I" (see entry 365), and was probably a popular song. The author complains of the abuses of Henry VI's counselors, charging that the king has been beggared by their excesses, the commons oppressed, etc. Suffolk, Lord Say, and others are mentioned, and the king is urged to control and punish them, for they are traitors who will never be true.

367. Aleyn, Charles. *The Historie of that Wise and Fortunate Prince, Henrie of that Name the Seventh, King of England. With that famed Battaile, fought betweene the sayd King Henry and Richard the third named Crook-backe, upon Redmoore neere Bosworth.* London: Printed by Tho. Cotes, for William Cooke, 1638. 156pp.

This paean to Henry VII is a history in verse of his reign, from his defeat of the evil usurper Richard III at Bosworth, until shortly before his death in 1509. Henry wins the hearts of his newly conquered countrymen by pardoning their support for the Yorkists, but his reign is plagued by rebellions by rogues who do not appreciate his generosity. He deals kindly with Lambert Simnel and his followers, but when Perkin Warbeck, a base imposter, leads a rebellion, the king decides that severity is the way to deal with rebels. Warbeck is captured, and Henry lures him and the innocent Earl of Warwick into a plot, and executes them both. Henry's grasping ways and heavy taxation alienate the country, but Aleyn praises him for bringing peace and prosperity to England.

368. Alley, Jerom. "The Widowed Queen; or, Elizabeth, Dowager of Edward IV, Delivering up her Second Son from Sanctuary: and Philippa to Edward III, in favour of the Burghers of Calais, being a poem and oration to which Prizes were adjudged by the Provost and Senior-fellows of Trinity College, Dublin, in Hilary Term, 1777." Dublin: Printed by R. Marchbank, 1777.

Not available for review.

369. *Ancient Songs and Ballads.* Collected by Joseph Ritson. London: Reeves and Turner, 1877. xc+436pp.

This is a collection of old songs and ballads first published in 1790, under the title *Ancient Songs from the time of King Henry the Third to the Revolution.* The collection contains several about the Wars of the Roses. See entries 392, 430, 441, 495.

370. "Arrest of the Duke of Suffolk." (Cotton Rolls ii.23) *Historical Poems of the XIV and XV Centuries.* (See entry 430.) pp. 186-187.

The gloating tone of this one stanza, thirty-line poem indicates the hostility of the commons toward Suffolk, who is blamed for Henry VI's unpopular marriage to Margaret of Anjou, the loss of English possessions in France, the death of the popular John Talbot, embezzlement, and other grievances. Robbins dates this poem in February, 1450, since no mention is made of Suffolk's return to royal favor at the Easter parliament in 1450.

371. Baldwin, William. *A Myrroure for Magistrates.* London: Thomas Marshe, 1559.

This is a collection of verse tragedies, most of them written by Baldwin and George Ferrers. See entries 372-378,

372. _____. *A Mirrour for Magistrates*. London: Thomas Marshe, 1563.

This edition adds eight tragedies to the 1559 edition. See entry 371.

373. _____. "How king Henry the syxt a vertuous prince, was after many other miseries cruelly murdered in the Tower of London." *Mirror for Magistrates*. 1559 ed. Campbell, ed. (See entries 371, 452.) pp. 211-218.

Henry tells how he hated sin and spurned worldly fortune, but despite this he was the most unfortunate of men. He relates the history of his family, both before his birth and during his lifetime. He accuses Edward IV of the murder of Edward of Lancaster, and Richard of Gloucester of his, Henry's, murder. He warns all men that princes who who break the law will suffer, along with their friends, and hopes that his sad story will teach them how frail is honor, and brittle worldly bliss.

374. _____. "How sir Richard Nevell Earle of Warwike, and his brother John Lord Marquise Mountacute through their to much boldnes wer slayne at Barnet field." *Mirror for Magistrates*. 1559 ed. Campbell, ed. (See entries 371, 452.) pp. 203-210.

Baldwin asks the reader to imagine Warwick lying in St. Paul's church with his brother Montague, and speaking the lines of the poem. He relates how he helped both the Duke of York and his son Edward in their quest for the crown. When Edward became king, he embarrassed Warwick by sending him to France to negotiate for a bride, and then turned around and married Elizabeth Woodville. Warwick then went over to the Lancastrians, and this caused his fall. He assures Baldwin that he was no hypocrite, but worked always for the country, rather than his own gain. He tells the poet to teach by his example, that if men would secure the people's love they must make their words and deeds agree, care only for the people's good, and be upright in their dealings.

375. _____. "The infamous ende of Lord John Tiptoft Earle of Wurcester, for cruelly executing his princes butcherly commaundmentes." *Mirror for Magistrates*. 1559 ed. Campbell, ed. (See entries 371, 452.) pp. 197-202.

Tiptoft chastises some chroniclers for omitting the reasons men did their

deeds, and cautions Baldwin to write the complete story. He notes that
he was often called Edward IV's friend, counsellor, and butcher, but he
was merely doing the king's will. He admits that that is no excuse for
doing evil, even though to refuse the king's command would result in his
own death. His greatest regret is the murder of the young sons of the
Earl of Desmond, and though the command was Edward's, he must
accept the blame as well. When he was attainted by parliament after the
restoration of Henry VI, he was blamed for all of Edward's misdeeds.
He warns all men to avoid high office, unless they can forsake their king
if he is wrong.

376. _____. "How the lord Clyfford for his straunge and abominable
cruelty, came to as straunge and sodayne a death." *Mirror for
Magistrates*. 1559 ed. Campbell, ed. (See entries 371, 452.) pp. 192-
195.

Clifford admits his shame and guilt for the cruel murder of the young
Rutland, who pleaded for his life. He declares that he did the deed to
avenge his father, slain at St. Albans by Rutland's father, the Duke of
York, but the boy was innocent. Clifford believes he was justly punished
when he was shot through the throat by an arrow while fighting against
York's eldest son, Edward.

377. [_____]. "Howe Collingbourne was cruelly executed for making a
foolishe rime." *Mirror for Magistrates*. 1563 ed. Campbell, ed. (See
entries 372, 394, 452.) pp. 346-348.

Collyngbourne, the author of the infamous couplet (see item 394), warns
that certain subjects are off-limits to poets. Describing his grisly death,
the one suffered by all traitors at the time, he insists that he meant no
harm to the king, and that he neither intended nor committed treason.
Since, however, the guilty are always suspicious, and consider vicious
anyone who notes their faults, they call their critics traitors. He urges
Baldwin to warn poets to avoid extremes, for by staying in the middle
they will be safe.

378. [_____]. "How Sir Anthony Wudvile Lorde Rivers and Skales,
Gouernour of prince Edward, was with his Neuew Lord Richard Gray
and other causeles imprisoned, and cruelly murdered." *Mirror for
Magistrates*. 1563 ed. Campbell, ed. (See entries 372, 452.) pp. 245-
266.

In one of the longest of the *Mirror* tragedies, Anthony Woodville, following More's version of the events surrounding the death of Edward IV, laments the earlier deaths of his father and brother at the hands of Warwick, and the enmity that the rise of his family caused among the old nobility, whose jealousy brought down many good men. Clarence, instead of rejoicing at the rise of the Woodvilles, was angry when Anthony was named governor of the royal children, but God punished the duke's sins when Gloucester smothered him. After Edward's death, the evil Gloucester, Hastings, and Buckingham captured the new king, and arrested and executed the innocent Rivers, Grey, and Vaughn, without trial. Rivers admits he earned his death for not executing Gloucester for murdering Henry VI and Clarence, and warns therefore that those in power should execute murderers, whoever they may be, or else be slain by them.

379. "Ballade Set on the Gates of Canterbury." (John Speed Davies Ms.) *An English Chronicle of the Reigns of Richard II., Henry IV., Henry V., and Henry VI.* Ed. by John Silvester Davies. London: The Camden Society, 1856. pp. 91-94. *Historical Poems of the XIV and XV Centuries.* (See entry 430.) pp. 207-210.

In this poem of ten eight-line stanzas, the poet laments the state to which England has fallen. He prays to God to reform the English and return them to goodness and purity, and to restore the Duke of York to his rightful position. York and his supporters, the Earls of March, Warwick, and Salisbury, are praised.

380. "The Battle of Barnet." (Trinity College Dublin MS. 601) *Historical Poems of the XIV and XV Centuries.* (See entry 430.) pp. 226-227.

This poem of four eight-line stanzas presents the popular London view of Edward IV in 1471, as having been unjustly deprived of his inheritance by Henry IV after the death of Richard II. The writer urges the people to accept the return of Edward IV as king, and referring to the death of the divisive Warwick, declares that it is now time for reconciliation with Edward, for he is worthy to be loved and feared.

381. "The Battle of Northampton." (Trinity College Dublin MS. 432) *Historical Poems of the XIV and XV Centuries.* (See entry 430.) pp. 210-215.

This poem of twenty eight-line stanzas was probably written between June 10, the day of the battle, and September 8, 1460, the day the Duke of York returned from Ireland. The writer tells of the nobles, to whom he refers by their badges, e.g., the rose is York, who was not at the battle, the fetterlock is Edward, Earl of March, the eagle is Salisbury, and the bear Warwick, who have returned from exile. When they hear the laments of the people, they go to Northampton and chase the dogs, Talmadge, Beaumont, and Egremont, who are killed by Warwick. The king is captured, but the victorious Yorkists kneel before him to assure him of their loyalty, and he accepts their vows.

382. "The Battle of Towton." (Trinity College Dublin MS. 432) *Historical Poems of the XIV and XV Centuries*. (See entry 430.) pp.215-218.

This poem of fifteen five-line stanzas was written in 1461, and relates the victory of Edward of Rouen, proclaimed Edward IV after his victories at Mortimer's Cross and Towton, over Margaret of Anjou's forces. The pro-Yorkist writer calls Edward the 'chief flour of this lond' who saved England from Margaret and her army of northern men, who planned to destroy the south of England. As in other poems of this sort, the writer refers to the nobles by their badges. (See entry 381.) He writes that when Edward returned victorious from Towton, having made England safe for men, women, and children, two archbishops crowned him king.

383. Beaumont, Sir John. *Bosworth Field: With a Taste of the Variety of Other Poems*. London: Printed by Felix Kyngston for Henry Seile, 1629. 208pp.

The Battle of Bosworth is portrayed as a battle between good, in the person of Henry Tudor, and evil, in that of Richard III. On the night before the battle, the king is haunted by dreams of his victims, while Henry is visited by an angel who urges him to fight for the crown, his victory assured by heaven's blessing. Richard is doomed, and Henry, with God on his side, slays the evil king and claims the crown.

384. "The Bisson Leads the Blind." (Harley MS. 5396) *Historical Poems of the XIV and XV Centuries*. (See entry 430.) pp.127-130.

This poem of ten eight-line stanzas is missing several of its lines. It is a lament for the terrible conditions that prevailed in the reign of Henry VI, when the bisson (purblind, or nearly blind) led the blind, evil ruled the land, truth was not valued, the clergy sold pardons, etc.

385. B[radock, or Blore] R. *The Preservation of King Henry VII*. London: Sold by G. Patten, 1599.   104 pp.

The author devotes the first part of this book to an argument of the superiority of verse over prose as a means of written expression, and a sycophantic dedication to Queen Elizabeth, the grand-daughter of Henry VII. The poem itself is divided into two parts, with an intervening section setting forth Richard, Duke of York's, title to the throne. In the first section, Henry Tudor goes into exile in Brittany, but Edward IV sends ambassadors laden with gifts, in an attempt to persuade the Duke of Brittany to yield the fugitive. The duke agrees, but Henry is saved by the arguments of a courtier, and Edward is satisfied, since he believes that Henry, who will be placed in sanctuary, will pose no threat. The second part tells of Edward's death and the murder of his two young sons and other claimants to the throne by the evil tyrant Richard of Gloucester. The author fills in the plot with many biblical and classical comparisons, and expresses his debt to Thomas More.

386. [Brereton, Humphrey]. "Bosworth ffeilde." *Percy's Folio MS.* (See entry 463.) Vol. III, pp.233-259.

Generally attributed to Humphrey Brereton, author of "Ladye Bessiye" (see entry 387), the edition in Percy contains additions written in the reign of James I. The ballad begins with words in praise of Henry VII, the savior of England, and the Stanleys, who supported him. Richard III, who tried to rule wisely, is persuaded by evil counselors to take Lord Strange hostage, to ensure his father's loyalty. The Stanleys are enraged by the action, and decide to fight against the king, but many knights and nobles come to the king's aid. Sir William Stanley meets secretly with Henry Tudor, hails him as king, and urges him to fight for his rightful crown. At Bosworth, Richard orders Strange's death, but convinced that he will soon have all the Stanleys in his grasp, rescinds the order. During the battle, one of Richard's knights urges him to flee, since the Stanleys have betrayed him, but he vows he will die king of England. After his death, Lord Stanley delivers the crown to Henry, and they ride to Leicester, bringing the late king's naked body for public display.

387. [_____.] "Ladye: Bessiye." *Percy's Folio MS.* (See entry 463.) Vol. III, pp.319-363.

This poem, attributed to Humphrey Bereton, a retainer of the Stanleys and the narrator, was written early in the sixteenth century, although this version was probably copied during the reign of James I from a transcription written in the reign of Elizabeth I. It is one of two ballads attributed to Brereton, which glorify the Stanleys and their contribution to Henry Tudor's victory at Bosworth. (See entry 386.) This ballad tells about the role of Elizabeth of York in the plot to bring Henry Tudor to England to claim the throne. Elizabeth, who lives with Lord Stanley in London after Bosworth, tells him that Richard murdered her brothers and planned to kill his wife, so that he could marry her. She asks Stanley's aid for Tudor, but he refuses because of the danger. She is adamant, and he finally relents. Bessie sends letters to supporters by Brereton, the only messenger she can trust, and meets with supporters, maps out strategy, and in general takes over the management of the campaign. The last part of the ballad repeats the story of the Battle of Bosworth in entry 386, adding that when Bessie sees her uncle's corpse at Leicester, she jeers him for the murder of her brother. She and Henry are married, and crowned by Sir William Stanley.

388. [Brooke, Christopher.] *The Ghost of Richard the Third*. London: Printed by G. Eld for L. Lisle, 1614. unpaginated.

Divided into three parts, His Character, His Legend, and His Tragedie, this poem is obviously based on Shakespeare's plays, despite the author's promise to tell more of Richard's character than could be learned from chronicles, plays, or poems. It is similar in style and content to the narrative poems of *The Mirror for Magistrates* (see entries 371-382, 452), and serves the same purpose of demonstrating to the reader God's punishment for a sinful life.

389. "Buckingham Betrayd: by Banister." *Bishop Percy's Folio Ms*. (See entry 463.) Vol. II, pp.253-259.

Buckingham raises his servant Banister to a high degree, and gives him lands and a rich wife. When Richard III comes to the throne and murders his nephews, Buckingham raises men to fight him. His men desert, and the duke flees to the protection of his old servant Banister, who promises to hide him. Buckingham dons poor workingman's clothes, and goes into the woods to labor like a common drudge, but when Banister learns that the king has offered 1000 marks and a knighthood to whomever will turn over Buckingham, he betrays him, and the duke is executed. When Banister claims the reward, he is cast into prison, where he is reviled by all, and he loses everything, including his children, who all meet terrible fates. Banister himself lives a long shameful life, suffering God's punishment for his treachery. (See also entries 439,455.)

390. "The Children in the Wood: Or, The *Norfolk* Gentleman's last Will and Testament." To the tune of Rogero, &c. *Collection of Old Ballads*.

(See entry 393.) Vol. 1, pp.221-226. Percy's *Reliques*. Third Series, Book II. (See entry 464.) pp.374-375.

A Norfolk gentleman, given the guardianship of his rich young niece and nephew, hires two assassins to murder them for their inheritance. The men take the children into the woods, where one of the assassins, moved by their plight, tries to persuade his companion to spare their lives. The other refuses, the two fight, and the soft-hearted assassin kills his partner. He leaves the children, promising to return, but when he fails to do so, they starve to death. Years later, when the fortunes of the wicked uncle have fallen, the assassin is arrested for theft, and he confesses the plot against the children, implicating the uncle, who then dies. The compiler of the *Collection* disputes the widely-held theory that the ballad was written about Richard III and the two princes, noting that if this were so, the Tudors, who lost no opportunity to blacken Richard's name, would have stressed the connection. He adds that the ballad may have been written during Richard's reign, but certainly no more than a hundred years after his death.

391. Churchyard, Thomas. "Howe Shores wife, Edwarde the fowerethes concubine, was by king Richarde despoyled of all her goodes, and forced to do open penance." *Mirror for Magistrates*. 1563 ed. Campbell, ed. (See entries 372, 452.) pp.373-386.

In the prose bridge preceding this poem, the author criticises Seager's poem on Richard III (see entry 474) as not being vehement enough for so violent a man. In this poem, Jane Shore bemoans the life she has led, deceived by the appeal of wealth and high living, only to be thrown down by fortune. Her beauty, which caught the king's eye and led to her rise, caused the loss of her honor. Although she blames herself, she shares the blame with her parents, who forced her to marry at an early age, against her will. She became Edward's mistress because of her beauty and wit, and gained great power over him, but used it to help those in need. As soon as Edward was dead, the Protector accused her of poisoning him, and forced her to do open penance. She curses the evil tyrant Richard, and calls down God's vengeance on him who murdered his way to the throne and despoiled her of all her possessions. She cautions the reader to learn from her fate, and to defy the world and all its wanton ways.

392. Chute, Anthony. *Beawtie dishonoured written under the Title of Shores Wife*. London: John Wolfe, 1593. 54pp.

This elegy on the death of Jane Shore laments her undeserved reputation for immorality. On her deathbed, she relates the story of her life, her low birth, great beauty, humility, honor, and chastity. Despite her purity, her great beauty led everyone to assume that she was wanton, and so she was married, against her will, to a wealthy, elderly goldsmith. She was so admired for her beauty, that she soon came to the notice of the king, whose advances she at first resisted. This only inflamed his desire, and she became his mistress. Jane used her privileged position to help others, but when Edward died, his brother, 'prowd Richard Gloster,' accused her of using witchcraft to wither his arm. He had her arrested, ravished her, and forced her to undergo public penance. After depriving her of all her property, he turned her out into the streets to beg or die, swearing to destroy anyone who helped her. Poor Jane expires after relating her sad tale, beautiful even in death.

393. *A Collection of Old Ballads*. 3 Vols. London: J. Roberts, 1723, 1724, 1725.

This is a comprehensive collection of old ballads and songs from the 16th and 17th centuries, including several about the events and personalities of the Wars of the Roses. The anonymous compiler wrote introductions to the works, many of them quite humorous. See entries 390, 439, 441, 445, 447, 453, 481,482, 487, 488, 494, 500.

394. Colyngbourne, William. "The Cat, the Rat, and Lovel our dog ruleth all England under the Hog." London, 1484.

This couplet, which refers to Catesby, Ratcliffe, Lovel, and Richard III, was found pinned to the door of St. Paul's Cathedral in July, 1484. Colyngbourne, the author, was an agent of Henry Tudor, and a commission comprised of the greatest lords in England convicted him of treason, and sentenced him to death. He was convicted because of his activities on Tudor's behalf, not for his literary efforts, and he died the horrible death reserved for that crime.

395. Cooper, Maria Susanna. *Jane Shore to Her Friend: A Poetical Epistle*. London: Printed for T. Becket. 1776. vii + 16pp.

Jane asks her friend if there is any hope for her. Her forced marriage caused her fate, but a wife, though she does not love her husband, swears to honor and obey him. She does not blame her husband, because she fell victim to the king's wiles and sinned against God. Her virtue, had she clung to it, could have saved her, but she was lost to reason, and a slave of passion. Her husband adored her, but she was seduced by the luxury of the court, and learned too late that there were thorns in the pleasure garden, and now she is alone and friendless, abandoned by her former friends. She prays for Edward's soul, but all that is left for her is a harlot's name, shame, and scorn. She fears most for the fate of Edward's sons, and will endure any torture to save them. She knows she will be found guilty and sentenced to death, but looks forward to going to heaven.

396. Daniel, Samuel. *The Civile Warres betweene the Howses of Lancaster and Yorke*. In 8 books. Books 1-4. London: P. Short for Simon Waterson, 1595. *The Civile Wars . . .corrected and continued*. Books 1-8. London: Simon Watersonne, 1609.

This epic poem in eight books is comprised of about 900 eight-line stanzas. The first book covers the period from the Conquest to the rebellion against Richard II, and the remaining seven, the Wars of the Roses, ending with Warwick's decision to rebel against Edward IV. Daniel was both a poet and an historian, and this is considered one of his finest works.

397. "The Day Will Dawn." (B.M. Additional MS. 40166) *Historical Poems of the XIV and XV Centuries*. (See entry 430.) pp.62-63. *Early English Carols*. (See entry 414.)

This poem of three four-line stanzas is a prayer for better times, written about 1445, when the wars in France were ending. The author laments the fact that returning soldiers found famine and unemployment.

398. "The Death of the Duke of Suffolk." (Cotton MS. Vespasian B.xvi) *Historical Poems of the XIV and XV Centuries*. (See entry 430.) pp.187-189. Sharon Turner. *History of England in the Middle Ages*. London, 1815. Vol.II, pp.169-170. Printed in *Ancient Songs and Ballads* (see entry 369) as "Requiem to the Favourites of Henry VI." (See entry 465.)

This ballad of nine eight-line stanzas recounts the horrible death of Suffolk in 1450. Turner, in his *History of England*, notes with regret the "exulting levity which shews the barbarous unfeelingness of political rancor," but finds it interesting that the writer, a cleric to judge by the use of so many Latin phrases, names the friends of Suffolk most hated by the commons. He notes also that the ballad contains the first use of the term 'jackanapes' or knave, in print. The ballad itself is a pro-Yorkist attack on Suffolk, and accuses the clergy of Lancastrian leanings.

The writer assigns to priests and peers, including the Archbishops of
York and Canterbury and the Duke of Buckingham, parts of the service
for the dead, declaring that they should pray for Suffolk's soul, hoping
and that there will never be such another as he.

399. "The Death of Edward IV." (Rylands Lib. Manchester, Eng. Ms. 113)
Historical Poems of the XIV and XV Centuries. (See entry 430.) pp.111-
113.

This poem, which is composed of ten seven-line stanzas, was written
probably in 1483, shortly after Edward IV's death, in praise of his life
and lamentation for his death. See also entry 444.

400. Deloney, Thomas. "A New Sonnet, containing the Lamentation of *Shores*
wife, who was sometime Concubine to King *Edward* the fourth, setting
forth her great fall, and withall her most miserable and wretched end."
To the tune of "The Hunt is Up." *The Garland of Good Will*. London:
Robert Bird, 1631. 128 pp.

The Garland of Good Will was entered in the *Stationers' Register* of
1592-3. Deloney is believed to have died in 1600, but the 1631 edition
of the *Garland* is the earliest extant. "Shores wife," the second poem in
the collection, is a twelve stanza work of six lines each, in which the
unhappy Jane warns other women to avoid her fate. As a young beauty,
she was married against her will to a goldsmith, but tempted by the
blandishments of the king, she became his mistress. After his death, the
protector, Richard of Gloucester, expelled her from the court, and against
all law and right, took all her possessions, so that she was forced to beg
for her bread. She had to undergo public penance, and she, who had
lived in luxury, died in poverty and disgrace. Though much shorter, the
poem is similar to Chute's "Beawtie dishonored." See entry 392.

401. "A Dialogue Between the D. of C. and the D. of P. at Their Meeting in
Paris with the Ghost of Jane Shore." Colophon. London: Printed for J.
Smith, 1682? 4pp.

Barbara Villiers, Duchess of Cleveland, and Louise de Keroualle,
Duchess of Portsmouth, mistresses of Charles II, meet in Paris and revile
each other, each jealous of the other's power over the king. The ghost
of Jane Shore, the favorite mistress of Edward IV, appears to them and
urges them to repent their sinful ways, or they will surely burn in Hell,
as she has done since her death.

402. Dolman, John. "Howe the Lord Hastynges was betrayed by trustyng to much to his evyl counsayler Catesby, and vilanously murdered in the tower of London by Richarde Duke of Glocestre." *The Mirror for Magistrates*. 1563 ed. Campbell, ed. (See entries 372, 452.) pp.267-296.

Hastings laments his fall, from an honorable and loyal friend to Edward IV, to a dishonorable death, brought about because of his disloyalty to Edward's queen. He relates how he accompanied Edward to the Continent when Warwick chased him from the country, and on their return defeated the earl. At Tewkesbury, after the capture of Edward of Lancaster, the king smote the youth with a gauntlet, but he was murdered by Clarence, Gloucester, Dorset, and himself, Hastings. All except Gloucester, whom he had helped to seize the crown, were punished, Clarence by drowning, and Dorset and himself by beheading. Hastings' greatest regret is that Catesby, whom he had loved and raised to greatness, betrayed him. His story of the protector's usurpation follows More's version.

403. Douglas, Alfred, Lord. "Perkin Warbeck." *The Complete Poems of Lord Alfred Douglas including the Light Verse*. London: Martin Secker Ltd., 1928. 226pp. pp.19-28.

On the night before his execution, Perkin Warbeck, the son of a weaver of Tournai, laments the fate that brought him to death by hanging. He was the only tall, fair, blue-eyed child in a family of dark siblings, and when he was fourteen, an English knight came to his town and declared him to be the image of an English king. He took him to Margaret of Burgundy, who trained him to play the part of Richard of York. In Scotland he was honored by the king, who gave him Katherine Gordon in marriage. He was not made for wars and strife, he declares, for though he had a king's body, he had the heart of a weaver's son. He enjoyed the sport of being a prince, but not the necessity of fighting for the crown. After his capture at Exeter, he confessed his imposture, and had almost persuaded his guards to let him escape, but his plan was discovered, and now his life is forfeit. He wishes that he had never been born, but hopes that the end will be quick. This poem of forty-one four-line stanzas was written in 1893 or 1894.

404. Drayton, Michael. *England's Heroical Epistles, written in Imitation of the Stile and Manner of Ovid's Epistles*. With Annotations. London: Printed by J. K. for N. Ling, 1597.

This is a collection of verse letters from historical figures in England, and the replies of the recipients. Several of the poems involve people in the period of the Wars of the Roses. See entries 405-412.

405. _____. "Queen Katherine to Owen Tudor." *England's Heroical Epistles*. (See entry 404.) pp.41-45.

Queen Katherine, the widow of Henry V, tells Owen Tudor that she had loved her husband, but now that he is dead, her love belongs to Owen.

406. _____. "Owen Tudor to Queen Katherine." *England's Heroical Epistles*. (See entry 404.) pp.45-48.

Owen Tudor replies to Queen Katherine (see entry 405) with a defense of the name of Tudor, which is as ancient and noble as that of Plantagenet. He declares that the great Merlin had foretold that he and Katherine would found a line of great kings and queens of England.

407. _____. "William de la Pole, Duke of Suffolke, to Queene Margaret." *England's Heroical Epistles*. (See entry 404.) pp.59-63.

Suffolk writes this epistle supposedly after he was sentenced to be banished for five years by the parliament at Bury for malfeasance in office. He bemoans his separation from the queen, for "where thou art not present, it is ever night,/ All be exil'd that live not in thy sight." He blames Warwick for his disgrace, for the earl blamed him for the loss of Maine and Anjou, thus winning favor with the commons. Warwick used treason to bring Suffolk down, raise the Nevilles, and advance the claims of York. Warwick accused Suffolk of murdering Duke Humphrey, but, he declares, they should question Eleanor Cobham and her necromancer to learn how he died. He praises his own exploits and devotion to the queen, whom he chose for Henry's bride, and for whose wedding he himself spent large sums. Though he loved her, he gave her to the king for her own good, and he promises to be patient in exile.

408. _____. "Queene Margaret to William de la Pole, Duke of Suffolke." *England's Heroical Epistles*. (See entry 404.) pp.63-67.

Queen Margaret, in her reply (see entry 407), mourns Suffolk's exile. Her heart, once so merry, is now a desert wilderness. Suffolk is nature's perfect work, a diamond with "Angell-eyes," and an eloquent spokesman for the king. She criticizes York's claim to the throne, and his hateful duchess, who is telling her 'brats' that they are the true heirs to the crown, and if she loses her first three sons she will crown the fourth, "That foule, ilfavored, crookback's stigmatick," who is like his mother. Who, Margaret asks, will curb York's and Warwick's power when he is gone? Even now they are in the ascendant, and she is alone in a sea of enemies. It was foretold that Suffolk would die in the sea, and every night she sees him in danger, cast upon the land and dead in the sand. She warns him of danger and prays he will return in better times.

409. _____. "Eleanor Cobham to Duke Humfrey." *England's Heroical Epistles*. (See entry 404.) pp.49-54.

Eleanor writes from the Isle of Wight, where she has been banished for sorcery, begging Humphrey to forgive her for shamimg him. She has been slandered for being his paramour, and indeed practiced magic, but did not win him by its use. Why did he not protect her when she was forced to do public penance? He was Lord Protector and next in line to the throne, yet Margaret of Anjou was given precedence by Suffolk. She regrets that Suffolk and Margaret had not both died before reaching England, for all that Henry V had won, Margaret had given away or would lose. She rages as well against Cardinal Beaufort for charging her with plotting the king's death by witchcraft, and prays she will not live to see her husband's ruin at the hands of her three enemies.

410. _____. "Duke Humphrey to Elinor Cobham." *England's Heroical Epistles*. (See entry 404.) pp.55-58.

Humphrey replies to Elinor Cobham (see entry 409) that, though he would like to, he cannot forget her. He upbraids her for thinking he was uncaring of her fate, for he had publicly lamented her loss. He blames Beaufort, who wants to rule through the king, for his fall, and for raising up the Duke of York to undermine his, Gloucester's, claim to the throne. He apologizes for neglecting her to serve his country, and assures her of his love, looking forward to the day when his enemies shall fall as low as he and Elinor. Until then, they must bide their time, for things can get no worse.

411. _____. "Edward IV, to Shores Wife." *England's Heroical Epistles*. (See entry 404.) pp.68-72.

Edward tells Jane that he didn't believe reports of her beauty until he saw her. Her husband cannot appreciate her, and her beauty would shine brighter were she adorned with "a Kingly State." In her husband's shop he has seen many jewels, but craved only her. It is unfit that her beauty should be hidden, for she belonged in a royal setting, where she would learn the difference between kingly and vulgar love.

412. _____. "The Epistle of Shores Wife to King Edward IV." *England's Heroical Epistles*. (See entry 404.) pp.73-76.

Jane replies to Edward IV (see entry 411), wondering why he, who has his choice of women, should choose her. Although she was married before she knew what love is, should she not be faithful to her husband? She has scorned suitors before, should she then surrender to him because he is a king? Men know what women like to hear, and flatter them. Does he blame husbands, then, for hiding their wives to keep them safe? Men want mercy, and women strength, for though they resist meaner men, kings will conquer. Edward is the reason she no longer desires her husband. Edward has conquered her heart, and made her love him, "even in the midst of hate."

413. _____. *Poly-olbion or A Chorographicall Description of All the Tracts, Rivers, Mountains, Forests, and Other Parts of this Renowned Isle of Great Britain*. London: Printed for John Marriott, John Grismand, and Thomas Dewe, 1622.

This work, which consists of thirty 'songs' of 300-500 lines each, written in hexameter couplets, is a chorographical description of England and Wales, part history, part topography, and part antiquary. The Twenty-second 'song' gives an account of the Wars of the Roses, with a description of the terrain on which the battles were fought. The word 'Poly-Olbion' is from the Greek, meaning 'having many blessings.'

414. *The Early English Carols*. Edited by Richard Leighton Greene. Oxford: Clarendon Press, 1935. 461pp.

This collection of early English songs and carols includes several written about the Wars of the Roses. See entries 397, 415, 435, 476, 491, 496, 498.

415. "Edward Dei Gratia." (Lambeth Palace MS. 306) *Historical Poems of the XIV and XV Centuries*. (See entry 430.) pp.221-222. Printed in *Early English Carols* (see entry 414) as "In Honour of King Edward IV." (See entry 435.)

In this poem of eight four-line stanzas, written probably in 1461, the writer gives thanks to God for restoring Edward IV to the throne.

416. Elizabeth of York. "My Heart is Set Upon a Lusty Pin." *The Women Poets in English: An Anthology*. ed. by Ann Stanford. New York: McGraw Hill Book Company, 1972. pp.16-17.

This poem of six stanzas of six lines each is attributed to Elizabeth of York, the daughter of Edward IV and wife of Henry VII. In it she prays to Venus to continue her in her happy state, delivered from sorrow into pleasure.

417. "Epitaph for the Duke of Gloucester." (Harley MS. 2251) *Historical Poems of the XIV and XV Centuries*. (See entry 430.) pp.180-183.

This poem, written in 1447, was incorrectly attributed to Lydgate by Stow, but a later authority noted that the work "is certainly not by Lydgate. It is a very feeble thing indeed, written in his manner, but has no MS. support for Lydgate's name, or any accordance with a known poem of his." (McCracken, quoted by Robbins, pp.346-347.) The poem contains thirteen eight-line stanzas, and is a prayer for the soul of Humphrey, the 'Good Duke of Gloucester,' murdered at St. Albans, despite all the good he had done for his country.

418. "Examples of Mutability." (MS. Rawlinson C. 813 Bodleian. Sum. Cat. No. 12653) *Historical Poems of the XIV and XV Centuries*. (See entry 430.) pp.184-186.

Written around 1460, this poem of eight eight-line stanzas relates the unfortunate fate of mighty nobles, in order to show the mutability of fortune. Among them are Eleanor Cobham, the wife of Humphrey of Gloucester, who was convicted of treason, John, Duke of Somerset, who, according to the author, was killed by a bull after his fall from power, and Humphrey of Gloucester, whose confession to a treacherous bishop was revealed to the king. The king then had Humphrey arrested for treason, and the shame and anguish of his arrest caused his death.

419. Ferrers, George. "How Humfrey Plantagenet Duke of Glocester Protector of England, during the minoritie of his Nephue kinge Henrye the sixt, (commonlye called the good Duke) by practise of enemies was brought to confusion." *Mirror for Magistrates*. 1578 ed. Campbell, ed. (See entry 452.) pp.444-459.

This tragedy, like the one about Eleanor Cobham, was intended for the 1559 edition, but was omitted. In it, Humphrey notes that all who climb to the top ranks of power are never free of the danger of falling. It is

vain to trust either in fortune or one's royal blood as a shield against
danger, as he can prove, who was son, brother, and uncle of kings.
Indeed, it was his very nearness to the crown that proved his undoing.
He rails against the Bishop of Winchester, who hated Humphrey for
opposing his grab for power, and Margaret of Anjou, who feared him
because she was childless, and he was next in line for the throne. It was,
however, her favorites, Exeter, Buckingham, and Suffolk who planned
his death, and as a result the conspirators lost their lives, and the House
of Lancaster was destroyed. Humphrey warns that, in order to be safe
from danger, all who are in line for the throne would be wise to keep a
low profile, and not to court the people's love.

420. _____. "How Richard Plantagenet duke of York was slayne through
his over rash boldnes, and his sonne the earle of Rutland for his lack of
valiauns." *Mirror for Magistrates*. 1559 ed. Campbell, ed. (See entries
371, 452.) pp.182-190.

Richard of York relates how his ancestor's rightful claim to the throne
was usurped by the Lancastrian line. With the help of his sons and his
wife, he planned to seize the throne, but although he fought three battles
against Somerset, Henry, and Margaret, "This spiteful duke, his silly
king and queen," and won the first two, he lost his life at Bosworth (sic).
The poem covers all of York's career, including his exile in Ireland, his
return to claim the throne, and his death, and he concludes that it is
better to lose part of one's right, than life and limbs fighting for it.

421. _____. "The tragedie of Edmund duke of Somerset, slayne at the first
battayle at Saynct Albanes, in the tyme of Henrye the sixte." *Mirror for
Magistrates*. 1563 ed. Campbell, ed. (See entry 452.) pp. 388-401.

Somerset bemoans the fact that he was born unfortunate, failing in all
endeavors. His hatred of the Duke of York only increased his enemy's
power and popularity, and his complicity in the murder of Humphrey of
Gloucester resulted in the destruction of the House of Lancaster. When
the Yorkists defeated the Lancastrians and captured the king at St. Albans
in 1450, Somerset lost his life, along with many other lords of his party.
As a result, Henry VI became a pawn of the Yorkists. Somerset blames
himself and others of the queen's faction, and warns that to avoid future
conflicts of this sort, wise councellors will put out such sparks when they
are small, and not listen to the advice of self-servers. He blames himself
for his fate, because he yielded when he should have stood firm against
false friends.

422. _____. "How Dame Elianor Cobham Duchesse of Glocester for practising of witchcraft and Sorcery, suffred open penance, and after was banished the realme into the yle of Man." _Mirror for Magistrates_. 1578 ed. Campbell, ed. (See entry 452.) pp.432-443.

Originally intended to be part of the 1559 edition, this tragedy tells the story of Eleanor Cobham, wife of Duke Humphrey, who was murdered at St. Albans. Eleanor's rise caused jealousy among the nobility, but she was protected by her powerful husband until she, in her pride, desired to be queen. She resorted to sorcery to discover the fate of Henry VI, intending him no harm, but Cardinal Beaufort used it as an excuse to destroy Humphrey. Eleanor was forced to do open penance, and banished to the Isle of Man. She curses Beaufort, "Bastard preest of the house of Lancaster," and wishes she were indeed a witch so that she could have taken revenge. She mourns her fate, not because it was totally undeserved, but because her actions caused the death of her innocent husband.

423. [_____]. "How Jacke Cade traiterously rebelling agaynst his Kyng, was for his treasons and cruell doinges wurthely punyshed." _Mirror for Magistrates_. 1559 ed. Campbell, ed. (See entries 371, 452.) pp.171-177.

Jack Cade, calling himself Mortimer, and pretending to be of that noble house, persuaded the men of Kent to rebel against Henry VI in 1450. He was victorious against the Staffords' army, and marched on London, where he had Lord Say and his son-in-law beheaded, set prisoners free, and terrorized the merchants and citizens. A large price was put on his head, and he was betrayed and captured. He enjoins Baldwin, the editor, to warn all men that a bad end awaits traitors.

424. _____. "How Lorde William Delapole Duke of Suffolke was worthily punyshed for abusing his Kyng and causing the destruction of good Duke Humfrey." _Mirror for Magistrates_. 1559 ed. Campbell, ed. (See entries 371, 452.) pp.162-169.

Suffolk relates his rise to power by winning battles in France, only to lose all that was won. He was responsible for Henry's marriage to Margaret of Anjou, although he had to cede much English territory in France to her father, and she brought no dowry. Humphrey of Gloucester opposed the marriage, but his advice was ignored, and Suffolk was rewarded, while Humphrey earned the queen's enmity. He bemoans the fact that his deeds, so highly praised and rewarded, were soon denounced as treason. He was blamed for Humphrey's murder, and the king was forced to exile him. On his way to France, his ship was captured, and he was seized and executed by the Earl of Devonshire, who accused him of Gloucester's murder, the king's marriage, and bringing the country to ruin.

425. _____. "How George Plantagenet third sonne of the Duke of Yorke, was by his brother King Edward wrongfully imprisoned, and by his brother Richard miserably murdered." *Mirror for Magistrates*. 1559 ed. Campbell, ed. (See entries 371, 452.) pp. 220-234.

Clarence, maintaining his innocence of any wrongdoing, claims that his desire to marry Mary of Burgundy angered Edward and caused his fall. Richard, who coveted the crown, used the tale that G would destroy Edward's children, and spread false rumors to prevent a reconciliation between Clarence and Edward. Clarence was arrested and imprisoned, and Richard stole into the Tower and drowned his brother in a butt of Malmsey wine.

426. "The Five Dogs of London." (Trinity College Dublin MS. 516) *Historical Poems of the XIV and XV Centuries*. (See entry 430.) pp. 189-190.

Written in 1456, this poem is an attack on the Duke of York. Five dogs, representing servants of the duke, are killed by their faithless master, who paid them for their services with death. The origin of the poem is given in Bale's *Chronicle* (*Six Town Chronicles*. Ed. by Ralph Flenley. Oxford: Clarendon Press, 1911. p.144), in which the author tells of "certain dogges hedes wt Scriptures in the mouthes balade wise," which were set upon the Standard in Fleet Street in front of the Duke of York, and which had been "slayn vengeably in the same nyght."

427. Fletcher, Giles. "The Rising to the Crowne of Richard the Third." *Licia, or Poemes of Love, in Honour of the admirable and singular Vertues of his Lady, to the imitation of the best Latin Poets, and others, whereunto is added the Rising to the Crowne of Richard the Third*. London: George Stevens, 1593. 80pp.

Richard III tells the reader that, although Jane Shore, Fair Rosamund, and others had fallen from great heights, their fall was nothing compared to his, and he scorns those who write of the fall of women. He, the son of a duke and brother of a king, rose quickly, and as quickly fell. Men say that he slew Clarence and Henry VI, but though he had no right to the crown, he cared not whom he killed to gain it. His brother the king died, leaving two sons, and Richard was named Protector, but he could not rest until he had the crown. Rivers was named guardian of the young king, but the protector accused him and Grey of Treason, and ended their lives. When the queen learned of this, she went into sanctuary with her children, but the Archbishop of York visited her to calm her fears, assuring her that if her elder son lost his life, the younger would be crowned. Richard destroyed his enemies and raised his friends, which made the people flock to him as a strong ruler. The account of his rise follows More's *History of Richard III*, and the poem ends with Richard's assertion that he does not repent his actions, for others have done more for less. His only regret is that he could not keep what he had won.

428. "God Amend Wicked Counsel." (Bodl. MS. Lat. misc. e. 85) *Historical Poems of the XIV and XV Centuries*. (See entry 430.) pp.196-198.

In this poem of fourteen stanzas of four lines each, written in 1464, Henry VI is heard to lament his troubles, which began with his marriage to Margaret of Anjou, who turned the common people against him by her enmity to the Yorkist lords.

429. Henry VI. "Untitled Poem." *Monarchs and the Muse*. Intro. by C. V. Wedgwood. Ed. by Sally Purcell. Illus. by Priscilla Eckhard. Oxford: Carcanet Press, 1972. pp.15-16.

This three stanza poem of four lines each is believed to have been written by Henry VI during the time of his imprisonment in the Tower, from 1464 to 1469. In it, the king disdains all worldy goods and pleasures as snares for the unwary.

430. *Historical Poems of the XIV and XV Centuries*. Ed. by Rossell Hope Robbins. New York: Columbia University Press, 1959. 440 pp.

This is a collection of historical and political poems of the late middle ages, in the original Middle English, including nearly thirty relating to the period of the Wars of the Roses. See entries 365, 366, 370, 379-382, 384, 397-399, 415, 417, 418, 426, 428, 437, 440, 443, 461, 463, 465, 468, 472, 476, 484, 485, 487, 492.

431. Holford, Margaret. *Margaret of Anjou; A Poem*. Philadelphia: M. Carey, 1816. 292 pp.

In this ten canto poem, Margaret is portrayed as a cruel, vengeful woman who scorns her husband, Henry VI, and her son, Prince Edward, for their weakness. After the battle of Hexham, she and her wounded son are rescued by Rudolph, a robber, who takes them to his hut, where Edward is healed by the youth Gerald. Gerald turns out to be Geraldine, a beautiful Irish noblewoman, and she and Edward fall in love. Margaret is not pleased, and asks Rudolph to arrange for a sorcerer to show her the future. She sees the evil, deformed Richard of Gloucester crowned, and her son wed to Warwick's daughter. Meanwhile, Edward and Geraldine meet a hermit, who turns out to be Henry VI, and he blesses their betrothal. In France, Warwick offers Margaret his aid, if her son will marry his daughter. The reluctant Edward is reminded of his duty, and when Geraldine decides to enter a convent and renounces their betrothal, he agrees. Warwick is killed at Barnet, and at Tewkesbury the Lancastrians are defeated. The wounded Edward is brought before the king and his evil brothers, and when he refuses to kneel, the king strikes him, and his brothers stab the prince to death. When Margaret sees her dead son, and the destruction of her hopes, she falls to the ground in a swoon.

432. Hull, Thomas. *Richard Plantagenet: A Legendary Tale*. London: J. Bell, 1774. iii + 30pp.

This narrative poem of eighty-one four-line stanzas is dedicated to David Garrick, "to whom we owe a livelier Idea of Richard the Third, than either Historian or Painter ever gave." Richard Plantagenet, the illegitimate son of Richard III, is hidden in a cloister by his father. He learns of his parentage on the eve of the Battle of Bosworth. After his father's death, he flees, and lives until 1546 as a bricklayer on the estate of Sir Thomas Moyle in Kent. In that year, Moyle gave him a piece of land and permission to build himself a house, and the poem opens as Richard is supposed to have finished the house. Several nineteenth century novels were based on this poem. See entries 138, 154, 238, 253, 522.

433. "Humpty-Dumpty."

This well-known Mother Goose rhyme is believed to have been written about Richard III after the Battle of Bosworth, when "Not all the King's horses/ Not all the King's men/ Could ever put Humpty Dumpty together again." See Katherine Elwes Thomas. *The Real Personages of Mother Goose*. London: Lothrop, Lee & Shepard Co., 1930. pp.38-39.

434. "I Love Sixpence."

This rhyme is a jibe at Henry VII's well-known love of money. See
Katherine Elwes Thomas. *The Real Personages of Mother Goose*.
London: Lothrop, Lee & Shepard Co., 1930. pp.42-43.

435. "In Honour of King Edward IV." *Early English Carols*. (See entry 414.)
pp.291-292. See also entry 415.

436. "Jane Shore." *Reliques of Ancient English Poetry*. (See entry 464.) pp.
262-263. Also published as "The Lamentation of Jane Shore." in *Ancient
Songs and Ballads*. (See entries 369, 447.) pp.259-264.

Jane Shore laments her decadent life as the paramour of Edward IV, and
the cruel punishment she suffered at the hands of Richard III. This
version is a copy of the first part of the ballad, found in the *Roxborough
Ballads*. (See entry 476.) Vol. II, pp.108-121.

437. "Jane Shore to the Duke of Gloster, an Epistle." London: R. Dodsley,
1749.   27 pp.

Jane Shore, cleared of the charge that she plotted against Richard III, is
now threatened with public shame for her sins. Jane censures Richard
for defiling his dead brother's name, whose soul is at that moment
probably praying for him. She urges Richard to relent before Edward's
ghost vindicates his name, and to punish her less harshly. She loved
Edward, but now that her guilty pleasures are over, she cries to heaven,
which allows lawless passions to enslave mankind. Then she admits that
heaven was not to blame, for she should have listened to reason. She
apologizes to Richard, but declares that if he knew her sufferings, he
would forgive her crime. She begs him to spare his brother's reputation,
and pardon her, and promises to retire to a convent and pray unceasingly
for his soul, as well as Edward's.

438. Johnson, Richard. *A Crowne-Garland of Golden Roses; consisting of
Ballads and Songs*. London: Printed by G. Eld for John Wright, 1612.
Part II, 1659. *The Crown Garland of Golden Roses*. Ed. by W.
Chappell. London: The Percy Society, 1842 and 1854.

This collection of ballads, probably written before 1612, includes several
about important figures of the Wars of the Roses. The 1612 edition
includes "A Princely Song Made of the Red Rose and the White" (see
entry 440) and "The Life and Death of the Great Duke of Buckingham."
(See entry 439.) Part II, from the edition of 1659, reprinted by the Percy
Society in 1854, contains "An Excellent Song Made of the Successors of

King Edward the Fourth." (See entry 441.) These ballads were frequently reprinted, and appear in several other collections, without attribution, and ofter with changes and/or additions.

439. _____. "The Life and Death of the Great Duke of Buckingham: who came to an untimely end for consenting to the depositing of two gallant young princes, King Edward the Fourth's children." *The Crown Garland of Golden Roses*. (See entry 438.) Part I, pp.25-29.

The powerful Duke of Buckingham allies himself with the Duke of Gloucester, in the hope that when he becomes king he will reward his faithful retainer. Buckingham had a hand in Clarence's death, and hated the queen and her two sons. When he claims his reward from Richard, however, he is met with disdain. He rebels, but his men desert him, and he flees to the protection of his servant Bannister, who turns him into the king for the reward. When Bannister tells the king how he betrayed his master, Richard banishes him instead of rewarding him, and he is forced to beg for his bread. His children suffer strange and terrible deaths, a punishment from heaven for their father's shameful act.

440. _____. "A Princely Song Made of the Red Rose and the White, Royally United Together by King Henry the Seventh and Elizabeth Plantagenet, etc." *The Crown Garland of Golden Roses*. (See entry 438.) Vol. I, pp.1-8.

Henry Tudor, a paragon of virtue, and a faithful and affectionate husband, is the hero of this ballad. During the strife between York and Lancaster, when father fought against son and kinsmen against king, many Englishmen were slain, but at length, "by Henries lawfull claime," the wars were ended and peace restored, for Richard the tyrant was dead. In a true love match, Henry took Elizabeth to wife, and the red rose and the white were united in love and peace. Henry, with "his princely liberall hand," gave more gifts and wealth to England than any previous king, but his greatest gift was to his queen, who bore so many children to bless the kingdom. Her death in childbirth left her husband desolate, and determined to remain a widower for the remainder of his life.

441. _____. "An Excellent Song Made of the Successors of King Edward the Fourth." to the tune of "O, man in desperation." *The Crown Garland of Golden Roses*. Part II. (See entry 438.) pp.50-55.

Gloucester and the Duke of Buckingham plot to murder the young sons of Edward IV after the king's death. Buckingham is plagued by guilt after Tyrell, Dighton, and Forrest murder the boys, and he and Richard III fall out. Richmond comes to England to claim his rightful throne, and at Bosworth, God causes Richard to be slain for his evil deed. Richmond, the instrument of God's will, is rewarded with the crown. He then founds a line of glorious monarchs, except for Mary, whose reign was marred by "blind ignorance against gods truth." An almost exact version of this ballad is found in *Bishop Percy's Folio Manuscript*, (see entry 383) Vol. III, pp.162-167, and in the *Collection of Old Ballads*, (see entry 393)Vol. III, pp.131-138.

442. _____. "A Courtly New Song of the Princely Wooing of the Fair Maid of London by King Edward," and "The Fair Maid of London's Answer to King Edward's Wanton Love." both to the tune of "Bonnie Sweet Robin." *The Crown Garland of Golden Roses*. (See entry 438.) Part II, pp.34-38.

King Edward woos a lovely maid with promises of advancement, a life of luxury, and even a crown, but she rejects his pleas and promises, declaring that she values her good name above all. Although Edward IV is not specifically named in the ballads, the theme fits very well with what is known of his amorous nature and adventures.

443. "The Kentish Insurrection." (Magdalen Coll. Oxford Charter Misc. 306) *Historical Poems of the XIV and XV Centuries*. (See entry 430.) p.63.

The writer of this seven line poem ask God's help in the rebellion against traitors, led by Jack Cade to protest the acquittal of the Duke of Suffolk in 1450 of the murder of the Duke of Gloucester. The rebels sought the removal of the 'traitors' surrounding Henry VI.

444. "King Edward IV. and the Tanner of Tamworth." Percy's *Reliques*. (See entries 464, 385, 466, 564.) 2nd Series, Book I, pp.199-202.

King Edward, out hunting with his lords, meets a well-dressed tanner mounted on a good horse, and asks him the way to Drayton Bassett. The tanner fails to recognize the king, and answers him rudely, thinking he and his companions are thieves. After having some sport with the tanner, the king reveals his identity, and the tanner fears that he will hang for insulting him. Instead, the king makes him an esquire and awards him Plumpton Park and tenements worth three hundred marks a year. Other versions of this ballad are found in Pepys *Ballads* (see entry 456) and *The Roxburghe Ballads* (see entry 471), where it is entitled "A Pleasant New Ballad betweene King Edward the Fourth and a Tanner of

Tamworth, in two Parts." (See entry 460.) The tale was well known during the 16th century, and the author of the *Art of English Poesie*, printed in 1589, believed it was based on fact.

445. "King Edward and Jane Shore." In Imitation, and to the Tune of, St. George and the Dragon. *Collection of Old Ballads*. (See entry 393.) Vol. I, pp.153-158.

The compiler warns ladies not to read this risqué ballad unless they are alone. He notes that it contains some expressions which nearly caused him to omit it from the collection, but since it is really old, he decided to include it. Jane Shore is compared to women of legend and history who had seduced and conquered heroes of old, but the compiler observes that it was probably written by a wag, rather than an enemy to her memory.

446. "The Lament of the Duchess of Gloucester." (Cambridge Univ. MS. Hh.4.12) *Historical Poems of the XIV and XV Centuries*. (See entry 430.) pp.176-180.

In this seventeen stanza poem of eight lines each, written in 1441, Eleanor Cobham, Duchess of Gloucester, who has been convicted of using witchcraft in order to destroy Henry VI and place her husband on the throne, warns other women to avoid her fate. The duchess was forced to do public penance, and was then exiled to the Isle of Man.

447. "Lamentation of Jane Shore." *Ancient Songs and Ballads*. (See entry 369.) pp.259-264.

See entry 392.

448. Le Guin, Ursula. "Richard." *Hard Words, and other Poems*. New York: Harper & Row, 1981. p.41.

In eleven lines the author, a well-known writer of science fiction, conveys the pathos of Richard III's betrayal and death, and the destruction of his reputation.

449. "The Lily White Rose." (B.M. Addit. M.S. 5465) *Historical Poems of the XIV and XV Centuries*. (See entry 430.) pp.93-94.

The author of this poem of two six-line stanzas and a refrain tells of seeing a queen in a garden. She picks a white rose, declaring, "The white rose is most true, & should by law, rule the garden." Robbins dates the poem in 1486, but notes it may have been written earlier as a companion piece to "The Roses Entwined" (see entry 474) in 1461, when Edward IV was proclaimed king, or in 1471, when he was in exile. He argues, however, for 1486, in the belief that the queen is Elizabeth of York, rather than Elizabeth Woodville, as some authorities believe.

450. Lydgate, John. "The Lament of the Soul of Edward IV." (B. M. Addit. MS. 29729, fol. 8ro).

See entry 483.

451. MacDonagh, Donagh. "The Ballad of Jane Shore." Illus. by Eric Patton. Dublin: Dolmen Press, 1954. 2 pp.

This ballad of eight four-line stanzas describes the penance performed by Jane Shore after the death of Edward IV. All of London watches in pity as the lovely young woman, naked to the waist and carrying a taper, walks through Lombard Street.

452. *The Mirror for Magistrates.* Edited by Lily B. Campbell. Cambridge: Cambridge University Press, 1938. vii+554pp.

This is a collection of verse tragedies inspired by Lydgate's translation of a Boccaccio work. The first edition appeared in 1559, and there were succeeding editions containing some revisions and additional material in 1563, 1578, and 1587. The editor of the *Mirror* was William Baldwin, and the work contained eighteen tragedies by several authors, including Baldwin, pertaining to personages involved in the Wars of the Roses. See entries 373-378, 391, 396, 419-425, 479, 481.

453. "The most cruel Murther of Edward the Vth, and his Brother the Duke of York, in the tower, by their Uncle Richard Duke of Glocester." *Collection of Old Ballads.* (See entry 393.) Vol. II, pp.100-105.

Richard of Gloucester, the Protector, persuades his two nephews to come to the Tower, where he promises they will be well taken care of. The very first night they are there, he hires Tyrell to murder them so he can seize the crown. Tyrell gets Dighton and Forrest to do the deed, and bury the bodies under some stones at the foot of a stair in the Tower. All the villains are punished for the crime when Richard is defeated at Bosworth by 'stout Richmond.' The compiler of the *Collection* suggests that readers consult both the Tudor chronicles and George Buck's defense of Richard before they make up their minds about whether he murdered the princes.

454. *The Most Pleasant Song of Lady Bessy; and how she married King Henry the Seventh, of the House of Lancaster.* Ed. by James Orchard Halliwell. London: The Percy Society, 1847.   79pp.

The text contains two versions of the ballad of the Lady Bessie, differing in language rather than content, but both are similar to the one printed in *Percy's Folio Ms.* (See entries 387, 462.)

455. "A most sorrowfull Song, setting forth the miserable end of *Bannister*, who betraied the Duke of *Buckingham*, his Lord and Master." To the tune of, *Live with me and be my Love. The Pepys Ballads.* (See entry 456.) Vol. II, pp.134-138.

Bannister betrays his master, the Duke of Buckingham, who has raised him from nothing, to honor and dignity. Instead of the gold he has expected as a reward from Richard III, he is berated as a traitor, and he loses his house, land, and possessions, and he and his wife and three children are turned out. The second part of the ballad is addressed to Jane Shore, who had also fallen from her high place, but her fall was not due to any fault of hers. Bannister's disgrace, on the other hand, was his own doing, and his fate was well-deserved. No one will lift a hand to help him, he and his wife will suffer for his treacherous act, and his children all meet with terrible deaths. (See entries 389, 439.)

456. "The Murthering of Edward the ffourth his sonnes." *Percy's Folio MS.* (See entry 456.) Vol. III, pp.162-167.

A copy, with slight variations, of Richard Johnson's "An Excellent Song Made of the Successors of King Edward the Fourth." (See entry 441.)

457. Niccols, Richard. *A Winter Night's Vision: Being an addition of such Princes especially famous, who were exempted in the former Historie.* London: Felix Kyngston, 1610.

This is a revised edition of *The Mirrour for Magistrates* (see entries 371, 372, 452), which contains ten new tragedies written by Niccols and Michael Drayton, including two about Richard III. (See entries 458, 459.)

458. _____. "The Lamentable Lives and Deaths of the Two Young Princes, Edward the fifth, and his brother Richard Duke of Yorke." *A Winter Night's Vision*. (See entry 457.) pp.734-748.

Richard of Gloucester, the wicked uncle, usurps the throne from his nephew Edward, and has Tyrell, Forrest, and Dighton put the two princes to death.

459. _____. "The Tragical Life and Death of King Richard the Third." *A Winter Night's Vision*. (See entry 457.) pp.749-769.

Richard III, whose unnatural birth, feet first and with teeth and hair, prefigures his life and character, murders all who stand in his way to the throne. These include Henry VI and his son Edward of Lancaster, Rivers, Grey, Hastings, Buckingham, his two nephews, and his wife Anne, whom he poisons so that he can marry his niece Elizabeth. On the night before Bosworth, his dreams are haunted by the ghosts of his victims, but he nevertheless fights bravely the following day. After his death, his despoiled body is brought to Leicester for burial.

460. Peachey, Alfred W. "The Red Rose Boy." *The Red Rose Boy, Margaret of Anjou, and Other Poems*. Gloucester: H. Osborne, 1885. 63pp. pp.1-4.

Edward of Lancaster, the son of Margaret of Anjou and Henry VI, awaits the Battle of Tewkesbury, which he hopes will restore the crown to Lancaster. His army is defeated, and he is brought a prisoner before Edward IV. The king demands to know why he has invaded the kingdom, and Edward replies that he had come to regain his father's throne. The enraged king strikes, and his knights stab the prince to death.

461. _____. "Margaret of Anjou." *The Red Rose Boy, Margaret of Anjou, and Other Poems*. (See entry 460.) pp.5-20.

After the Battle of Tewkesbury, Margaret, in despair over the defeat of her army and the death of her son, goes to the house of her supporter, Payne. He attempts to help her escape, but they are captured and imprisoned in the Tower, where she remains for three years. The French king offers to ransom her, and the king allows her to go after she agrees to renounce her claim to the throne. She returns to Anjou, where, having lost her husband, son, and father, she dies of a broken heart.

462. *The Pepys Ballads*.   Ed. by Hyder Edward Rollins.   Cambridge,
Massachusetts: Harvard University Press, 1929. 6 Vols.

A collection of old ballads, including several relating to the Wars of the
Roses. See entries 444, 455.

463. Percy, Thomas, Bishop of Dromore. *Bishop Percy's Folio Manuscript:
Ballads and Romances*.   Ed. by John W. Hales and Frederick J.
Furnivall. London: N. Trubner & Co., 1867-1868. 3 Vols.

This collection of old ballads, compiled about 1650, possibly by a
Lancashireman, came into the hands of Bishop Percy, and he used them
extensively for his *Reliques of Ancient English Poetry*. (See entry 464.)
The manuscript is now in the British Museum. For ballads relating to the
Wars of the Roses see entries 386, 387, 389, 390, 441, 454, 456, 469,
480, 491, 497.

464. _____. *Reliques of Ancient English Poetry*. Philadelphia: Porter &
Coates, [187-?].   558pp.

First published in 1765, with editions containing additional material in
1767, 1775, and 1794, the ballads, songs, and sonnets in this collection
were taken mainly from the compiler's *Folio* (see entry 463), and it
contains several concerning the Wars of the Roses. See entries 390, 436,
444, 486, 487, 501.

465. *Plantagenet: a Poem. Being a Short Sketch of the Civil Wars Between the
Houses of York and Lancaster: Wherein the Horrors of Those Times are
Endevoured to be Described. With explanatory notes*. London: Printed
by J. Almon, 1785. 19pp.

Not available for review.

466. "A Pleasant new Ballad between King Edward the Fourth and a Tanner of
Tamworth, as hee rode upon a time with Nobles on Hunting, towards
Drayton Basset." *Roxburghe Ballads*. (See entries 477, 444, 565.) pp.
163-169.

This is a shorter, slightly different, version of entry 444.

467. "A Political Retrospect." (Society of Antiquaries MS. 101) *Historical
Poems of the XIV and XV Centuries*. (See entry 430.) pp.222-226.

This poem, written in 1462, celebrates the victory of Edward IV, and reviews the past misdeeds of the Lancastrians who usurped the throne from the rightful heir of Richard II.

468. "A Prayer to Henry VI in English Verse." *Henry the Sixth: A Reprint of John Blacman's Memoir*, with translation and notes by M. R. James. Cambridge: Cambridge University Press, 1919. pp.50-51.

This prayer in verse, printed originally in *Ushaw Magazine* of 1902, p. 279, is a plea to Henry, the "blessed king so full of vertue," to intercede with Christ and the Virgin Mary in times of trouble. The prayer of six eight-line stanzas, was found inscribed in the flyleaf of a Primer of 1408, but is obviously of a much later date.

469. "Prelude to the Wars." (Cotton Rolls ii.23) *Historical Poems of the XIV and XV Centuries*. (See entry 430.) pp.201-203.

This political song of nine four-line stanzas "paved the way for the popularity of the house of York." (Thomas Wright, *Political Poems and Songs*. London, 1859, 1861. 2 Vols. Vol. II, pp.221-223.) The writer uses badges rather than names to refer to specific nobles, but identifies them in marginal notes; e.g., swanne (Bedford), bear (Warwick), eagle (the king), and white hart (Arundel). He writes of the decline or defeat of the great lords of England's past glory, and the dismal situation of the country in 1449, with the future of the falcon, the Duke of York, uncertain.

470. Radcliffe, Mrs. Anne (Ward). *St. Alban's Abbey. The Poetical Works of Anne Radcliffe*. London: Published for H. Colburn by R. Bentley, 1834. 2 Vols.

This long poem, which the author, a popular Victorian novelist, termed a metrical or poetical romance, is in ten cantos. After giving a brief history of the abbey, the author turns to the dreadful day in 1455, when the first battle of the Wars of the Roses took place within its sacred precincts. The forces of the cruel, devious, and deceitful Duke of York confront those of the king and his noble Lancastrian supporters. The duke wants the king to turn over his evil counselors, but he knows that Henry will refuse, and without warning he attacks the royal forces. The slaughter is great on both sides. Florence Fitzharding, the wife of a Lancastrian baron, goes to the abbey to find her husband, who, in turn, is looking for his father among the dead and dying. The Lancastrian abbot protects Fitzharding from York's vengeance, and the baron is reunited with his wife and father. They remain in hiding in the abbey until the triumphant Yorkists take their royal prisoner to London, and the three return to their home. The author has included 94 pages of notes on the history of the abbey and the battle.

471.   "Reconciliation of Henry VI and the Yorkists." (Cotton Ms. Vespasian B. xvi) *Historical Poems of the XIV and XV Centuries*. (See entry 430.) pp.194-196.

This poem of eight eight-line stanzas was written by a Lancastrian Londoner in 1458 to give thanks that civil war has been averted by the reconciliation of the Lancastrian lords Somerset, Northumberland, Clifford, and Egremont, to York, Warwick, and Salisbury. He prays that peace may continue, but it was short-lived. A slightly different version of the poem is found in Sharon Turner's *History of England in the Middle Ages*. (London, 1815. Vol. III, pp.211-213.)

472.   "Requiem to the Favourites of Henry VI."

See entry 350.

473.   "The Rise of the House of York." *The Faber Book of English History in Verse*. Ed. by Kenneth Baker. London: Faber and Faber, 1988. p.86.

This verse of three eight-line stanzas, written in 1461, is a celebration of the coronation of Edward IV and the House of York. The writer likens England to a garden that has for many years been overgrown with weeds (the House of Lancaster), and now will be put right by Edward IV, who with God's help overcame those who would destroy him.

474.   "The Roses Entwined." (with music) (B. M. Addit. M.S. 5465) *Historical Poems of the XIV and XV Centuries*. (See entry 430.) pp.94-95.

This poem, dated by Robbins 1486, consists of six six-line stanzas and a refrain. Although some authorities believe it may have been written in 1460, before the Yorkist victory at Northampton, the 1486 date seems more appropriate. The writer declares: The rose it is a ryall floure./ The red or the white? shewe his colour! Both be full swere & of lyke savour:/. . . I love the rose both red & white, etc. See entry 491.

475. "The: rose of Englande:" *Percy's Folio Ms.* (See entry 463.) Vol. III, pp. 187-194.

One of the pieces that compose the Bosworth Field and Stanley Cycle (see entries 384, 386, 387, 482), this is an allegorical poem about how the Earl of Richmond returned to proclaim his right to the throne. (The eponymous rose is Richmond.) The work was probably written by a Lancashire or Cheshire-man who admired the Stanleys, before Sir William Stanley's execution in 1495, but the version in *Percy's Folio* was probably written in the reign of Henry VIII. It tells of a rose which grows in a lovely garden. A boar destroys and buries the bush, swearing it will never bloom, but an eagle rescues one branch and takes it to his nest. The rose is exiled, but returns to Milford Haven with the Blue Boar (the Earl of Oxford) to fight the White Boar. Lord Stanley supports him, and Wales rises to his aid. Joined by the men of Lancashire and Cheshire, Henry, the Stanleys, Oxford, and Talbot defeat and slay Richard III at Bosworth, and now the red rose, Henry VII, flourishes in the garden of England.

476. "The Rose of Rouen." *The Early English Carols.* (See entry 414.) pp. 292-294.

This poem was printed as "The Battle of Towton" in *Historical Poems of the XIV and XV Centuries.* See entry 382.

477. *The Roxburghe Ballads.* Ed. by Charles Hindley. London: Reeves and Turner, 1873. 11 vols.

This collection of songs and ballads, printed between 1560 and 1700, is a reprint of a work published in London in 1774. They were collected by Robert, Earl of Oxford, and added to by others, especially the Duke of Roxburgh, whose manuscripts were bought by the British Museum after his death. Included are several ballads about the Wars of the Roses. See entries 444, 466, 494.

478. Ryman, James. "A Remembrance of Henry VI." (Cambridge Univ., MS./Ee. 1.12) *Historical Poems of the XIV and XV Centuries.* (See entry 430.) pp.199-201.

This poem of eight seven-line stanzas, a panygyric to Henry VI, may have been written before May, 1471, since it makes no mention of his murder. Robbins, however, dates it 1492.

479. Sackville, Thomas. "The complaynt of Henrye duke of Buckingham."
Mirror for Magistrates. 1563 ed. (See entry 452.) pp.318-345.

Buckingham warns that fortune, which lifts princes up, will then cast
them down, and his tale is proof of the uncertainty of life. Born to a
high position, and endowed with great gifts, he squandered everything by
supporting Richard of Gloucester's bid for the throne. When the usurper
murdered his nephews, however, Buckingham turned against him, and
raised an army to attack him, but his men were cowards, and deserted
him. He was betrayed for a large reward, taken to Salisbury, and
beheaded.

480. "Scotish: ffeilde:" *Percy's Folio Ms*. (See entry 463.) Vol. I, pp.199-234.

This is one of several poems written to glorify the Stanleys for their two
great achievements, Bosworth Field and Flodden. (See entries 386, 387.)
It begins with the landing of Henry Tudor at Milford Haven, and goes
on to describe his victory at Bosworth and marriage to Elizabeth of York,
always led and supported by the Stanleys. The second part of the poem
is devoted to an equally inaccurate account of the battle of Flodden in
1513, and is the author's attempt to justify the cowardly flight from the
battle by many of the Cheshire, Lancashire, and Yorkshire men, on the
grounds that they could not fight without a Stanley at their head. The
feud between the Stanleys and the Howards, begun at Bosworth, is still
very much in evidence at Flodden. Another poem written by a supporter
of the Stanleys, "Fflodden ffeilde" (*Ibid.*, pp.313-340), attempts to show
how the family had triumphed over the malice of the Howards, despite
the lies spread after the battle of Flodden by the Earl of Surrey, the son
of the Duke of Norfolk who died fighting for Richard III at Bosworth.

481. Seager, Fraunces. "How Richard Plantagenet duke of Glocester, murdered
his brothers children usurping the crowne, and in the third yeare of his
raygne was most worthely deprived of life and kingdome in Bosworth
playne by Henry Earle of Richemond after called king Henry the .vii."
Mirror for Magistrates. 1563 ed. (See entry 452.) pp.359-370.

The reader is asked to imagine Gloucester, tormented by devils in the
deep pit of Hell, howling the lines of the poem. Gloucester admits to the
murders of Clarence, his two nephews, and Buckingham, all of whom
stood in his path to the throne. His account of the death of the princes,
like others in the *Mirror*, follows More's version. As a result, nobles
and commons turn against the king, and Buckingham revolts to avenge
the princes' deaths. Gloucester expresses the hope that his story will be

a mirror to other princes, who by ruling wisely and justly, can avoid his fate.

482. "The Ship of State." (Trinity College Dublin MS. 516) *Historical Poems of the XIV and XV Centuries*. (See entry 430.) pp.191-193.

This poem of ten eight-line verses, written in 1458, compares the chief Lancastrians to the parts of a warship. The entire ship is represented by Henry VI, the mast by his son Edward, the lantern by the Duke of Exeter, the stern by Somerset, etc.

483. Skelton, John. "The Lament of the Soul of Edward IV." (Harley MS. 4011) *Religious Lyrics of the Fifteenth Century*. Ed. by Carleton Brown. Oxford: The Clarendon Press, 1939. pp.250-53.

This poem was attributed to Skelton by Stow, who owned the manuscript, and it was included in a collection of Skelton's works published in 1568. It is elsewhere attributed to Lydgate. (See entry 404.) The work consists of eight twelve-line stanzas, in which Edward IV, speaking from his grave, laments the mutability of fortune, which allowed him to rule for so short a time, pleasing some and displeasing others. He fortified towns, built or improved castles, and amassed great wealth, all of it now gone, for, he notes, no matter how high a man may rise, he will be food for worms in the end.

484. _____. "Of the deth of the noble prynce Kynge Edward ye forth." *Here after foloweth certayne bokes compiled by Mayster Skelton /Poet Laureat/ whose names her after shall appere*. London: Printed for Richard Lant by Henry Tab., ca. 1545. Unpaginated.

This is a slightly different version of entry 483.

485. _____. "How king Edward through his surfeting and untemperate life, sodainly died in the mids of his prosperity." *Mirror for Magistrates*. 1559 ed. (See entry 365.) pp.235- 239.

This is the same as entry 484, under a different title.

486. _____. "Upon the Dolour[u]s Dethe and Muche Lamentable Chaunce of the Most Honorable Erle of Northumberlande." (British Museum MS. Reg. 18. D ii Fol. 165) *Reliques of Ancient English Poetry*. (See entry 464.) Vol. I, pp.82-85.

This long elegaic poem mourns the murder of the fourth Earl of Northumberland by the citizens of Yorkshire. The noble, brave, loyal, and kindly earl was attempting to collect a large tax imposed by Henry VII in 1489, when the rebellious men of the north pulled him from his horse and killed him, while his own men fled like ungrateful cowards. Skelton does not mention Northumberland's betrayal of Richard III at Bosworth, the probable cause of his murder by men loyal to the late king.

487. "A Song of the Life and Death of King *Richard* the Third, who after many Murthers by him committed upon the Princes and Nobles of this Land, was slain at the Battel of Bosworth in *Leicestershire*, by *Henry* the Seventh, King of *England*." To the Tune of *Who list to lead a Soldier's Life. Collection of Old Ballads.* (See entry 393.) Vol. III, pp.47-53, and *Reliques of Early English Poetry.* (See entry 464.) Vol. III, pp.524-525.

The evil tyrant Richard murders all who stand in his way to the throne, excepting only Henry Tudor, who raises an army in France and comes to claim his rightful inheritance. After a long combat between the two at Bosworth, Henry kills the tyrant. With the usurper dead, Henry weds Elizabeth of York, unifies the kingdom, and brings peace.

488. "A Song of the Wooing of Queen *Catherine*, by *Owen Tudor*, a young Gentleman of Wales." Translated out of the *Welsh. Collection of Old Ballads.* (See entry 393.) Vol. III, pp.32-37.

A duet between Owen Tudor, a Welsh gentleman "of no great birth or fortune," and Catherine, widow of Henry V. Tudor pays suit to the queen, but she is unwilling at first to consider a match with one so far beneath her in rank, wealth, and culture. She is overcome, however, by Tudor's sweet words, and agrees to marry him and go to Wales with him. Henry Tudor, later Henry VII, was the grandson of the pair.

489. "A Songe Made in Edward the Fourthe, his Tyme, of Ye Battele of Hexhamme, in Northomberlonde; Anno M.CCCC. lxiv." Newcastle-upon-Tyne: Richardson, 1849. 20 pp.

Not available for review.

490. "Take Good Heed." (Trinity Coll. Dublin MS. 432) *Historical Poems of the XIV and XVth Centuries.* (See entry 430.) pp.206-207.

This forty-eight line poem is a warning to the Yorkist lords to beware of treachery from false friends who would betray them. The date of the work is uncertain, possibly between late 1457 and March 1458, when York and Lancaster were ostensibly reconciled. Other possibilities are late 1460, before Wakefield, or February 1454, when York was appointed Protector.

491. "The Tudor Rose." *The Early English Carols*. (See entry 414.) p.295.

This verse was printed as "The Roses Entwined" in *Historical Poems of the XIV and XV Centuries*. See entry 474.

492. Turner, Sharon. *Richard the Third, A Poem*. London: Longman, Brown, Green, and Longmans, 1845. xxiii + 278pp.

Not available for review.

493. "Twelve Letters Save England." (Trinity Coll. Dublin MS. 432) *Historical Poems of the XIV and XV Centuries*. (See entry 430.) pp.218-221.

This poem of eighteen four-line stanzas celebrates Edward IV and three other Yorkist lords who were responsible for his victory: his father, the Duke of York, and the Earls of Warwick and Salisbury. The writer tells of seeing, in summer, a gentlewoman sitting in Cheapside, embroidering twelve letters on a vestment, and these letters shall save England. They are the three R's for the Richards (York, Warwick, and Salisbury), E for Edward, etc.

494. "The Union of the Red Rose and the White, by a Marriage between King *Henry* VII. and a Daughter of King *Edward* IV." *Collection of Old Ballads*. (See entry 393.) Vol. II, pp.106-114.

This is another version of "A Princely Song Made of the Red Rose and the White" (see entry 440), with a few changes in words.

495. [Vincent, Augustine, Rouge-croix, Pursuivant of Armes.] "Right thus did cese of the Marchis blode." *A Discoverie of Errours in the First Edition of the Catalogue of Nobility, Published by Raphe Brooke, Yorke Herald, 1619*. London: William Jaggard, 1622. pp.622-623.

The eight stanza poem of seven lines each describes the lineage of the House of York, giving the births, marriages, and deaths of its members, from Sir Roger Mortimer to Richard, Duke of York and his children. It is published, without attribution, in Vincent's *Discoverie of Errours*, which he wrote to correct an earlier work on the peerage by Raphe Brooke.

496. "The White Rose." *The Early English Carols*. (See entry 408.) p.294.

This poem was printed as "The Lily White Rose" in *Historical Poems of the XIV and XV Centuries*. See entry 449.

497. "White rose & red:" *Bishop Percy's Folio MS*. (See entry 463.) Vol. II, pp.312-319.

This poem is substantially the same as Richard Johnson's "A Princely Song Made of the Red Rose and the White" (see entries 440, 494), but it was revised and expanded after 1619, since James I's queen, Anne of Denmark, who died in that year, is referred to in the past tense.

498. "Willikin's Return." (B.M. Addit. Ms. 19046) *Historical Poems of the XIV and XV Centuries*. (See entry 430.) pp.198-199. *The Early English Carols*. (See entry 414.) p.292.

Written in 1470, this carol of four three-line stanzas was discovered in a book of late 15th and early 16th century Latin proverbs and grammatical rules, possibly owned by Sir Thomas Stanley. The carol anticipates the return of Warwick to restore Henry VI to the throne. Robbins notes that the use of the 'Nowell' refrain may indicate that the carol was written at Christmas 1470, after Henry's restoration the previous October.

499. W[incoll], T[homas]. *Plantagenet's Tragicall Story: or, The Death of King Edward the Fourth: With the Unnatural Voyage of Richard the Third, Through the Red Sea of his Nephews Innocent Bloud, to His Usurped Crowne*. London: Printed for M.F for Richard Tomlins, 1649. 127pp.

In this long poem in iambic pentameter, the author employs numerous classical and biblical references to tell the story of Edward IV's reign and death. Edward's only fault was his lust, but his brother Richard is a study in evil, drawn from More's *History*. The poem ends with Elizabeth Woodville learning of the cruel death, at the hands of Tyrell, Dighton, and Green, of her sweet, innocent sons. The author wonders, at the end of his tale, whether Buckingham might have had some part in the murder of the princes, since he was guilty of so much else in helping Richard gain the crown.

500. "The Woful Lamentation of Mrs. Jane Shore, a Gold-smith's Wife of London, sometime King Edward the Fourth's Concubine, who for her Wanton Life came to a Miserable End. Set forth for the Example of all wicked Livers." To the Tune of *Live with me*. *The Roxburghe Ballads*. (See entry 477.) Vol. II, pp.108-121. The first part of the ballad is also found in *Collection of Old Ballads*. (See entry 393.) Vol. I, pp.145-152.

In the first part of this two part ballad, Jane Shore laments the sinful life she led as the mistress of Edward IV, which resulted in the grievous punishment she suffered at the hands of Richard III, and the loss of her possessions, reputation, husband, and friends. "The Second Part of Jane Shore wherein her sorrowful husband bewaileth his own Estate and Wife's Wantoness, the wrong of Marriage, the Fall of Pride; being a Warning for Women," tells Matthew Shore's tale of his betrayal by his wanton wife, whom he had loved to distraction, and denied nothing. He is forced by shame to exile himself abroad, returning only after her miserable death. His final undoing is brought about by his conviction for clipping coins, and he too dies in disgrace, brought about by the behavior of his unconstant wife.

501. Woodville, Anthony, Earl Rivers. "Balet." *Ancient Songs and Ballads*. (See entry 369.) pp.149-151. Percy's *Reliques* (See entry 464.) pp.185-186.

This five stanza poem of four lines each was written by Rivers, the brother of Elizabeth Woodville, during his captivity at Pontefract in 1483, and preserved by Rous. Rivers laments, but accepts his fate, knowing his life is shortly to end.

❖

Plays

502. Almar, George. *Peerless Pool! A Melo Drama in Two Acts*. London: J. Duncombe & Co., 1833. 36 pp.

Richard of Gloucester lusts after Verity, a pure, beautiful maiden who lives at Peerless Pool. His two evil Italian retainers hire ruffians to kidnap her, to please Richard and destroy the power of his mistress Matilda Clifford. Verity is in love with Warwick Kent, Richard's head bodyguard, and Andreas Marco, the younger Italian, loves Matilda, who is grieving for her husband, who she believes killed in battle, and their lost child. Verity's adopted father Wat attempts to rescue her, and when all the misunderstandings and mistaken identities are sorted out, Matilda has found her husband and child, Verity and Warwick are wed, the villains are punished, and Duke Richard has pardoned everyone, as he reminds the audience that history has judged him unfairly.

503. Anderson, Maxwell. *Richard and Anne. A Play in Two Acts*. Introduction and notes by Roxane C. Murph. Jefferson, N. C.: McFarland & Company, Inc., 1995. 152 pp.

The ghost of Richard III's jester interrupts the opening night performance of a New York production of Shakespeare's *Richard III*, intending to force its cancellation. Although he creates havoc among the cast and crew, he cannot achieve his objective. He does, however, succeed in bringing back from their graves Richard III, Anne Neville, Henry Tudor, and others, in order to show the audience the true facts about his beloved master and the ignoble and cowardly Henry Tudor. Like most of Anderson's plays, *Richard and Anne* is partly in verse.

504. Arnold, Samuel. *The Battle of Hexham: A Comedy in Three Acts*. Libretto by George Colman. Dublin: [Printed by P. Byrne], 1790?   46 pp.

A musical version of entry 511.

505. Binyon, Laurence. *Brief Candles*. With engravings by Helen Binyon. London: The Golden Cockerel Press, 1938.   50pp.

Written at the suggestion of H. B. Irving, the son of the famous actor-manager Henry Irving, this one act play takes place in a single twenty-four hour period at Fotheringhay Castle.   Cecily, Duchess of York, awaits the visit of her son Richard, who is on his way to London after the death of Edward IV.   Never reconciled to the marriage of Edward to Elizabeth Woodville, which she believes was illegal, Cecily urges Richard to do away with Edward's two sons and take the crown for himself.   He reluctantly agrees, but when he leaves, Cecily regrets her advice, and attempts to call him back, but it is too late.

506. Burnand, F. C. *The Rise and Fall of Richard III; or, A New Front to an Old Dickey. A Richardsonian Burlesque*. London: Phillips, 1868.   45pp.

This burlesque is based on Colley Cibber's version of Shakespeare's *Richard III* (see entry 510), and relies heavily on puns for its humor. The songs are set to popular contemporary tunes and operatic melodies, and there are references to other plays by Shakespeare, including *Macbeth* and *King Lear*.   Anachronisms, as in Shakespeare's plays, abound; Henry Tudor speaks broken English, smokes cigarettes and cigars, and the characters dance the can-can.   The editor notes that Burnand was parodying the melodramatic style of actor John Richardson.

507. By, William. *Richard III Travestie, in Three Acts, with Annotations*. London: Sherwood, Neely, and Jones, 1816.   91pp.

This burlesque of Cibber's version of Shakespeare's *Richard III* (see entry 510) employs many prizefight terms, nineteenth century slang, and not a few vulgarisms, and contains songs set to contemporary popular tunes.   Although it follows the general outline, and there are glimpses of some of the dialogue of Shakespeare's play, there are many of the anachronisms found in Burnand's play.   (See entry 506.)   The characters smoke and drink gin, and indeed Anne Neville is portrayed as quite a toper.   The music hall humor is continued in the author's endnotes.

508. Caryll, John. *The English Princess; or, The Death of Richard III.*
London: Thomas Dring, 1667. 74pp.

Richard III and Elizabeth Woodville attempt to persuade Elizabeth of
York to marry Richard. She, however, is in love with Henry Tudor.
Fearing that Elizabeth will slip through his fingers, Richard hires an
assassin to murder her, in order to prevent her marriage to Henry.
Henry kills Richard at Bosworth, thus foiling the plot, and he is then
persuaded to accept the crown.

509. Chenevix, Richard. *Henry the Seventh. An Historical Tragedy in Five
Acts. Two Plays.* London: J. Johnson & Co., 1812. pp.147-319.

In this play, written mostly in verse, Henry Tudor's victory at Bosworth
is marred by jealousy of the popular Yorkists. Short of money, he tries
to wring it from his unwilling subjects, confiscates the estates of all
Yorkists who fell at Bosworth, and insists that parliament confirm his
title in his own right. He decides not to marry Elizabeth of York until
he is crowned, and confines the Earl of Warwick in the Tower in fear
that men will rally round him. Lord Clifford, a loyal Lancastrian, is
repelled by Henry's jealousy, and joins Perkin Warbeck in Burgundy,
where they convince the duchess that Warbeck is the younger son of
Edward IV. The Londoners rise against Henry because of his treatment
of Elizabeth, but the expected support for Warbeck, when he invades
with Scottish, help does not materialize, and the pretender is captured.
Henry lays a plot to seduce Warwick and Warbeck to attempt an escape,
so that he can execute them. Elizabeth bears Henry a son, but when she
learns that her mother, whom Henry had imprisoned, has died, she
realizes that Henry will always hate their son for his Yorkist blood, and
she dies. Henry now believes that he has rid himself of all Yorkists, but
he learns that many of his subjects want him to abdicate in favor of his
son.

510. Cibber, Colley. *The Tragical History of King Richard III. As it is Acted
at the Theatre Royal.* London: for B. Lintott, 1700. 56pp.

This five act play by the eighteenth century actor is a revised version of
Shakespeare's play. Cibber added to, changed, and many critics believe,
generally butchered the original, inserting many speeches, omitting
others, and including scenes from *Henry VI, Part III*. Cibber's version
was very popular throughout the nineteenth century, and is the one
parodied by several writers of the period. (See entries 506, 507.) In his
preface the author complains that the licensing authorities, despite the

favorable revues of "several persons of the first Rank and Integrity," had
refused to allow the performance of the first act, which he believed was
the best in the play. He notes that there is no danger of readers
confusing his lines with Shakespeare's, but to avoid any unjustified
praise, he has printed Shakespeare's lines in italics, and done his best to
imitate the bard's style and manner of thinking.

511. Colman, George, the Younger. *The Battle of Hexham. A Comedy in Three
     Acts*. Dublin: Printed by P. Byrne, 1790.   57pp.

Adeline, disguised as a man, and her servant Gregory, have travelled to
Hexham to find her husband, who has deserted her and their children to
join the Lancastrian forces. After the battle, many of the defeated
Lancastrians, including Adeline, Gregory, Queen Margaret, and her son,
escape to the forest, where they are captured by a band of robbers led by
Gondibert. Adeline recognizes Gondibert as her husband, and the two
are reunited. The loyal Lancastrian robber king then arranges for
Margaret and her son to escape to safety in Scotland, to await the day
when Henry VI can reclaim his throne. The comedy referred to in the
title is provided by the robbers and common soldiers. See entry 504.

512. Conrad, Robert Taylor. *Aylmere, or, The Bondman of Kent. Aylmere, or,
     The Bondman of Kent, and Other Poems*. Philadelphia: E. H. Butler &
     Co., 1852.   308pp.

The author incorporates some incidents from the Peasants' Revolt of 1381
in his verse play, in which Jack Cade, who has lived in exile in Italy
since his father's murder by Lord Say, returns to Kent under the name
of Aylemere, with his wife Mariamne and their son. He finds that Say
is hated for his tyranny, and decides to win freedom for the bondsmen.
Lord Clifford makes unwelcome advances to Mariamne, Say has Cade's
mother murdered and orders Cade's arrest, and the commons rebel,
declaring that Cade is Lord Mortimer, the rightful king. Cade's son
starves to death, but Clifford promises Mariamne that he will save her
husband if she will marry him. She stabs him to death as the rebels
break her husband out of prison. The mob enters London, where Cade
attempts to keep order. Say is captured, and Cade insists on a royal
pardon before the rebels will leave London. Say taunts Cade, telling him
Mariamne has gone mad with grief over her son's death, the two men
fight and Cade is stabbed with a poison blade. Mariamne regains her
sanity, but both she and Cade die as the charter of freedom for the
bondsmen is proclaimed.

513. _____. *Jack Cade, The Captain of the Commons*. London: T. H. Lacy, 1869? 65pp.

A later, slightly shorter version of entry 512.

514. Coyne, J. Stirling [pseud.]. *Richard III. A Burlesque. In One Act*. London: William Barth, 1844. 18pp.

The characters in this play, which was first performed at the Theatre Royal, Adlephi, include the ghost of Henry VI, Buckingham, and Norfolk. The play opens with the courtship scene in which Richard woos Anne Neville, and like others of its genre, has many puns and songs set to popular tunes of the day.

515. Crowne, John. *The Misery of Civil War. A Tragedy, as it is Acted at the Dukes Theatre*. London: R. Bentley and M. Magnes, 1680. 72pp. Reprinted in 1681 as *Henry the Sixth. The Second Part. or the Misery of Civil War*. London: R. Bentley and M. Magnes.

This five act play, which condenses and confuses the events of twenty years into a few weeks or months, has a cast of villains and one saint, Henry VI. The play opens with Jack Cade's rebellion of 1450, in a scene with overtones of the Peasants' Revolt. Young Clifford kills Cade, an agent of the Duke of York, and immediately afterward at St. Albans (1455) York kills Clifford's father. York is accompanied by his three older sons, Edward, George, and Richard the hunchback. Young Clifford then kills York's youngest son, the toddler Rutland. After the battle, Warwick meets Elizabeth Woodville, grieving over her husband's corpse. He falls in love with her, but must leave for France to arrange a marriage for Edward, now king. Warwick returns to find Edward marrying Elizabeth, whom he has just met. The enraged earl throws his support to Henry, but Richard knows that Edward had earlier married Eleanor Butler, and decides to use this knowledge to seize the crown. Eleanor, disguised as a man, attacks Edward, and he kills her. Warwick is killed in the battle in which Henry's son is captured and killed by George and Richard. The evil Richard then goes to the Tower and murders Henry, who realizes that he must pay for his grandfather's usurpation of the throne from Richard II.

516. _____. *Henry the Sixth; or, The Murder of the Duke of Gloucester*. London: R. Bentley and M. Magnes, 1681. 70pp.

As this four act verse play opens, Eleanor Cobham urges her husband

Duke Humphrey of Gloucester to seize the throne from his nephew Henry VI, because the weak, pious Henry dislikes being king, and would prefer to be a monk, and Humphrey would be doing him a favor. Humphrey refuses, swearing loyalty to Henry. The queen hates both Eleanor and Humphrey, whose influence over Henry she fears, and she and her lover Suffolk plot to entrap Eleanor in sorcery, and so discredit both. Their plan succeeds, Eleanor is banished, and Humphrey arrested, with the king's reluctant assent. To ensure that Humphrey will not be a danger to them, Suffolk, the queen, and Cardinal Beaufort decided to have him murdered, the cardinal declaring that it is no sin to kill a man so dangerous to the kingdom. After Gloucester's murder, the cardinal's conscience drives him mad, and he dies. Suffolk is murdered by sailors as he goes into exile, and the distraught queen realizes that she must fight to preserve the throne for her son. The play ends as Henry announces that Jack Cade has led his rebels to the gates of London.

517. Daviot, Gordon [Elizabeth Mackintosh]. *Dickon. Plays by Gordon Daviot*. Foreward by John Gielgud. London: Peter Davies, 1953. pp.155-240.

In this two act play by Josephine Tey (pseud.), the author of *The Daughter of Time* (see entry 323), Richard is portrayed as a noble man surrounded by greedy and unscrupulous enemies. He takes the crown in order to save the country from their selfish ambition, and pardons them for their opposition., but his trust in Buckingham, Stanley, and others, who he believes to be his friends, proves his undoing. He is rewarded by betrayal and the loss of his life and reputation.

518. *A Dialogue Between King Richard III and his Adopted Son Richard IV*. Dublin, 1744. Reprinted, London: J. Warner, 1744.

A humorous dialogue, not available for review.

519. Dumont, Frank. *Richard the Three Times*. New York: M. Witmark & Sons, 1905. 12 pp.

This burlesque of Shakespeare's *Richard III* is not available for review.

520. Edgar, David. *Dick Deterred*. New York and London: Monthly Review Press, 1974. 112pp.

The characters in this two act play, which satirizes the Watergate scandal, include Nixon (Richard of Gloucester), Eugene McCarthy (Clarence), and Haldeman (Buckingham). The dialogue parodies that of

Shakespeare's *Richard III* in scenes which range from the Republican convention, Key Biscayne, Florida, and the Democratic convention in Chicago.

521. Edison, John Sibbald. *Henry of Richmond: A Drama in Five Acts. Part I.* London: Rivingtons, 1857. 236pp.

This verse play opens as Henry Tudor has defeated Richard III at Bosworth. Maud Herbert, Henry's childhood sweetheart, is in Wales, awaiting word that he will marry her, but both her mother and Margaret Beaufort, Henry's mother, believe it is necessary for Henry to marry Elizabeth of York, in order to unify the country. Against their own inclinations, and despite the pleas of well-meaning family and friends, who believe that Maud and Henry should marry, they reluctantly agree to part, and Henry sends a proposal of marriage to Elizabeth. His duty to his country and to his domineering mother have won over Henry's love for Maud, as Margaret convinces him that he has never been formally betrothed to her, or indeed made, by word or gesture, any indication of his feelings.

522. _____. *Henry of Richmond: A Drama in Five Acts. Part II.* London: Rivingtons, 1860.

It was the author's intention to publish this play in the same volume with Part I, but, as he explains in the preface to that work, it would have made the book too large. Not available for review.

523. _____. *Northumberland: An Historical Dramatic Poem.* London: Rivingtons, 1866. 256 pp.

The Earl of Northumberland, Henry VII's Lieutenant of the North, has been ordered by the king to collect a subsidy to pay for the war with France. The kindly earl informs the king that the tax would impose a great burden on the poor people of the area, but the council convinces Henry that his law must be obeyed, or chaos would result. Insurgents, led by Lord Egremond, plot to murder Northumberland, whom they hate for betraying Richard III at Bosworth, as well as for collecting the subsidy. The rebels attack and mortally wound Northumberland, who dies in his wife's arms, knowing he has done his duty to the king, who will send an army to crush the rebels. Northumberland's wife was the same Maud Herbert who expected to marry Henry Tudor. (See entry 521.) This play in four acts, here called parts, is in verse.

524. Ford, John. *The Chronicle Historie of Perkin Warbeck: A Strange Truth*. London: Printed by T.P. for Hugh Beeston, 1634. Unpaginated.

Perkin Warbeck, supported by Margaret of Burgundy, attempts to wrest the throne from Henry VII by claiming to be the younger son of Edward IV. Although based on Bacon's *History of Henry VII*, Ford's treatment of Warbeck is sympathetic.

525. Francklin, Thomas. *The Earl of Warwick, a Tragedy in Five Acts*. London: J. Dicks, n.d. *The Earl of Warwick, a Tragedy, as it is perform'd at the Theatre Royal in Drury-Lane*. Printed for T. Davies, R. Baldwin, and W. Griffin, 1766. 72 pp.

This verse play bears a striking resemblance to Hiffernan's *The Earl of Warwick*. (See entry 531.) The plot concerns Margaret of Anjou's attempt to prevent the marriage between Warwick and Elizabeth Gray, and to arrange that Edward IV marry the lady instead. Margaret hopes that when Warwick, who has been sent to France to arrange a marriage between Edward and Bona of Savoy, learns that the king is in love with Elizabeth, he will be so humiliated that he will turn against Edward and help to restore Henry VI to the throne. Edward fears Warwick's anger, but even the threat of civil war will not dissuade him from marrying Elizabeth. Margaret, who intends to use Warwick and then destroy him, fuels his anger at Edward, and he joins her cause. When Edward learns that Warwick is his rival in love, they quarrel, but Elizabeth tries to make peace between them. Warwick has raised an army for Margaret, but on the battlefield he and the king are reconciled, and the earl pursues Margaret. When he reaches her, she stabs him, and dying, he asks Elizabeth to marry Edward in atonement for his betrayal of the king. Edward promises to pattern himself on Warwick, and he and Elizabeth are married.

526. Fripp, Robert S. P. *Dark Sovereign: The True Tragedy of King Richard III. The Last Great Play Written in the Language of the English Renaissance*. Toronto: Printed by the author, 1991. 199pp.

This five act play, with two inductions and a glossary, is not, declares the author, revisionist history, but his interpretation of the true history of Richard III, written in the language of 16th and 17th century England. The plot follows mostly anti-Ricardian sources, such as More, Mancini, and Vergil, with some more sympathetic ones as well. As the play opens, in 1483, the young princes in the Tower are murdered in their beds. The scene then flashes back to 1471, as Anne Neville mourns the death of Edward of Lancaster, while Richard of Gloucester seeks her hand in marriage. She agrees to marry him, despite his hand in Edward's death. The characters of Truth and Rumour then describe the quarrel which follows between Richard and Clarence over the Wawick estates. The plot moves on toward the death of Edward IV and the disasters which followed, to the death of Richard III at Bosworth. The author gives Richard the benefit of the doubts about his motives and character.

527. Gent, Thomas. *The Contingencies, Vicissitudes or Changes of this Transitory Life: set forth in a long and pathetick Prologue, spoken for . . . Jane Shore, Concubine to the goodly King Edward IV, and the sufferings of Princess Elizabeth.* Illus. York: Printed by the author, 1761. 24 pp.

Not available for review.

528. Gilmore, Thomas H. *Margaret of Anjou; An Original Play.* Fullerton, Calif.: California State University, 1973. Ann Arbor, Mich: University Microfilms Inc., 1973. iv+93pp

This three act play in blank verse, with some internal rhymes, was written as a master's thesis, and purports to tell the story of Margaret of Anjou's life from the time she came to England as the bride of Henry VI, until the death of her lover, and the father of her son, the Duke of Suffolk, during Jack Cade's rebellion. The author takes enormous liberties with historical fact, distorting chronology and inventing quite unbelievable situations in the furtherance of the convoluted plot.

529. Grindrod, Charles. *King Edward V. Plays from English History.* London: Kegan Paul, Trench & Co., 1883. pp.268-352.

In this four act verse play, Jane Shore warns Hastings not to trust Gloucester, and her fears are realized when, with Buckingham's help, Gloucester arrests and executes Rivers and Grey, and takes control of the king. Hastings now regrets his support of Gloucester, and swears to protect the king, but the queen, who has fled into sanctuary, is forced to yield her younger son to Gloucester. The duke accuses Hastings of treason, has him executed, and seizes the throne. He asks Brackenbury, the Constable of the Tower, to kill the two princes, but when Brackenbury refuses, the king declares that it was only a jest to test him. He then hires Tyrell and his henchmen to do the deed. Brackenbury discovers the bodies and attacks Tyrell, and the king enters, and feigning horror at the murders, denies Tyrell's accusation that he ordered them. Richard tells Brackenbury that he played the same jest on Tyrell, never dreaming that he would be taken seriously. He begs the Constable not to reveal the boys' deaths, for the country's sake, but when he refuses, Richard accuses Brackenbury of the murders and has him arrested. He then orders the burial of the bodies, and promises to reward the murderers.

530. Heywood, Thomas. *The First and Second Parts of King Edward the Fourth*. London: J. W. for J. Oxenbridge, 1599. Unpaginated.

This play covers the period between the marriage of Edward IV to Elizabeth Woodville in 1464, to the quarrel between Richard III and Buckingham in 1483, frequently condensing the action of many years into a few weeks or months. Heywood drew heavily on More's *History of Richard III*, popular ballads, and a vivid imagination in writing this dramatic, but historically inaccurate play.

531. Hiffernan, Paul. *The Earl of Warwick, or The King and Subject; a Tragedy*. London: G. Kearsley, 1764. 63pp.

In the dedication to this play, apparently inspired by *The Amours of Edward IV* (see entry 13), the author refers to Warwick as the "born enemy to oppression of every sort, and strenuous assertor of the 'Rights and Liberty of Man.'" The play itself is taken from a French work entitled *Le Comte de Warwick*, and was obviously the basis of Francklin's *Earl of Warwick*. (See entry 525.) Warwick and Elizabeth Woodville are in love, and plan to marry, but when Warwick goes to France to arrange a marriage between Edward IV and the French king's sister, Edward falls in love with Elizabeth. When Warwick learns of the king's betrayal, he agrees to help Margaret of Anjou put Henry VI back on the throne. Elizabeth attempts to repair the rift between Warwick and the king, but both men are too proud to reconcile. When Warwick finally decides, however, to return to his Yorkist loyalty, the enraged Margaret stabs him. Elizabeth then stabs herself, and throws herself on her lover's body.

532. *Humpty Dumpty, Crook'd Back Dick & Jane Shore, or, Harlequin, Pearl Prince and Grape Queen*. Hull: J. Temple, 1857. 16 pp.

Not available for review.

533. Jamieson, Percy David. *Richard IV, an Historical Play in Five Acts.*
Cambridge: Fabb & Tyler, Limited, 1910.   110 pp.

Perkin Warbeck, the hero of this verse play, is a young Fleming who is
used as a tool by Margaret of Burgundy to unseat Henry VII. She has
rumors spread in England that he is the younger son of her brother,
Edward IV, and then has Perkin coached to play the part. He is
introduced to her court as a stranger who convinces her of his identity,
and he is then accepted by the kings of France and Scotland. Perkin
marries Catherine Gordon, the cousin of James IV of Scotland, who joins
him in an invasion of England. The expected help from the English fails
to materialize, and after the battle at Exeter the ghost of the true Richard
of York appears to Perkin to admonish him for his deception. Overcome
with remorse, Perkin flees to sanctuary, but is eventually captured and
sent to the Tower, where he meets the Earl of Warwick. The two plan
to escape by bribing their guards, but the plot fails and both are
sentenced to death. The ghost appears again, to tell them that a better
life awaits them after death.

534. Jesse, John Heneage. *The Last War of the Roses. Memoirs of King
Richard the Third*. London: John Bentley, 1862.   pp.377-496.

When Master Henry, the ward of shepherd Hugh Bartram, but actually
the son of Lord Clifford who was killed at Towton, learns from his
friend Trafford, the illegitimate son of a powerful noble, that Henry
Tudor has landed in Wales, he plans to join him. Henry and Trafford
are both in love with Lady Anne St. John, Margaret Beaufort's niece,
and Trafford plans to betray Henry's true identity to Richard III for the
reward. The treacherous Trafford tells Anne that Henry loves another,
and so she spurns him. Margaret Beaufort begs her husband Stanley to
abandon the cruel Richard III, who has murdered his nephews, but
Stanley refuses, for the king is holding his son Lord Strange hostage.
The king intends to force Elizabeth of York to marry him, but she wants
to marry Henry Tudor. All ends well, however, when Northumberland
rescues Lord Strange, enabling Stanley to come to Tudor's aid at
Bosworth, Trafford is unmasked and killed in a duel by Clifford, the
lovers are reunited, and Tudor pledges to make his reign one of peace,
love, and plenty.

535. Keteltas, Caroline M. *The Last of the Plantagenets: A Tragic Drama, in
Three Acts; Founded on the Romance of that name by William Heseltine*.
New York: Printed by R. Craighead, 1844.   56pp.

This play was inspired by Heseltine's novel. (See entries 138, 154, 238, 253, 432.) Richard Plantagenet, the son of Richard III, is ignorant of his parentage. He loves, and is loved by, Bridget, Edward IV's youngest daughter, who is destined for the convent. Richard III, preparing to fight Henry Tudor, wants his son to reign should he die in the battle. On the day before Bosworth, De Mountford, one of the king's supporters, takes Richard to meet his father, who gives him a ring which will reveal his identity. Elizabeth Woodville, however, decides to destroy Richard because she believes that he is the son of Edward IV and Clara, her former lady-in-waiting, who was really his mother. Elizabeth bribes the abbot, who had been in love with Clara, to murder the boy. Richard opens the ring and learns his true identity. Elizabeth Woodville, angry that the abbot has let both Bridget and Richard escape, threatens him, but he declares that he will reveal that she had murdered Clara. She threatens him with death if he doesn't kill Richard and return Bridget to the convent. Before Bosworth, the king acknowledges Richard as his son and heir, but the abbot attempts to stab the boy, who seizes the dagger and kills the abbot. Richard joins his father in the battle, but the king is killed, Tudor is crowned, and the play ends as de Mountford carries in the corpse of young Richard, who has died in the battle, as Bridget dies in the convent.

536. *King Richard III, or, The Battle of Bosworth Field. A Drama in Five Acts, adapted to the theatrical characters and scenes in the same.* London: Hodgson's Juvenile Drama Series, 1800? 24pp.

This play, apparently written for young people, is a pastiche of parts of Shakespeare's and Cibber's *Richard III*, with some additional lines by the unknown author. Although he used many of the original lines, this is a prose play, with a few short passages of verse.

537. *King Richard III. Travestie, a Burlesque, Operatic, Mock Terrific Tragedy, in Two Acts.* London: E. Duncombe, 1823. 52pp.

This Travestie is composed largely of songs to tunes ranging from music hall ditties to *Don Giovanni*, and speeches which paraphrase, in parody employing contemporary slang, some of those of Shakespeare's play, and which frequently refer to events of interest at the time.

538. Luce, Margaret. *The Kingmaker*. London: Home & Van Thal, 1946. 144 pp.

With her mother's help, Elizabeth Woodville plots to seduce Edward IV into marriage, as Warwick is negotiating a French marriage for the king. The Kingmaker is humiliated when Edward announces his marriage to Elizabeth, and outraged by the greed of the queen's relations. The popular Warwick, with the help of Edward's brother Clarence, gets control of the king, but Edward regains the upper hand and forces Warwick into exile, where he joins forces with the Lancastrians. He returns to England and drives Edward into exile, but Clarence turns his coat again, and helps Edward in his bid to regain the throne. At Barnet, Warwick is wounded and captured, and the treacherous Clarence stabs him in the back. Edward, who had revered his cousin Warwick, mourns even in victory, the loss of his proud but patriotic cousin.

539. Macklin, Charles. *King Henry the VII. or The Popish Imposter, A Tragedy*. London: Printed for R. Francklin, 1746. 96pp.

This five act play takes place at the court of James IV of Scotland, where Sevez, the Papal legate, plans to use Perkin Warbeck as a tool to oust Henry VII from the English throne. He must first destroy the Earl of Huntley and other Scottish nobles, who have turned against Rome. Perkin is in love with with Katherine Gordon, Huntley's daughter, but she loves another. When Huntley is arrested for treason, James promises to spare his life if Katherine will marry Perkin, and she agrees. Lord Clifford, who repents his earlier support of Warbeck, tells Henry that the pretender has made a pact to secure the support of France and Rome. He will yield all English trade and possessions to France, obey all decrees from France and Rome, and pay any tribute demanded of him. In exchange, France and Spain will invade England, and the pope will send priests to poison and seduce the minds of Englishmen. Huntley and other Scots defect to the English, Perkin loses his courage when he sees the death and destruction he has caused, and the expected help from English traitors fails to materialize. At Exeter, Perkin is arrested and executed, the Scots and English then agree to be friends in future, and James will wed Henry's daughter Margaret.

540. MacLeod, K. Ramsey. *Gloucester: A Tragedy in Two Acts*. Lake Charles, La.: Published by the Author, 1960. 83 pp.

Not available for review.

541. Macready, William Charles. *The Life and Death of King Richard III. A Tragedy: Restored and Re-arranged from the Text of Shakespeare: as performed at the Theatre Royal, Covent Garden*. London: Printed for R. and M. Stodart, 1821. 70pp.

In his preface, the actor-playwright Macready declares it his intention to "restore the *Character of Richard and the language of Shakespeare*" which Colley Cibber had destroyed. (See entry 510.) Despite this intention, he retained many of Cibber's revisions, and added several of his own, although he did restore many of the lines that Cibber had cut. These include Richard's opening speech, which Cibber had placed toward the end of the first act. Macready decries Cibber's alteration of the character of Richard III from the one depicted by Shakespeare, More, and the chroniclers, and criticizes him for omitting the humor which they had stressed as an integral part of that character. Nevertheless, this version did not receive either the critical or popular acclaim accorded Cibber's version during the 19th century.

542. Morand, Eugene, Vance Thompson, and Marcel Schwob. *Jane Shore. Drama in Five Acts*. Paris, 1901. 115 pp.

Jane Shore, the beautiful wife of a goldsmith, is kidnapped by Edward IV, and taken to court. They fall madly in love, and the kind, brilliant Jane becomes the dominant member of the council, replacing the evil Richard of Gloucester. When the king dies, Gloucester plans to kill his nephews, and he executes anyone who opposes him. Smitten by Jane, he proposes marriage, promising to aid the poor and rule well. When Jane learns that Richard has executed Earl Rivers, she turns against him, and is thrown into the Tower. She stabs her jailer, escapes with the princes, and helped by the poor people of London, sends the boys aboard a ship which will take them to safety. Jane is arrested and forced to do penance by the church, and although she is mortally ill, she accepts this punishment for her sins. She dies happy, in the mistaken belief that she has saved the princes, who have actually been captured by their wicked uncle.

543. Morris, T. B. *Dark Betrothal: A Play in One Act*. London and New York: Samuel French, 1938. 28pp.

Elizabeth of York, awaits with dread the outcome of the Battle of Bosworth between Richard III and Henry Tudor. She does not want to marry either her uncle Richard, whom she believes to be both murderer and usurper, nor Henry, the heir of the hated Lancastrians.

544. Phelan, Agnes Vivien. *Margaret of Anjou. A Drama*. Chicago: Donohue & Henneberry, 1888. 48 pp.

The author of this three act verse play has condensed the action of ten

years into a few months. Margaret of Anjou, who has been forced from
the throne with her husband Henry VI by Edward of York, writes to her
father, King René, for aid to recover her rights. René, however, is more
interested in writing poetry than in warfare, and scorns Margaret's fierce
nature. Margaret then turns to Louis XI for help, but he will not lift a
finger unless he in convinced that France will profit by it. Margaret and
her son arrive at the French court uninvited, and she learns that her old
enemy Warwick has quarrelled with Edward and is now in France. She
accepts Warwick's offer of help, and hopes that Louis will aid her as
well, if only to avenge the insult he suffered at the hands of Edward,
who has spurned Louis' sister-in-law, and married Elizabeth Woodville,
Margaret's former lady-in-waiting. In the final act, René learns that
Margaret's forces have been defeated, and her son and Warwick slain.
He mourns his grandson's death and the ruin of Margaret's hopes, by
writing a dirge in their honor.

545. Phillips, Ambrose. *Humfrey, Duke of Gloucester. A Tragedy.* London:
J. Roberts, 1723. 100pp.

In this five act play, which owes much to Shakespeare and John Crowne
(see entries 515, 516, 552), York, Salisbury, and Warwick, unhappy that
Henry VI is ruled by Rome, decide that Gloucester is England's only
hope. The queen, Suffolk, and the evil Cardinal Beaufort plan to destroy
Gloucester, whose wife has been imprisoned on false charges of sorcery.
Gloucester is the favorite of the commons, and Beaufort decides that he
must be murdered, but the good duke's enemies pay a heavy price for
their treachery. Suffolk is exiled and murdered by a mob, to the great
distress of the queen, and Beaufort's guilty conscience drives him mad
before he dies.

546. Pownall, David. *Richard III Part Two.* With music by Stephen Boxer.
Motocar and Richard III Part Two. London and Boston: Faber and
Faber, 1979. pp.45-112.

This two act play opens on George Orwell, who is holding the
manuscript for *1984* and expounding his philosophy of government. The
time is 1948, and the author is concerned about the fate of historical
truth, which in his play is destroyed by a government which invents a
story for propaganda purposes, deliberately believes it, forgets it created
it, and then accepts it as history. The creators of Betrayal, a board
game, take over the stage. The action, which switches back and forth
between 1485 and 1948, opens on Cecily Neville, who has hired a
Moorish artist to create a stained glass window depicting the true Richard

III, just as Henry Tudor is about to invade. Elizabeth Woodville, who wants Tudor to win the coming battle, has paid the artist to subvert the project. When her son Edward dies of natural causes, Elizabeth persuades Richard to hide the fact, since she wants to reveal it in her own time to Henry, her intended son-in-law. The play is interspersed with musical numbers, and with several of the characters playing both 15th and 20th century parts, indicated by a simple change of costume. All the action is viewed as part of the Betrayal game, in which the honorable Richard, Orwell's alter ego, is sacrificed to the expediency of the state, as represented by Henry Tudor. The play ends with Cecily telling of her son's death at Bosworth, and the disgraceful treatment his corpse received at the hands of the victor.

547. *Richard the Third Travesty, a Comic Opera in Two Acts.* London, 1815. 26 pp.

Not available for review.

548. Rowe, Nicholas. *The Tragedy of Jane Shore. Written in Imitation of Shakespear's Style.* London: Bernard Lintot, 1714. 63pp.

Jane Shore, the heroine of this five act play, repents of her former sinful life as mistress of the late king Edward IV, and vows to die rather than yield to the importunities of Lord Hastings. She escapes the court, only to be discovered by the Protector, Richard of Gloucester. She is reconciled with her estranged husband, the goldsmith, before she dies, and he is led off to his execution.

549. St. George, Elizabeth Ann. *Richard III: a Play.* London: Spook Enterprises, 1978. 28 pp.

Not available for review.

550. Schaller, Mary W. *The Final Trial of Richard III.* Woodstock, Ill.: The Dramatic Publishing Company, 1986. 61pp.

This one act courtroom drama, which takes place five hundred years after the Battle of Bosworth, pits History and Rumor for the prosecution, against Charity for the defense, in the trial of Richard III. More, Shakespeare, Anne Neville, and others are called as witnesses, the audience serves as the jury, and alternate endings, depending on the verdict, are provided.

551. Selby, Charles. *Kinge Richard Ye Third or Ye Battel of Bosworth Field, Being a Familiar Alteration of the Celebrated History, by a Gentleman from Stratford, in Warwickshire, called Ye True Tragdies of King Richard Ye Third, etc. . .A Merrie Mysterie in One Act.* London and New York: Samuel French, 1844.

This is a burlesque of Shakespeare's *Richard III*, in which a few lines from the original play are generously interspersed with contemporary references and slang, and songs sung to popular tunes of the day, ranging from Bellini's *Norma* to "Yankee Doodle Dandy." The play is broad farce, ending with the ghost of Henry VI snatching the crown from Henry Tudor after the Battle of Bosworth, and Richard III rising from the dead to address the audience.

552. Shakespeare, William. *The First Part of King Henry the Sixt. Mr. William Shakepeare's comedies, histories and tragedies. Published according to the true original copies.* fol. London: Printed by Isaac Jaggard, and Ed. Blount, 1623. pp.96-119.

Although this five act play is generally attributed to Shakespeare, it is believed to be the work of several men. It was first acted in 1592, but had its first publication in 1623. As the play begins, England mourns the death of Henry V, who has left his infant son in the care of his feuding relations, his brothers Bedford and Gloucester, and his uncle Henry Beaufort, Bishop of Winchester. The disarray of the English commanders in France encourages the French, led by Joan of Arc, to regain much of the territory won by Henry V, while in London, Richard, Duke of York, and John, Earl of Somerset, initiate the Wars of the Roses with their enmity. York lays claim to the the the throne, but the young Henry VI appoints him Regent of France and Somerset commander of the horse. They refuse to cooperate with each other, and Talbot, attempting to hold the line against the French, is defeated and killed. Joan of Arc is taken prisoner, and Suffolk captures Margaret of Anjou. He falls in love with her, but since he is already married, he resolves to wed her to King Henry, and rule the king through her. His plan succeeds, and peace is agreed between England and France, as York foresees the loss of English possessions in France.

553. _____. *The First Part of the Contention of the Two Famous Houses of Yorke and Lancaster.* London: T. Creede for T. Millington, 1594.

An abridged and corrupt version of *The Second Part of King Henry the Sixt.* (See entry 554.)

554. _____. *The Second Part of King Henry the Sixt, with the Death of Good Duke Humphrey. Mr. William Shakespeare's comedies, histories and tragedies. Published according to the true original copies.* fol. London: Printed by Isaac Jaggard, and Ed. Blount, 1623. pp.120-146.

This five act play was first published in quarto in 1594, under the title *The First Part of the Contention of the Two Famous Houses of Yorke and Lancaster.* (See entry 553.) As with the *The First Part of Henry the Sixt*, there is some question of the authorship, but it is generally attributed to Shakespeare. As the play opens, Henry's bride, Margaret of Anjou, arrives in England, and it is revealed that the Duke of Suffolk, who arranged the marriage, has ceded Maine and Anjou to the French as part of the settlement, and that the bride has brought no dowry. Henry, however, is pleased with the bargain, and rewards Suffolk, while depriving the Duke of York of the regency of France. Gloucester, Warwick, and Salisbury are furious, and York awaits his opportunity to seize the throne. The queen and her faction plot Gloucester's destruction, and entrap his wife, Eleanor Cobham, into sorcery. They are aided by York, who believes that he will rise by Gloucester's fall. Suffolk, Cardinal Beaufort, and York convince Henry that Gloucester is a traitor, and he is arrested and strangled by agents of his acccusers. The enraged commons, who loved Gloucester, storm the palace and accuse Suffolk of the murder, and the duke is exiled and murdered by seamen. The cardinal dies, consumed by guilt, and Salisbury and Warwick agree to support York's claim to the throne. York, on his way to Ireland, encourages Jack Cade to rebel, and the rebels besiege London before they are dispersed, and Cade is killed. York returns from Ireland and declares himself king. His sons Edward and Richard join him, Warwick, and Salisbury, and at St. Albans they defeat the Lancastrians. York kills Lord Clifford, and the hunchbacked Richard slays Somerset, as the king and queen flee to London, pursued by the Yorkists.

555. _____. *The True Tragedie of Richard Duke of Yorke and the Death of Good King Henrie the Sixt.* London: P. S[hort] for T. Millington, 1595.

This is an abridged and mutilated version of *The Third Part of King Henry the Sixt.* (See entry 556.) Most authorities agree that both this version and *The First Part of the Contention, etc.* (see entry 552) are corrupt acting versions, and that Shakespeare, using corrected copies, revised and expanded the plays, which were then published in the First Folio.

556. _____. *The Third Part of Henry the Sixt, with the Death of the Duke of Yorke. Mr. William Shakespeare's Comedies, Histories and Tragedies. Published according to the True Original copies.* fol. Printed by Isaac Jaggard, and Ed. Blount, 1623. pp.147-172.

An early, abridged, and mutilated version of this play, whose authorship, like that of both parts one and two is disputed (see entries 551, 553), was published in 1595 as *The True Tragedie of Richard Duke of Yorke, and the Death of Good King Henrie the Sixt.* (See entry 555.) The story continues where *Henry VI, Part Two* leaves off, as the king and his followers arrive in London after their defeat at St. Albans, to find the Duke of York seated on the throne, surrounded by his adherents. York insists that his title is stronger, and Henry agrees to disinherit his son, if he can retain the crown for his lifetime. The furious queen raises an army, and at Sandal Castle defeats and kills York. Warwick and York's sons, Edward and Richard, then defeat Margaret's forces at Towton, and she and her son flee to France, while Henry seeks safety in Scotland. Edward is declared king, Henry is captured, and Warwick goes to France to secure Edward a bride. Edward, however, marries Elizabeth Woodville, and the humiliated Warwick defects to the Lancastrians, and marries his daughter Anne to Margaret's son. The rebels invade England and depose Edward, who returns with an army, defeats and kills Warwick, and in a rout of Margaret's forces at Tewkesbury, the three Yorkist brothers stab Prince Edward of Lancaster to death. Richard, who has been created Duke of Gloucester, then hurries secretly to the Tower, where he murders King Henry.

557. _____. *The Tragedy of King Richard the Third. Containing, His treacherous Plots against his brother Clarence: the pittiefull murther of his innocent nephewes: his tyrannicall usurpation: with the whole course of his detested life, and most deserved death. As it hath beene lately Acted by the Right Honourable the Lord Chamberlaine his servants.* London: Printed by Valentine Sims, for Andrew Wise, 1597. 48 leaves.

This first quarto edition of the play, probably written in 1593, is generally considered the most authoritive text. The work draws heavily on More, through Holinshed's *Chronicles*, and shows evidence of Shakespeare's familiarity with *The True Tragedy of Richard the Third* (see entry 561), and set for all time the picture of the evil hunchbacked king in the minds and hearts of writers and the public. Gloucester plots the murder of Clarence, confesses that he killed Henry VI, Edward of Lancaster, and Warwick, and woos the latter's daugher over the coffin of her father-in-law. After he seizes the throne, he has the princes murdered, and then causes a rumor to be spread that his wife is mortally ill, in preparation for his intended marriage to his niece Elizabeth. The night before Bosworth, the king is haunted by the ghosts of his victims, and the battle itself is a fight between evil, in the person of Richard III, and angelic savior, in the person of Henry Tudor, who defeats Richard and takes his rightful place as England's king.

558. Sisson, Rosemary Anne. *The Queen and the Welshman: A Play in Three Acts.* Illus. London and New York: Samuel French, 1958. 73pp.

This play about the romance between Katherine Valois and Owen Tudor is not available for review. The author wrote a later novel on the subject, with the same title. See entry 307.

559. _____. *The Dark Horse: A Play.* London and New York: Samuel French, 1979. 79pp.

Edward IV sends Bishop Stillington to Brittany to bribe Duke Francis into turning over Henry and Jasper Tudor. After accepting the money, Francis changes his mind, but the near betrayal turns Henry from a sweet-natured, naive young man, into a suspicious, grasping tyrant, determined to trust no one. When he wins the crown from Richard III, he decides to blacken the late king's memory to ensure his own safety, and he spreads the rumor that Richard had his two mephews murdered. Henry had reluctantly promised to marry Elizabeth of York, and although she has been attracted to his portrait, his arrogance and cruelty give her pause. Her half-brother Dorset attempts to persuade her and Stanley to prevent Henry's coronation, but she finally decides that her only safety lies in marriage to him. Henry institutes the first royal bodyguard in English history, and demands that everyone, including Jasper, call him Your Highness. Jasper, hurt and angry by his nephew's ingratitude, decides to return to Wales, but Margaret Beaufort convinces him that her son needs him. He decides to stay when he sees signs of remorse in Henry for his uncaring treatment of his old followers.

560. Tate, Gerald A. *Elizabeth Wydeville, A Play in One Act.* Oxford: Printed at the Shakespeare Head Press, 1933. 24pp.

This play takes place at Grafton Regis in June 1464. Edward IV has secretly married Elizabeth Woodville, a Lancastrian widow with two small children, and Edward's mother, the Duchess of York is furious at what she perceives as an insult to the Yorkist cause, and to the Earl of Warwick, who has been arranging a French marriage for the king.

Elizabeth's kindness and generosity have won over Richard of Gloucester and Lord Howard, and she finally wins the duchess' approval as well.

561. Thompson, C. Pelham. *The King's Command. A Farce in two Acts.* Frontispiece--an engraving by Mr. Findley. London: J. Duncombe & Co., [1835?]. 26pp.

In this short play with musical accompaniment, Lord Berkeley, a favorite of Edward IV, plans to marry Lady Edith Butler, Countess of Pembroke. Simon, her gardener, wants to wed her maid Lucy. Edith fears that the king will be angry at Berkeley for leaving the court, and urges him to return, promising to follow. He tells her he cannot, for when news of her beauty had reached the court, Edward had sent him to confirm the report. He fell in love with her, and told the philandering king that the reports were exaggerated. Edward and his courtiers arrive, and fearing the king's reaction, Edith and Lucy exchange clothes and identities. When Edward discovers the deception, he plans to punish the miscreants by forcing Edith to marry Simon, and Lucy to wed Berkeley, but he relents and both pairs of lovers are reunited.

562. *The True Tragedie of Richard the Third: Wherein is showne the death of Edward the fourth, with, the smothering of the two yoong Princes in the Tower: With a lamentable ende of Shores wife, an example for all wicked women. And lastly the coniunction and ioyning of the two noble Houses, Lancaster and Yorke. As it was playd by the Queenes Maiesties Players.* London: Printed by Thomas Creede, 1594. Unpaginated.

Written partly in verse and partly in prose, this one act play is believed to be the first historical tragedy printed in English. It gives the standard Tudor portrait of the evil hunchbacked murderer, who is slain at Bosworth by the noble Henry Tudor. The epilogue has a chorus, which includes Elizabeth Woodville and Elizabeth York, who catalogue the glorious achievements of the Tudor monarchs. The play was obviously known to Shakespeare, for there are striking similarities of dialogue and incident between it and his *Richard III.*

563. [Valpy, Dr. Richard]. *The Roses, or King Henry the Sixth; A Tragedy.* Reading: Smart and Cowslade, 1795. 48pp.

After the battle of Towton, where Richard of Gloucester kills Clifford, Edward IV marries Elizabeth Grey, which turns Warwick against him. In one of the passages taken from Shakespeare, Richard tells of his plans to detroy all who stand in his way to the throne. Warwick rebels, joins the Lancastrians, and Richard and Clarence agree to help Edward, as Clarence recites John of Gaunt's speech from *Richard II* (III,i). Warwick captures Edward and puts Henry VI on the throne, but Richard and Hastings rescue Edward, as Margaret of Anjou and her army arrive from France. Warwick is killed at Barnet, and the victorious Yorkists then defeat the remaining Lancastrian forces, imprison Margaret, and Richard and Clarence murder her son. Richard then hurries to London, where Henry VI, after reciting part of a speech from Shakespeare's *Richard II* (III, ii), is stabbed to death by the evil duke, as Edward and Clarence enter the palace in triumph.

564. Vaughan, Stuart. *The Royal Game*. Chicago: The Dramatic Publishing Company, 1974. 103pp.

This two act play takes place after Bosworth, when Henry Tudor and Bishop Morton discover that the sons of Edward IV, purportedly murdered by Richard III, are still alive. Henry orders them killed, but the younger boy escapes, to surface as Lambert Simnel. His mother, Elizabeth Woodville, coaches him, since a blow to his head has destroyed his memory, but their attempt to overthrow Henry fails. The king agrees to spare the young prince after Elizabeth of York officially rejects him as her brother, and the hopes of the Yorkist to reclaim the throne appear at an end.

565. Waldron, Francis Godolphin. *A King in the Country. A Dramatic Piece, in Two Acts*. Acted at the Theatres-Royal at Richmond and Windsor, 1788. London: Printed for the Editor, 1789. 28pp.

The plot, which is based on "The Tanner of Tamworth" (see entries 444, 466), an underplot of Heywood's *First Part of King Edward the Fourth* (see entry 530), tells how Hobbs, the tanner, meets Edward IV in the forest at Drayton-Basset, and not recognizing him, speaks disrepectfully to him. Edward offers his steed for the tanner's mare, and pumps him for his opinion of the king. Hobbs praises Henry VI's piety and Edward's wit and courage, declaring that he is Yorkist or Lancastrian as the wind blows. Edward meets the tanner's beautiful daughter, and proposes marriage. In the second act, the king asks the commons for a loan for war with France, but the wealthier citizens plead poverty. Hobbs shames them into contributing, and Edward pardons the tanner's son, who has been sentenced to death for theft, and the tanner for his initial disrespect, giving him a hundred marks a year.

566. Wills, William Gorman. *Jane Shore. A Play.* London: Tinsley Brothers, 1876. iv + 70pp.

Not available for review.

Index

❖

References are to entries, except where otherwise indicated.

About the Compiler

ROXANE C. MURPH is an independent researcher and free-lance writer specializing in 15th-century English history and the Wars of the Roses. She is the author of *Richard III: The Making of a Legend* (1977).

ISBN 0-313-29709-6

90000>

EAN

9 780313 297090

HARDCOVER BAR CODE